BUSINESS ETHICS

A MANAGERIAL, STAKEHOLDER APPROACH

BUSINESS ETHICS

A MANAGERIAL, STAKEHOLDER APPROACH

Joseph W. Weiss
Bentley College

Wadsworth Publishing Company
Belmont, California
A Division of Wadsworth, Inc.

Business Publisher: Larry Alexander
Editorial Assistant: Karen Mandel
Production Editor: Carol Carreon Lombardi
Managing Designer: Kaelin Chappell
Print Buyer: Diana Spence
Art Editor: Nancy Spellman
Permissions Editor: Peggy Meehan
Copy Editor: Melissa Andrews
Cover: Jeanne Calabrese
Compositor: Joan Olson
Printer: Malloy Lithographing, Inc.

*This book is printed on
acid-free recycled paper.*

International Thomson Publishing
The trademark ITP is used under license.

Printed in the United States of America.

1 2 3 4 5 6 7 8 9 10—98 97 96 95 94

Library of Congress Cataloging-in-Publication Data

Weiss, Joseph W.
    Business Ethics : a managerial, stakeholder approach / Joseph W.
Weiss
        p.   cm.
    Includes bibliographical references and index.
    ISBN 0-534-92512-X (alk. paper)
    1. Business ethics.   2. Social responsibility of business.
I. Title.
HF5387.W45   1994
    174′ .4—dc20   93–27746

CONTENTS

PREFACE

Read any major newspaper or business journal, and you will find an event, crisis, or issue that relates a corporation's activities to ethics. Questions are quickly asked: "Who is right? Who is wrong? Who stands to gain or lose? Who is hurt or liable? Who should pay for the damages? Who should have acted responsibly? Will justice be served?"

Students and professionals need straightforward frameworks to help sort out complex issues and make ethical decisions—about their own actions, about the organizations in which they work, and about the cases they study.

Business Ethics: A Managerial, Stakeholder Approach was created as a first course in business ethics and was written with four goals in mind:

- to cover major contemporary and international topics in business ethics;

- to present stakeholder analysis—a practical method for studying news-breaking events in the business world;

- to present the material in a straightforward, "reader friendly" way; and

- to offer succinct ethical tests and guidelines for making decisions in realtime.

The mission of this book is to present thoughtful and accessible frameworks for understanding and making decisions about ethical dilemmas in business. The book uses questions and discussions that encourage the reader's participation in the decision-making process. Ethical decision making involves a person's own value judgments as well as the content of the situations. This book helps students see and understand their own ethical decision-making styles, assumptions, and premises.

A Proactive Approach

Although business ethics issues change daily, classic ethical principles remain constant. This book shows that contemporary business topics can be analyzed by using traditional ethical principles in a stimulating way. The reader is put in the decision-maker's seat, with thought-provoking cases and discussion questions that ask "What would you do if you had to decide a course of action?" Readers will also be able to examine changing ethical issues and business problems as they appear in *The Wall Street Journal, 60 Minutes, 20/20, The New York Times, Business Week,* and other news media.

Stakeholder Analysis

Stakeholder analysis is not the only method used to examine ethical dilemmas and problems in business, but it is the major method illustrated in this book. Why? Stakeholder analysis is one of the most comprehensive, orienting approaches for identifying issues, groups, strategies, and outcomes (potential or realized) in complex ethical dilemmas. Other approaches introduced in the book (for example, issues management and crisis management) can be used with a stakeholder analysis. The nature of the situation or problem determines which approach is more useful. Stakeholder analysis is presented here as a starting point for mapping the "who, what, when, where, why, and how" of ethical problems that involve organizations and their constituencies.

Features of the Book

Throughout the text, the presentation is clear and understandable: principles, concepts, and examples are written to minimize jargon and maximize meaning. The content is intended to contribute to courses in these areas: introduction to business, business law, business and society, and business policy.

Additional features of this book include:

- A contemporary approach for examining international moral issues regarding competitiveness. Japanese and U.S. cultural and decision-making approaches that affect ethical outcomes are discussed.

- Cross-disciplinary topics relating to philosophy, law, ethics, business and society, and management. Discrimination and sexual harassment are presented in a multidisciplinary way, from management and ethical perspectives.

- Concept coverage to examine standalone cases. Small cases are written into the text, but users can adopt any cases they wish.

- A focused approach is used with concrete examples when examining controversies in business ethics; for example, AIDS in society and the workplace is discussed.

Objectives of the Book

- To introduce basic ethical concepts, principles, and examples to enhance understanding and use of ethical precepts and frameworks in solving moral dilemmas;

- To introduce the stakeholder approach as a strategic and practical method for mapping corporate, group, and individual relationships so readers can understand and apply ethical reasoning in the marketplace and in workplace relationships;

- To expand readers' awareness of what constitutes ethical and unethical practices in business at the individual, group, organizational, and multinational levels; and

- To instill a confidence and competence in the readers' ability to think and act according to moral principles as they create, manage, and study stakeholder relationships.

Structure of the Book

Chapter One defines business ethics and familiarizes the reader with examples of ethics in business practices, levels of ethical analysis, and what can be expected from a course in business ethics.

Chapter Two introduces the stakeholder approach and its use in studying social responsibility relationships at the individual employee, group, and organizational levels. This method can incorporate principles and concepts from the entire book.

Chapter Three contains a discussion of the "micro-level" approach to ethical decision making: moral principles and concepts derived from both classical and more contemporary ways of thinking and acting ethically are presented. Individual styles of moral decision making are also discussed in this section. Although this section is a micro-level approach, these principles can be used to examine and explain corporate strategies and actions as well. (Executives, managers, employees, coalitions, government officials and other external stakeholder groups are also individuals.)

Chapter Four presents the corporation as stakeholder and discusses contemporary moral and conceptual issues that organizations face in stakeholder relationships. It also addresses the nature of corporations as moral actors and environments.

Chapter Five presents ethical issues and problems that firms face with external consumers, government, and environmental groups. The question "How moral can and should corporations be and act in commercial dealings?" is examined.

Chapter Six addresses the individual employee stakeholder and examines the kinds of moral issues and dilemmas individuals face in the workplace.

Chapter Seven aggregates the level of analysis to domestic and multinational corporations (MNCs) and discusses ethical issues between MNCs, host countries, and other groups. Ethics and industrial competitiveness within and between nations is also discussed, using the United States and Japan as examples.

Chapter Eight outlines emerging ethical issues that employees, managers, corporations, and multinational stakeholders must manage in the 1990s and in the rapidly approaching twenty-first century.

Acknowledgments

This book has been "in the making" throughout several years of teaching MBA students. I would like to thank them for their questions, challenges, and class contributions that stimulated the research and presentation of this text. I thank The Center for Business Ethics at Bentley College and Michael Hoffman and his staff for providing resources that helped make this book possible. I also thank my colleagues with whom I have met and worked over the years in the Academy of Management and the Organizational Behavior Teaching Society. Their suggestions are reflected in the book. I also thank my colleagues in the Management Department of Bentley College who contributed to idea generation and motivation for executing the writing of the text. Kathy Rusiniak, my graduate assistant, helped enormously with Chapter 8 and the Glossary. Kristin Galfetti helped with the original research and construction of discussion questions. I recognize and extend thanks to those who reviewed and offered valuable revision suggestions, including Robert Giacalone, University of Richmond; John James, University of Florida; Susan Jarvis, University of Texas—Pan American; Dr. Lisa Newton, Fairfield University; Joan Ryan, Lane Community College; and William Wines, Boise State University.

BUSINESS ETHICS

A MANAGERIAL, STAKEHOLDER APPROACH

1

Business Ethics Defined

The fate of America lies in the success of its businesses. As one of the most fundamental social institutions, business impacts on the lives of most of us. It shapes the nature of our workplaces, determines how much we get paid, and defines career routes and career possibilities that help us plan the future. Thus, changes in business practices have major social as well as economic consequences, both positive and negative.

(Kanter 1989, 3)

Recent business crises and scandals have had societal, even global, consequences and have awakened the interest of media, government, and public group stakeholders in business ethics. The following sample of recent business crises indicates that business has not been conducted "as usual" between business leaders and their stakeholders, outside and inside firms. For example,

- The Savings and Loan scandals cost taxpayers over an estimated $200 to $500 billion. The scandals involved irresponsible and unethical actions by government and business professionals in a variety of occupations who exceeded their mandates and responsibilities. Who should pay? Taxpayers?

- Union Carbide's gas leak in Bhopal, India, resulted in 2,000 deaths and over 200,000 injuries. The company still faces lawsuits. Would reaction have been the same if this had happened in the United States?

- The Manville Corporation filed for bankruptcy as a strategy to gain court protection to remain solvent and to avoid paying millions in liability suits to thousands of asbestos claimants, many of whom have died or are permanently disabled. Who is liable? Who should pay?

- Carl Icahn, T. Boone Pickens, Irwin Jacobs, and other corporate raiders have bought, sold, and restructured corporations for quick profit at the cost of local jobs and even of national long-term economic interests. Should corporations be bought, sold, and restructured as a competitive strategy? Who wins? Who loses in this game?

Inside corporations, moral issues and problems are also under greater scrutiny. For example,

- Corporations are increasingly implementing sexual harassment programs as more women enter the workplace and as complaints grow; the U.S. Supreme Court has ruled to protect employees from such harassment at work. How should managers deal with issues of sexual harassment at work?

- Acquired immunodeficiency syndrome (AIDS) in the United States and in the workplace is a serious problem. It is estimated that 1% of the U.S. health care budget was spent on AIDS in 1991. This estimate continues to increase as the decade advances. To what extent is company management responsible for screening and educating employees about AIDS? Should certain professionals and employees be required to be tested for AIDS?

These crises and other moral issues in the workplace involve business leaders, managers, and employees as invested **stakeholders***. Ethical principles and guidelines are being sought by business leaders to understand and manage these and other legal and moral dilemmas.

Although business ethics is not new, there is a renewed and growing interest in the subject. Major corporations such as Johnson and Johnson, Boeing, General Mills, GTE, Hewlett Packard, Xerox, and others have created ethics codes, instituted social responsibility audits, and included ethics in their training. A 1989–1990 follow-up survey of *Fortune 500* industrial firms and 500 service corporations by Bentley College's Center for Business Ethics showed that 46% of the 244 firms responding were expanding efforts to incorporate ethics into their companies—this compares to 19% of companies surveyed in 1984. In this same study, 49% of companies surveyed had also adopted some form of ethics training, compared to 35% in 1984; 91% reportedly had a written code of ethics, compared to 75% in 1984. Nearly 87% of those surveyed in 1990 believed the public is more aware of ethical issues in business, and 84% listed "being a socially responsible corporation" as a main goal in their ethics program, as compared to 27% who said that increased profit is a main goal (see Carroll 1989; Hoffman & Frederick 1990).

The Wall Street Journal, Business Week, Forbes, Fortune, Business Horizons, and other business journals frequently feature surveys and articles on ethical issues that range from global dumping to sexual harassment. Moreover, nationally accredited business schools require business ethics topics in their curriculum. Ethics is now being included in accounting, business policy, strategic and international management, law, and organizational theory and behavior courses.

---

*Key terms that appear in **boldface** will be found in the Glossary of this text.

1.1 BUSINESS ETHICS: A STAKEHOLDER APPROACH

> Schools of business administration have moved over the past 25 years from
> teaching the basic principles useful in operations management, to the quan-
> titative models applicable in the functional departments, to the computer
> systems needed for the technical areas, to the competitive concepts required
> for strategic planning. In the next five years I forecast that these schools will
> move even further to the ethical principles required for stakeholder com-
> mitment. *(Hosmer 1991, 50–51)*

We present a stakeholder approach in this book for understanding
and studying a corporation's moral responsibilities and obligations
toward the individuals, groups, and institutions it serves. A stakeholder
approach is also critical to meet what Sethi, Namiki, and Swanson (1984)
have called "the Management Challenge." In their book *The False Promise
of the Japanese Miracle,* they note that the five areas that determine the
success or failure of an enterprise have been financial, manufacturing,
human resource, management, marketing, and strategic management.
They stated:

> To this must be added a sixth: the management of external relations—that
> is, business–government relations and dealing with other external con-
> stituencies. For in a hostile external environment, sociopolitical factors often
> have as much, if not more, impact on a firm's performance as the economic
> and market factors. *(Sethi et al. 1984, 279)*

The stakeholder approach is explained in detail in Chapter 2. For
purposes of introduction, we note at the outset that the stakeholder
approach views a corporation's ethical responsibilities in terms of its
moral and economic obligations to the stakeholders (that is, constituencies) with whom it does business. Corporations are dependent to
a large extent on their stakeholders to execute business goals successfully in society. For example, Exxon's stakeholders include its stockholders, customers, suppliers, employees worldwide, political and
environmental groups that influence its transactions, unions, and international governments. Exxon (a corporate stakeholder) also depends
and is obligated to each of these groups in different ways to achieve its
aims. Exxon is primarily obligated economically to its stockholders;
however, a stakeholder approach argues that if Exxon does not meet its
moral, social, political, and legal obligations to its other stakeholders, it
will not be able to function effectively or to serve its shareholders fairly
and justly in a democratic social system. The *Exxon Valdez* oil spill and
the resulting ecological crisis showed that Exxon deals with numerous
stakeholders.

A stakeholder analysis can also focus on key actors other than corporations. A focal or key stakeholder can be an individual or a group as well as an institution. For example, Clarence Thomas, the recent Supreme Court nominee—now justice—was a focal stakeholder who had to defend not only his judicial credentials but also his personal integrity after Professor Anita Hill accused him of sexual harassment. Who were the stakeholders in this incident? What was at stake for each? Who was right, and who was wrong? Who was morally responsible or irresponsible? While this example does not directly involve a business corporation, it does focus on the business of the Supreme Court, the U.S. Senate, voters, and a number of important groups in society. The stakes may well include future business decisions, since Thomas, as a Supreme Court judge, will certainly be involved in making decisions affecting business. This situation calls for a stakeholder analysis, since so many parties, issues, and stakes were involved. The incident was complex, and the outcomes were not easily predicted. The moral responsibility of each party had to be weighed and judgments made.

The stakeholder approach addresses these types of ethical dilemmas for individuals, managers, and corporations. It is an approach that provides (1) a pragmatic means of understanding the social and moral obligations of business to each of its stakeholders and stockholders; (2) a method for mapping the complex relationships between a focal stakeholder and other constituencies; (3) a method of identifying strategies that each stakeholder can use to interact with moral responsibility toward others in crises, critical incidents, or ethical dilemmas; and (4) a way of "keeping score" and assessing moral responsibility and responsiveness of focal and other key stakeholders to each other. In complex and ambiguous ethical situations, right and wrong decisions are not always clear. A stakeholder approach enables decision makers to clarify relationships, strategies, and events in order to describe and evaluate moral options that address issues of justice, fairness, and equity in all stakeholder interests.

The moral role of managers from a stakeholder perspective is also not limited to purely economic, scientific, or profit motives. Society has evolved to a point of complexity such that business owners and managers must understand their moral obligations and their interdependencies with governments, consumers, the media, and a host of external constituencies in order to succeed in their stakeholder relationships. As one author noted:

> The ethical manager will be realistic about both the situation and the roles and functions of business, government and other institutions in dealing with

it. He will also bear in mind the long-term interest of the persons and communities which he affects, having the courage to place those interests above his own short-term preoccupations. He will see his problems in the context of all of their relationships, employing his skills as a generalist to help produce appropriately systemic solutions. *(George Cabot Lodge, quoted in Hoffman 1990, 152)*

Before explaining this approach in greater detail in Chapter 2, we return to our discussion of defining and clarifying the following topics: business ethics, levels of ethical analysis, myths about business ethics, reasons why ethical reasoning is required in business, the nature of ethical reasoning in business, and whether business ethics can be taught or trained.

1.2 WHAT IS BUSINESS ETHICS?

Business ethics is the art and discipline of applying ethical principles to examine and solve complex moral dilemmas. Business ethics asks, "What is right and wrong? Good and bad?" in business transactions. Ethical "solutions" to business problems may have more than one "right" alternative and sometimes no "right" alternative may seem to be available. Logical and ethical reasoning is therefore required to understand and think through complex moral problems in business situations.

Although there is no one "best" definition of business ethics, there is a consensus that business ethics is an area that requires reasoning and judgment based on both principles and beliefs in making choices to balance economic self-interests against social and welfare claims.

Laura Nash (1990, 5) defined business ethics as "the study of how personal moral norms apply to the activities and goals of commercial enterprise. It is not a separate moral standard, but the study of how the business context poses its own unique problems for the moral person who acts as an agent of this system." Nash stated that business ethics deals with three basic areas of managerial decision making: (1) choices about what the law should be and whether to follow it; (2) choices about economic and social issues outside the law's domain; and (3) choices about the priority of one's self-interest over the company's.

In defining business ethics, it is also helpful to see how working professionals identify a wide range of issues that they experience in their professions and organizations. In an international survey of 300 companies worldwide, more than 80% of chief executive officers and senior managers stated the following as the top ethical issues facing businesses (Baumann 1987):

Employee conflicts of interest	91%
Inappropriate gifts	91%
Sexual harassment	91%
Unauthorized payments	85%
Affirmative action	84%

Also, in a national *Wall Street Journal* survey (1990, A1) of 1,400 working women, the following unethical practices were reported as occurring most frequently in business:

- Managers lying to employees
- Expense-account abuses at high levels
- Office nepotism and favoritism
- Taking credit for others' work

The same study reported that the most unethical behavior happens in the following areas:

Government	66%
Sales	51%
Law	40%
Media	38%
Finance	33%
Medicine	21%
Banking	18%
Manufacturing	14%

Other examples of questionable ethical activities that involve and also affect corporations include (Gordon 1990, 93):

- Receiving or offering kickbacks
- Stealing from the company
- Firing an employee for whistle-blowing
- Padding expense accounts to obtain reimbursements for questionable business expenses
- Divulging confidential information or trade secrets

- Terminating employment without giving sufficient notice
- Using company property and materials for personal use

These reported ethical issues in business suggest that any useful definition of business ethics must address social and economic problems in the workplace, including relationships between professionals at all organizational levels, and between corporate executives and external groups.

1.3 LEVELS OF BUSINESS ETHICS

Business ethics, then, is not simply a personal or an individual matter. Business ethics operates at multiple levels and perspectives. In this section, we review two illustrations of the different levels of analyzing ethical dilemmas in business. Because business leaders—and other invested business parties—must manage a wide range of stakeholders, inside and outside of organizations, understanding the different levels of stakeholders facilitates our understanding of complex relationships among the participants involved in ethical business dilemmas.

Carroll (1989, 110–112) discusses five levels at which business ethical issues can be addressed. Figure 1-1 illustrates *the individual, the organizational, the association, the societal,* and *the international* levels. Understanding moral dilemmas by identifying the level(s) at which moral issues originate and influence different stakeholder interests can add clarity for those who must decide what course of action to take. Also, as the film *Wall Street* illustrates, individual motivation and morality (or immorality) is linked to the organization, industry, and society. The themes of individual greed and unlimited ambition in the film were based on beliefs that brokerage firms (in the 1980s) could be vehicles for pursuing illegal activity: buying and selling stocks based on inside information to gain individual wealth. The view in the film that American society rewards individual wealth above all else is controversial but intriguing.

Ethical questions at the *individual level* address such issues as whether to cheat on an expense account, to call in sick when one is not, to accept a bribe, to follow one's conscience over an administrative order, to report a sexual harassment incident, or, as in the film *Wall Street,* to sacrifice legal standing for individual wealth. If an ethical issue involves or is limited to individual responsibilities, then a person must examine his or her own ethical motives and standards before choosing a course of action. (Chapter 3 deals with ethical individual stakeholder principles.)

Figure 1-1 Business Ethics Levels

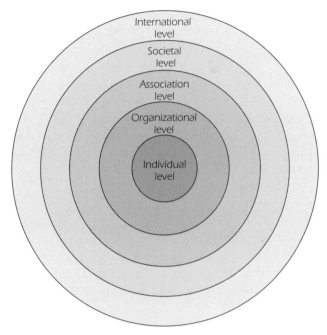

Source: Archie B. Carroll. "Linking Business Ethics to Behavior in Organizations." S.A.M. *Advanced Management Journal* 7 (Summer 1978): 110. Reproduced with permission of the publisher.

At the *organizational level,* ethical issues arise when, for example, a person or group is pressured to overlook wrongdoings of his or her peers in the interest of company harmony; or when an employee is asked to perform an unethical or illegal act to earn a division or work unit profit. In the film *Wall Street,* the brokerage firm director praised Bud, the young employee, when he succeeded and fired him when he was caught for insider trading. If an ethical issue arises at the organizational level, the organizational member(s) should examine the firm's policies, procedures, and ethics code—if one exists—before making a decision.

At the *association level,* an accountant, lawyer, medical doctor, or management consultant may refer to his or her professional association's charter or ethics code for guidelines on conducting business before, for example, advising a client to deduct questionable items for tax purposes, or offering a plea bargain, or risking harmful side effects from ordering a prescription, or advising a client to acquire a company that conducts illegal business transactions.

At the *societal level*, the laws, norms, customs, and traditions govern the legal and moral acceptability of behaviors. Business activities that are acceptable in Italy may be immoral or illegal in the United States. The 1977 Foreign Corrupt Practices Act (FCPA) made it illegal for a U.S. company or its officials to bribe foreign government officials and politicians. However, business customs in the Middle East, Asia, or certain other Mediterranean societies may view grease payments and bribery as acceptable negotiating tactics. It is advisable to consult with knowledgeable and trustworthy contacts in a foreign country to understand the legal and moral codes of conduct before doing business there.

At the *international level*, an example of an ethical issue would be whether an employee should work for or accept his or her company's policy of doing business with a government that supports apartheid when American social values and laws do not support racial discrimination. Ethical issues at this level can be more difficult to resolve, since a mix of cultural, political, and religious values often is involved in a decision. Constitutions, laws, and customs should be consulted to understand what are and are not acceptable practices with regard to a particular decision.

As can be seen, these levels can and often do overlap. It is helpful to identify the ethical level(s) when confronting a moral issue and to ask whose values, beliefs, and economic interests are at stake in the decision. Is there a moral basis or guide—an authority—for making decisions? Whose authority is more legitimate? Chapter 2 builds on these levels by explaining how to construct a stakeholder map that more specifically identifies interest groups at each of the levels discussed above.

A related set of three ethical business perspectives is offered in Figure 1-2.

These ethical perspectives also include the *person* and the *organization* and add a dimension referred to as the *system*. These levels are shown here because they distinguish among the domains of the national, political, economic, cultural, religious, and business "systems" in relationship to the person and the firm. When an individual is identifying or confronting a particular ethical dilemma, these perspectives force the decision maker to ask, "What are the values, customs, or mores of the *country*? Of the political and business system? Of my organization? What are my individual values? How congruent or incongruent are these ethical perspectives in deciding a course of action in a given moral dilemma?" For example when WGBH, a public Boston TV station, aired the controversial "docudrama" "Death of A Princess" in 1980, the Saudi Arabian government threatened to take action against the station and the government.

Figure 1-2   A Framework for Classifying Ethical Levels

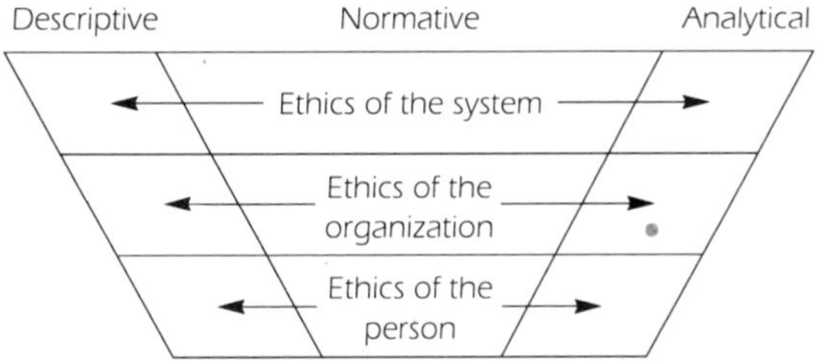

Source: John B. Matthews, Kenneth E. Goodpastor, and Laura L. Nash. *Policies and Persons: A Casebook in Business Ethics.* New York: McGraw-Hill, 1985, 509. Reproduced with permission of the publisher.

The film made public the Saudi government's execution of a Saudi princess and her alleged lover for their socially unacceptable relationship and love affair. The Saudi royal family believed that an international airing of the film misrepresented and violated their religious and cultural values. They viewed the showing of the Western docudrama to Western audiences as an embarrassment to them, their culture, and their privacy. The WGBH management claimed it was their right under the First Amendment to show the film. It was shown without drastic consequence but with loss of much international goodwill at the time (Matthews, Goodpastor, and Nash 1985, 392). When ethical levels conflict, as in this example, whose ethical imperatives should prevail in deciding a course of action? Whose policy and procedures should take precedence?

In Chapter 2, the "stakeholder approach" is presented as a method to assist decision makers in the identification of different interest groups who hold economic, political, social, and moral "stakes" or interests in particular business and ethical outcomes. In that chapter we will also discuss how to "rank" and evaluate the importance and effects of different economic, political, and moral stakes on a decision. International groups' stakes frequently enter into ethical conflict, as the above example illustrates, and when U.S. corporations operate across national borders, deciding whose stakes should prevail in a difficult moral dilemma is often not easy. As we discuss in Chapter 7, the American practice of **capitalism** differs from that of the Japanese. Recently, ethical conflicts have surfaced over these differences at the system level. We maintain that a stakeholder analysis can help the decision-making process by clarifying who the stakeholders are and what their stakes entail.

To this point we have defined business ethics and different levels of analysis for examining ethical dilemmas. Before discussing the nature of

Figure 1-3 Myths About Business Ethics

1. Ethics is a personal, individual affair.
2. Business and ethics don't mix.
3. Ethics is relative.
4. Good business means good ethics.

ethical reasoning, we turn to four common myths about business ethics, since these continually surface in discussions and arguments regarding this subject.

1.4 MYTHS ABOUT BUSINESS ETHICS

Not everyone agrees that ethics is a subject that is relevant or necessary in business education or dealings. Some say it is not. Although this book does not advocate or promote a particular ethical position or belief system, we argue that ethics is relevant to business transactions for reasons we will present throughout this book. However, certain myths persist about business ethics, which we discuss here and refute, along with other business ethicists.

A **myth** is "a belief given uncritical acceptance by the members of a group, especially in support of existing or traditional practices and institutions" (*Webster's* 1947). Myths regarding the relationship between business and ethics, in this discussion, do not represent truth but rather popular and unexamined notions. Four myths are presented (Figure 1-3) and refuted. Which myths have you accepted as unquestioned truth? Do you agree that the following myths are indeed myths?

First myth: "Ethics is a personal, individual affair, not a public or debatable matter."

This myth holds that individual ethics is based on personal or religious beliefs and that it is in the privacy of one's own conscience that one decides what is right and wrong. This myth has its notable advocates. For example, Milton Friedman (1970, 33), a well-known economist, views ethics as not suitable for business professionals to address or deal with seriously or professionally, since they are not equipped or trained to do so.

Although it is true that individuals must and do make moral choices in life, including business affairs, it is also true that individuals do not operate in a vacuum. Individual ethical choices are most often made and influenced in discussions, conversations, and group contexts. Individuals rely on organizations and groups for meaning, direction, and purpose. Moreover, individuals are integral parts of organizational cultures, which have norms, values, rules of conduct, and standards to govern what is acceptable and unacceptable. Therefore, to argue that ethics related to business issues is only or mainly a matter of personal or individual choice is to belittle the role organizational culture plays in shaping and influencing members' attitudes, perceptions, and behavior. One survey (Posner and Schmidt 1984) showed that 60% to 70% of managers in U.S. firms claimed they felt pressure to sacrifice their personal moral integrity for corporate goals. Another study (Carroll 1975) found that the lower a manager is in a hierarchy, the greater he or she perceives pressures toward unethical behavior. This evidence strongly suggests that business cultures and organizational pressures powerfully influence individual ethical choices and decisions. This is not to say that individual ethical decisions are not important; they are. The argument here is that business ethics is not primarily or only a private affair. It can also be a societal, organizational, and/or international affair, since business ethical decisions also involve these influential levels.

Second myth: "Business and ethics don't mix."

This popular myth (DeGeorge 1986) holds that business practices are basically amoral (not necessarily immoral), since businesses operate in a free market. This myth also asserts that management is based on scientific, not religious or ethical, principles.

Although this myth might have thrived in an earlier industrializing American society and even during pre-Vietnam 1960s America, the myth has been eroded over the past two decades given widespread accounts of bribery, kickbacks, unsafe products, oil spills, toxic dumping, air and water pollution, improper use of public funds, and the Savings and Loan scandals. The international and national basis for an infatuation with a purely scientific understanding of U.S. business practices, in particular, and of a value-free marketing system has been undermined by these events. As one saying goes "A little experience can inform a lot of theory."

The ethicist Richard DeGeorge (1986) has noted that the myth that business is amoral is a myth because this notion ignores the fact that business involves all of us. It is a human activity, not simply a scientific one, and as such can be evaluated from a moral perspective. If everyone in business acted amorally or immorally, as a pseudoscientific notion of business would suggest, businesses would collapse. Employees would steal from employers; employers would fire employees at will; contractors would openly violate obligations; chaos would prevail. DeGeorge also noted that business and society share the same American values: rugged individualism in a free-enterprise system, pragmatism over abstraction, freedom, and independence. It is when business practices violate these American values that society and the public are threatened or harmed.

Finally, the belief that businesses operate in "free markets" is debatable (Velasquez 1988). While the value or desirability of the concept and principles of a "free market" is not in question, practices of certain firms in free markets are. At issue are the unjust methods of accumulation and noncompetitive uses of wealth and power in the formation of monopolies and oligopolies (that is, small numbers of firms dominating the rules and transactions of certain markets). The breakup of AT&T is an example of how one powerful conglomerate could dominate and control the market. The U.S. market environment can best be characterized as a "mixed economy" based on, but not limited to or explainable only by, free-market mechanisms. Mixed economies rely on government policies and laws to control for deficiencies and inequalities. For example, protective laws are still required, such as those governing minimum wage, antitrust, layoffs from plant closings, and instances of labor exploitation. In such mixed economies where injustices thrive, ethics is a viable and lively topic.

Third myth: "Ethics in business is relative."

This is one of the more popular myths that holds that there is no right or wrong way of believing or acting. Right and wrong are in the eyes of the beholder.

There is some truth to the claim that ethics is not based solely on absolutes. However, to argue that all ethics is relative contradicts everyday experience. For example, the view that because a person or society believes something to be right makes it right is problematic when examined. As Hoffman and Moore (1990, 5–7) argued, many societies believed in and practiced slavery; however, in most contemporary individuals' experiences, slavery is historically and morally wrong. When these individuals and firms do business in societies that promote slavery, does that mean that the individuals and firms must also condone and practice slavery? Also, an employee may steadfastly believe that working over-time violates her beliefs in holding to an 8-hour day. This may be true for her, but it may harm the workgroup's and company's goals and needs in specific instances. Should she quit whenever a few weeks of overtime are required? The simple logic of relativism, as we discuss again in Chapter 3, gets complicated when seen in daily experience. Also, if ethical relativism were carried to its logical extreme, no one could argue or disagree with anyone about moral issues, since each per-son's values would be right and true for him or her. Ultimately, this logic would state that there is no right or wrong apart from an individual's or society's principles. How could interaction, communication, transac-tions, and negotiations be completed if ethical relativism were carried to its limit?

Fourth myth: "Good business means good ethics."

The reasoning here (Stone, 1975) is that executives and firms that main-tain a good corporate image, practice fair and equitable dealings with customers and employees, and earn profits by legitimate, legal means are de facto ethical. Such firms, therefore, would not have to be con-cerned explicitly with ethics in the workplace. Just do a hard, fair day's work, and that has its own moral goodness and rewards.

The faulty reasoning underlying this logic is that ethics does not provide solutions to technical business problems in marketing, account-ing, finance, research and development, and the like. Moreover, as Rogene Buchholz (1989, 28) argued, there is no correlation between being "good" and being successful materially.

Lisa Newton (1986, 249) and Buchholz (1989, 25) also argue that "excellent" companies and corporate cultures have created and pursued values and concern for people in the workplace that exceed the profit motive. Excellence seems to be related more to customer service, to main-tenance of meaningful public and employee relationships, and to corpo-rate integrity than just to the profit motive. The point is that ethics is not something value-added to business operations; it is integral, necessary, and central to managing successfully. A more accurate logic from busi-ness experience would suggest that "good ethics means good business." This is more in line with observations from successful companies that are ethical first and also profitable.

Finally, Michael Hoffman and Jennifer Moore (1990, 13) asked, "What happens, then, if what should be ethically done is not the best thing for business? What happens when good ethics is not good business?" They continued:

> The ethical thing to do may not always be in the best interests of the firm.
> . . . We should promote business ethics, not because good ethics is good
> business, but because we are morally required to adopt the moral point of
> view in all our dealings with other people—and business is no exception.
> In business, as in all other human endeavors, we must be prepared to pay
> the costs of ethical behavior. The costs may sometimes seem high, but that
> is the risk we take in valuing and preserving our integrity.

As we have indicated, there are many logical problems in these myths about business ethics. In many instances, these myths hold simplistic and even unrealistic notions about ethics in business dealings. In the following sections, we continue the discussion about the nature of business ethics by exploring two questions: (1) "Why use ethical reasoning in business?" and (2) "What is the nature of ethical reasoning?"

1.5 WHY USE ETHICAL REASONING IN BUSINESS?

Ethical reasoning is required in business for at least three major reasons: (1) Many times, laws are insufficient and do not cover all aspects or "gray areas" of a problem (Stone 1975). For example, should the Manville Corporation have paid millions to asbestos claimants if that would have bankrupted the firm? Or, should that company (as it did) have legally declared bankruptcy and faced ethical reaction from the media and the public? Many legal actions may be unethical and cause pain and physical or economic harm to others. What rules or guidelines can people turn to in these situations when laws are not enough? (2) Free-market and regulated-market mechanisms do not effectively inform owners and managers about how to respond to complex crises that have far-reaching ethical consequences; for example, should companies, as American Cyanamid did in the late 1970s, legally prohibit pregnant women from working in toxic areas to protect their unborn fetuses, even though the firm's policy had the effect of pressuring several women into unemployment and choosing sterilization? Later in the 1980s, the firm faced unanticipated discrimination charges and lawsuits from several interest groups. In 1991, the Supreme Court ruled in a 6–3 vote that such "fetal protection" policies are a form of sex bias that is prohibited by civil rights law. American Cyanamid may have acted legally in the 1970s, but did it act ethically? What reasoning and guidelines help us answer questions when or before enacted laws provide authoritative guidelines?

(3) A third argument holds that ethical reasoning *is* necessary because complex moral problems require "an intuitive or learned understanding and concern for fairness, justice, due process to people, groups and communities" (Carroll 1989). Company policies and procedures are limited in scope and detail in covering human, environmental, and social costs of doing business. On what grounds or reasoning did the U.S. Congress vote to authorize President Bush to use his authority to declare war on Iraq? Were ethics and moral principles involved? The point here is that law, formal policy, and written procedures may not always be sufficient in certain situations to enable those who must act to do so with clear, unquestionable authority. Ethics plays a role in business because laws are often absent or insufficient to guide morally complex decisions.

The Nature of Ethical Reasoning in Business

In addition to the reasons discussed above, LaRue Hosmer* offered five major characteristics of ethical problems that also show the complexity of managerial ethics and point out the nature of ethical reasoning:

1. **Most ethical decisions have extended consequences.** Managerial decisions, actions, and results have consequences whose effects extend beyond their control and organization into society. For example, bribes change governmental processes. Pollution affects environmental health. The consequences and effects should be considered before decisions are made.

2. **Most ethical decisions have multiple alternatives.** Simple "yes" or "no" choices do not adequately characterize the many alternatives that exist and that should be considered in such decisions as "Should a manager pay a bribe? Should a factory pollute the air?"

3. **Most ethical decisions have mixed outcomes.** As in the second point, outcomes and alternatives are not unambiguous; they have social benefits and costs as well as financial revenues and expenses associated with the ethical choices.

4. **Most ethical decisions have uncertain consequences.** Unanticipated and unknown consequences can follow ethical choices.

5. **Most ethical decisions have personal implications.** Such decisions can affect the lives and careers of the decision makers. Individual costs and benefits, in addition to financial and social ones, are associated with most alternatives in ethical decisions.

*Adapted from LaRue Tone Hosmer. *The Ethics of Management.* 2nd ed. Homewood, IL: Richard D. Irwin, 1991, 13–15. Used with permission of the publisher.

Hosmer's approach to using ethical reasoning in moral dilemmas is to (1) consider different alternatives to the problem, (2) do a legal analysis, and (3) think through a moral analysis, using several ethical principles that we discuss in Chapter 3.

George Steiner and John Steiner* list 10 reasons why moral problems are often complex and difficult and require reasoning from ethical principles:

1. **Managers confront a distinction between facts and values when making ethical decisions.** Facts are statements about what is; values are views individuals hold independently from facts. A full description of the facts in business problems does not automatically give a just answer.

2. **Good and evil exist simultaneously, interlocked.** The availability of Paraquat, a chemical manufactured by Imperial Chemical Industries in England and Chevron Chemical Company in America, increases crop yield but is toxic to humans and has led to illnesses and deaths in less developed countries. Should firms export this product to countries, even if some countries know the effects but still request the product?

3. **Knowledge of consequences is limited.** Results that owners and managers sometimes intend to happen often have very different effects on employees and customers. Facts often do not justify negative consequences of intended actions.

4. **The existence of multiple corporate constituencies exposes management to competing and conflicting ethical claims.** Tobacco farmers give ethical priority to the tobacco economy in the South, as do stockholders. The Surgeon General's office and the medical establishment argue against harmful effects of smoking. Managers in this industry must weigh these pros and cons in doing business.

5. **Multiple constituencies often use conflicting ethical arguments to justify their claims.** Who is right and who is wrong? Managers must be able to recognize conflicting premises and assumptions in moral arguments. In Niagara Falls, the Love Canal Homeowners Association charged Hooker Chemical Corporation with disregard for the health of residents near the canal because, during the 1940s, 22,000 tons of highly toxic, carcino-

*Adapted from George Steiner and John Steiner. *Business, Government, and Society.* 5th ed. New York: Random House, 1988, 373–376. Used with permission of McGraw-Hill Publishing Company.

genic chemical wastes were dumped. Birth defects, miscarriages, and nerve and respiratory illnesses resulted. Hooker's defense was that the country needed the chemicals. In 1990, health officials declared the area once again inhabitable, and residents are moving back to houses once condemned. Who is to be believed and on what grounds?

6. **Ethical standards change over history.** In the 1950s, U.S. firms made payoffs to foreign officials; with the 1977 passage of the Foreign Corrupt Practices Act, bribes and payoffs are illegal. In certain Arab, Asian, African, and Latin American countries, payoffs are still part of doing business. Ethically correct conduct is an elusive goal, and applying ethical standards is an art.

7. **Human reasoning is imperfect.** Well-intentioned managers make mistakes in their ethical judgment. When faced with the temptation for profit performance, honest managers may compromise their standards, as did Robert Beasley at Firestone Tire and Rubber Company when he embezzled over $500,000 from a $12.6 million slush fund he managed. He was caught by the IRS and served 4 years in jail.

8. **Ethical standards and principles are not always adequate in resolving conflicts.** No principles can replace human judgment in very complex cases.

9. **Twentieth-century [and we add twenty-first–century] managers are faced with new ethical problems that exceed traditional concerns such as honesty, charity, and modesty.** Now, managers must weigh and balance human life against economic factors in decisions. How should cancer studies that show that workers and residents exposed to plant emissions risk illness be balanced against costs of emission regulation, inflationary impact, capital investment reduction, and loss of jobs and economic benefits from closed plants?

10. **Managers in large organizations must now deal with ethical complexities.** These include moral problems such as organizational versus public interest loyalty, preferential hiring of certain classifications of individuals, and peaked performance of individuals before retirement.

Given the complexity of most ethical decisions, it is clear that simple "yes" and "no" answers are insufficient. Ethical reasoning should, therefore, help us sort out fact from fiction, assumptions and inferences, alternatives and options, and benefit and cost alternatives to help us make more informed, responsible moral decisions.

1.6 **CAN BUSINESS ETHICS BE TAUGHT AND TRAINED?**

Given the complexity and often vague nature of ethical problems and moral dilemmas, the question arises, "Can business ethics, then, be taught or instructed?" This ongoing debated question has no final answer. Studies continue to address the issue. One study, for example, that surveyed 125 graduate and undergraduate students in a business ethics course at the beginning of a semester showed that students did not reorder their *priorities* at the end of the semester on the importance of 10 social issues, but they did *change the degree of importance* they placed on the majority of the issues surveyed (Stead and Miller 1988). What, if any, value can be gained through teaching and training ethical principles and their uses in business?

We begin this discussion by stating what business ethics courses *cannot* or should not, in our judgment, do. Ethics courses should not advocate a single set of rules to play by or offer one best or only solution to specific ethical problems. There may, given the facts and circumstances of situations, be more and less desirable courses of action to take. Decisions will depend on facts, inferences, and rigorous, logical ethical reasoning. Neither should ethics courses or training sessions promise "superior" or absolute ways of thinking and behaving in situations. Rigorous, informed, and conscientious ethical analysis does not mean the best or only way to reason moral problems.

Ethics courses and training *can* do the following (Jones 1988–1989):

- Provide people with rationales, ideas, and vocabulary to help them participate effectively in the process of ethical decision making
- Help people "make sense" of their environments by "abstracting" and selecting ethical priorities
- Provide intellectual weapons to do battle with advocates of economic fundamentalism and those who violate ethical standards
- Enable employees to act as alarm systems for company practices that will not pass society's ethical tests
- Enhance conscientiousness and sensitivity to moral issues and commitment to finding moral solutions
- Enhance moral reflectiveness and strengthen moral courage
- Increase the ability of people to become morally autonomous ethical dissenters, and the conscience of a group
- Improve the moral climate of the firm by providing ethical concepts and tools to use for creating ethics codes and social audits

Other scholars argue that ethical training can add **value** to the moral environment of a firm and to relationships in the workplace in the following ways (Hanson 1987):

- Finding a match between an employee's and employer's values
- Managing the pushback point where one's values are tested by peers, subordinates, and superiors
- Handling an unethical directive from one's boss
- Coping with a performance system that encourages cutting ethical corners

Teaching and training business ethics, then, does not promise to provide answers to complex moral dilemmas, but thoughtful and resourceful business ethics educators can facilitate the development of *awareness* of what is and is not ethical; help individuals and groups realize that their ethical tolerance and decision-making styles decrease unethical blindspots; and enhance a curiosity and concern to discuss moral problems openly in the workplace. Figure 1-4 illustrates how this book will implement our plan of approach.

Before summarizing this chapter, we briefly summarize Kohlberg's six stages of moral development to illustrate a major theory in this field.

Stages of Moral Development

Lawrence Kohlberg's (1973) three levels with six stages of moral development offers a guide that can be used to observe our (and others') level of moral maturity, especially as we engage in different organizational transactions. Whether, and to what extent, ethical education and training contribute to one's moral development in later years is not known. Most individuals in Kohlberg's 20-year study reached stages 4 and 5 by adulthood. Only a few attained the sixth stage. The three levels and six stages include:

Level 1: Preconventional level (self-orientation)

Stage 1: Punishment avoidance: Avoiding punishment by not breaking rules. There is little awareness of others' needs.

Stage 2: Reward seeking: Acting to receive rewards for self. There is awareness of others' needs, but not of right and wrong as abstract concepts.

Figure 1-4 Plan of the Book

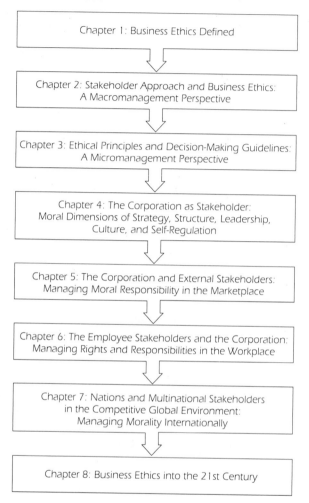

Chapter 1: Business Ethics Defined

Chapter 2: Stakeholder Approach and Business Ethics:
A Macromanagement Perspective

Chapter 3: Ethical Principles and Decision-Making Guidelines:
A Micromanagement Perspective

Chapter 4: The Corporation as Stakeholder:
Moral Dimensions of Strategy, Structure, Leadership,
Culture, and Self-Regulation

Chapter 5: The Corporation and External Stakeholders:
Managing Moral Responsibility in the Marketplace

Chapter 6: The Employee Stakeholders and the Corporation:
Managing Rights and Responsibilities in the Workplace

Chapter 7: Nations and Multinational Stakeholders
in the Competitive Global Environment:
Managing Morality Internationally

Chapter 8: Business Ethics into the 21st Century

Level 2: Conventional level (others orientation)

Stage 3: Good person: Acting "right" to be a "good person" and to be accepted by family and friends, not to fulfill any moral ideal.

Stage 4: Law and order: Acting "right" to comply with law and order and norms in societal institutions.

Level 3: Postconventional, autonomous, or principles level (universal, humankind orientation)

> Stage 5: Social contract: Acting "right" to reach consensus by due process and agreement. Person is aware of relativity of values and tolerates differing views.

> Stage 6: Universal ethical principles: Acting "right" according to universal, abstract principles of justice, rights. Person reasons and uses conscience and moral rules to guide actions.

Refer to these stages when attempting to resolve a moral conflict at work or in other settings. Observe and identify at which level and stage the individuals or groups are. At which level and stage are the arguments of those resolving a moral dilemma?

SUMMARY

Business ethics deals with what is "right and wrong" in business decisions, behavior, and policies. Business ethics provides principles and guidelines that assist in making informed choices to balance economic interests and social responsibilities.

Business ethics operates at several levels: the individual, the organizational, the association, the societal, and the international. These levels illustrate the complexity and linkages of ethical decision making in business transactions. This chapter introduces the stakeholder approach to ethical decision making, which identifies constituencies and their claims at these different levels of interaction in business environments.

Stakeholders include corporations, managers, individuals, groups, societal institutions, and nations. The stakeholder approach provides a means for mapping complicated relationships between the focal and other stakeholders, a means of identifying strategies of each stakeholder, and a means for assessing moral responsibility of the constituencies.

Four myths often held about business ethics are discussed. Each myth is illustrated and refuted.

Ethical reasoning in business is discussed with steps provided to guide decision making. Three reasons why ethical reasoning is necessary in business include the following: First, laws are often insufficient and do not cover all aspects or "gray areas" of a problem; second, free-market and regulated-market mechanisms do not effectively inform owners and managers about how to respond to complex crises that have far-reaching ethical consequences; and, third, complex moral problems require an intuitive or learned understanding and concern for fairness, justice, and due process to people, groups and communities. Ethical reasoning helps individuals sort through conflicting opinions and information in order to solve moral dilemmas.

Kohlberg's three levels and six stages of moral development are presented and discussed as a means to assist in ethical decision making by identifying the basis underlying moral arguments and motivations.

Ethical education and training can be useful in developing a broader awareness of the motivations and consequences of our decisions. Business ethics does not, however, provide superior or universally correct solutions to morally complex dilemmas. Principles and guidelines are provided that—with case analysis, role playing, and group discussion—can enhance insight and self-confidence in resolving moral dilemmas in which there often are two right (or wrong) solutions.

Questions

1. Why is there a renewed interest in business ethics?
2. What are three outstanding ethical issues facing businesses today?
3. What unethical practices occur most frequently in business?
4. Identify benefits for using the stakeholder approach in ethical decision making.
5. Which, if any, of the four myths in the chapter do you not accept as a myth?
6. Identify three reasons for using ethical reasoning in business situations.
7. Is the law sufficient to help managers/employees solve ethical dilemmas? Explain.
8. What are some important distinctive characteristics of ethical problems?
9. Briefly describe three or four of the benefits that can be gained through ethics courses and training.

Exercises

1. Invent and state your own definition of "business ethics." Do you believe that ethics is an important factor in business today? If you were the CEO of a corporation, how would you communicate your perspective on the importance of ethics to your employees, customers, and other stakeholder groups?

2. Conduct your own small survey of five people regarding their opinions of the importance of unethical practices in businesses today. Is more or less importance given by your interviewees to economic performance *or* to socially responsible behavior? Summarize your results.

3. You are giving a speech at a Rotary International meeting. You are asked to give an introduction to the members on business ethics. Give an outline of your speech.

4. Review Kohlberg's levels and stages of moral development. After careful consideration, briefly explain which stage predominantly, or characteristically, defines your ethical positions and arguments. Explain. Has this stage influenced a recent decision you have made or action you have taken? Explain.

5. You are applying to a prestigious business school. The application requires you to describe an ethical dilemma in your history and how you handled it. Describe the dilemma.

References and Suggested Readings

Baumann, Mary. "Ethics in Business." *USA Today* (1987). The original source for the statistics is the Conference Board.

Bowie, Norman, and Ronald Duska. *Business Ethics*. 2d ed. Englewood Cliffs, N.J.: Prentice-Hall, 1991.

Buchholz, Rogene. *Fundamental Concepts and Problems in Business Ethics*. Englewood Cliffs, N.J.: Prentice-Hall, 1989.

Carroll, Archie. "Managerial Ethics: A Post-Watergate View" *Business Horizons* (April 1975): 75–80.

————. *Business and Society: Ethics and Stakeholder Management*. Cincinnati: South-Western, 1989.

DeGeorge, Richard. *Business Ethics*. 2d ed. New York: Macmillan, 1986.

Freeman, R. E., and D. Gilbert, Jr. *Corporate Strategy and the Search for Ethics*. Englewood Cliffs, N.J.: Prentice-Hall, 1988.

Friedman, Milton. "The Social Responsibility of Business Is to Increase Its Profits." *New York Times Magazine* (September 13, 1970): 33.

Gordon, Judith, et al. *Management and Organizational Behavior*. Boston: Allyn & Bacon, 1990.

Hanson, Kirk O. "What Good Are Ethics Courses?" *Across the Board* (September 1987): 10–11.

Hoffman, Dr. Michael, and Dr. Robert Frederick. Unpublished summary of survey. Available upon request from Bentley College Center for Business Ethics. 1989–1990.

Hoffman, Michael, and Jennifer Moore. *Business Ethics: Readings and Cases in Corporate Morality*. 2d ed. New York: McGraw-Hill, 1990.

Hosmer, LaRue. "Managerial Responsibilities on the Micro Level." *Business Horizons* (July-August 1991): 49–55.

————. *The Ethics of Management*. Illinois: Irwin, 1987.

Jones, Thomas. "Ethics Education in Business: Theoretical Considerations." *The Organizational Behavior Teaching Review* XIII, no. 4 (1988–1989): 1–18.

Kanter, Elizabeth Ross. *When Giants Learn to Dance.* New York: Simon & Schuster, 1989.

Kohlberg, Lawrence. "State and Sequence: The Cognitive Developmental Approach to Socialization." In *Handbook of Socialization Theory and Research,* edited by D. A. Gosline, Chicago: Rand-McNally, 1969.

———. "The Claim to Moral Adequacy of a Highest Stage of Moral Judgement." *The Journal of Philosophy* LXX (1973): 630–646.

Matthews, John, Kenneth E. Goodpastor, and Laura L. Nash. *Policies and Persons: A Casebook in Business Ethics.* New York: McGraw-Hill, 1985.

Miles, Robert. *Managing the Corporate Social Environment: A Grounded Theory.* Englewood Cliffs, N.J.: Prentice-Hall, 1987.

Nash, Laura. *Good Intentions Aside, A Manager's Guide to Resolving Ethical Problems.* Boston: Harvard Business School Press, 1990.

Newton, Lisa. "The Internal Morality of the Corporation." *Journal of Business Ethics* (1986): 249.

Posner, Barry, and Warren Schmidt. "Values and the American Manager: An Update." *California Management Review* (Spring 1984): 202–216.

Semke, Ron. "Ethics Training: Can We Really Teach People Right from Wrong?" *Training HRD* (May 1977).

Sethi, S., Nobuaki Namiki, and Carl Swanson. *The False Promise of the Japanese Miracle.* Boston: Pitman, 1984.

Stead, Bette, and J. Miller. "Can Social Awareness Be Decreased Through Business School Curriculum?" *Journal of Business Ethics* 7, no. 7 (July 1988).

Steiner, George, and John Steiner. *Business, Government, and Society: A Managerial Perspective.* 5th and 6th eds. New York: Random House, 1988 and 1991.

Stone, C. D. *Where the Law Ends.* New York: Harper & Row, 1975.

Velasquez, Manuel. *Business Ethics, Concepts and Cases.* 2d and 3d eds. Englewood Cliffs, N.J.: Prentice-Hall, 1988 and 1992.

The Wall Street Journal, "Ethics are lacking in business" (August 21, 1990): A1.

Webster's Third New International Dictionary of the English Language Unabridged. Vol. II. Chicago: Encyclopedia Britannica, Inc., 1971.

2

A Stakeholder Approach and Business Ethics

"A year after the *Exxon Valdez* ripped open its bottom on Bligh Reef [off the Alaskan coast] and dumped 11 million gallons of crude oil, the nation's worst oil spill is not over. . . . Like major spills in the past, this unnatural disaster sparked a frenzy of reactions: congressional hearings, state and federal legislative proposals for new preventive measures, dozens of studies and innumerable lawsuits" (Dumanoski 1990). The grounding of the tanker on March 24, 1989, spread oil over more than 700 miles. "The disaster fouled waters and shorelines . . . damaging one of the world's major fisheries and killing more than 36,000 migratory birds including at least 100 bald eagles" (Rawkins 1990). A grand jury indicted Exxon in February 1990. At that time the firm faced fines totaling over $600 million if convicted on the felony counts. More than 150 lawsuits and 30,000 damage claims were reportedly filed against Exxon, and most were not settled by July 1991. The charge that the captain of the *Valdez,* Joseph Hazelwood, had a blood–alcohol content above 0.04 % was dropped, but he was convicted of negligently discharging oil and ordered to pay $50,000 restitution to the state of Alaska and serve 1,000 hours cleaning up the beaches. Exxon executives and stockholders have been embroiled with courts, environmental groups, the media, and public groups over the crisis. Exxon has paid $300 million in damages to 10,000 commercial fishermen, business owners, and native Alaskan villages. (In May 1991, Exxon's first-quarter profits were reported at $2.24 billion.)

2.1 WHY A STAKEHOLDER APPROACH TO BUSINESS ETHICS?

The *Exxon Valdez* incident illustrates the magnitude of problems and issues a large corporation faces in a crisis; this situation provides a window into the combined economic, political, environmental, and moral dimensions of interactions between a corporation and its stakeholders. Moreover, an incident that begins as an industrial problem can quickly escalate to societal and even international proportions. What method(s) can best be used to understand and evaluate who is right, who is wrong, and what costs must be incurred by whom in resolving issues of justice, rights, and fairness in such complex situations? "Rightness" and "wrongness" are not always easy to determine in moral dilemmas. As Abraham Lincoln stated, "The true role, in determining to embrace or reject anything . . . is not whether it have any evil . . . in it, but whether it have more evil than of good. . . . There are few things wholly evil or wholly good."

The **stakeholder approach** is an analytical way of observing and explaining how different constituencies are affected and affect business decisions and actions. The stakeholder approach as applied to the moral management of organizational stakeholders is based on the view that profit maximization is constrained by justice, that regard for individual rights should be extended to all constituencies of business that have a stake in the affairs of business (Bowie and Duska 1991).

Underlying the stakeholder approach is the ethical imperative that businesses are mandated in their fiduciary relationships to their stockholders and shareholders to act in the best interests and for the benefit of their customers, employees, suppliers, and stockholders and to respect and fulfill these stakeholders' rights (Evan and Freeman 1988). In this chapter, we use the stakeholder approach as a tool for analyzing complex ethical dilemmas that call for moral (as well as political and economic) judgment, as the *Exxon Valdez* case exemplifies. In Chapter 3, we present ethical decision-making principles and criteria that stakeholders can use to make choices and that observers can apply to examine decisions various stakeholders made or can make.

The stakeholder approach, then, is a method for mapping and managing the complex moral relationships between a corporation's strategic activities and those who affect and are affected by such actions (Freeman 1984). Why use a stakeholder approach? The stakeholder approach is a response to the growth and complexity of the modern corporation and its influence on the environment, the economy, and the public. A more familiar way of understanding corporations is a "stockholder" approach that focuses on financial and economic relationships; however, a stakeholder approach includes moral, political, ecological, and human welfare interests as well as economic factors. Both approaches inform management about the strategic and ethical status and direction of a company, division, or unit.

In this chapter, we focus on the stakeholder approach as a means of studying managers' social and moral responsibility strategies, actions, and outcomes toward other stakeholders. The stakeholder approach is a pragmatic way of understanding multiple, competing political, economic, and moral claims of a host of constituencies. The aim here is to familiarize you with the framework so that you can apply it in the classroom and in actual news-breaking events that appear in press and in the media. Even though you may not be an executive or manager, the framework can enable you to see and understand complex corporate dealings, events, and crises in the immediate environment more clearly. And, as will be discussed later in the chapter, the stakeholder analysis can be used in smaller units and groups within a company. In fact, individuals are also stakeholders in organizations. While this chapter focuses on upper-level and functional area managers as stakeholders who formulate and direct corporate strategy, in Chapters 3 and 5, we will discuss the individual employee and manager as stakeholders. Our first task is to understand the logic and use of the stakeholder approach in general. We will then discuss how this approach can be used in the moral management of organizational stakeholders, since this is the focus of this book. Chapter 3 provides ethical principles that you can use to evaluate the moral criteria of strategies managers use in responding to different stakeholders.

In an earlier industrial age, when business owners were concerned more with basic production relationships, there was less need for a framework to understand a company's dealings with a limited number of suppliers and customers. In the present technological and information age, corporate activities affect the public in wide-ranging ways. Corporate activities are under the scrutiny of the media, lobbying groups, and sophisticated consumers who can respond legally, morally, and economically to enterprises. The example of Exxon's oil spill illustrates how that firm's executives had to address a host of groups—and lawsuits—who had a wide range of "stakes" (that is, interests) in how the company handled the incident. The number of constituencies and stakeholders Exxon had to address reflects the complexity of the business environment in the 20th century.

The *Exxon Valdez* incident also shows that in a pluralistic, democratic society, power is diffused across groups, individuals, organizations, and institutions (Carroll 1989, 6, 7). There is, in fact, no one central or absolute source of authority to direct, unify, or evaluate competing interests between a company and its stakeholders, especially in a democratic, pluralistic, and capitalist society such as the United States. The government and legal systems often play roles in this process, but more often than not these roles operate after the fact. In an open-market system, special interests, lobbyists, and the media are significant forces that influence corporate decisions. In such a complex pluralistic society, corporate leaders and those who strive to understand and monitor corporate activities need a method that helps them understand and "keep score" with each of their stakeholder's strategies and power relationships in crises and events that affect the public and the business. The stakeholder analysis is one approach that is used for these purposes. Just as important, it is a method that can be used to identify the moral reasoning of managers and their stakeholders. Stakeholder welfare, rights, and responsibilities can be identified and monitored in given situations. Chapter 5 also presents "issues management" and "crises management" frameworks that can be used with the stakeholder analysis.

2.2 **STAKEHOLDER ANALYSIS DEFINED**

The **stakeholder analysis** is a framework that enables users to map and then manage corporate relationships (present and potential) with groups who affect and are affected by the corporation's policies and actions. A stakeholder analysis does not have to result from a crisis situation. It can be used as a planning method to anticipate actions and reactions over events and policy outcomes. As will be explained later, a stakeholder analysis is not limited in its use to large enterprises. One goal of a stakeholder analysis from a firm's perspective is to create "win–win" situations for itself and its stakeholder relationships. By "win–win" we mean moral decisions that are profitable for all constituencies within the constraints of justice, fairness, and economic considerations. In reality, this does not always happen.

Stakeholder Analysis: A Strategic and Moral Management Function

Stakeholder analysis is part of the strategic management function of a firm. The analysis can be used for a number of purposes: here, we emphasize the use of stakeholder analysis for identifying and managing social responsibility roles and relationships between a company and its constituents in a given or projected situation in which exchanges between the firm and external groups are concerned. As in the *Exxon Valdez* incident, using a stakeholder analysis forces and opens economic and political relationships into wider legal, moral and social responsibility issues (and vice versa). For example, the following questions regarding the *Valdez* crisis can be posed: What effect on the judicial system will this extended case have? Why was the initial settlement overturned? What are the limits of the tort system in the larger political system?*

The analysis usually begins with economic, political, or ecological issues and then evolves into social responsibility and ethical decisions when questions of human and social costs and benefits, equity, and justice are raised.

Stakes

A **stake** is any interest, share, or claim a group or individual has in the outcome of a corporation's policies, procedures, or actions toward others.

*Special thanks to Lisa Newton for suggesting these questions in an early review of the manuscript.

Stakes and claims can be based on legal, economic, social, moral, technological, ecological, political, or power interests (Carroll 1989, 57; Weiss 1986). Stakes of stakeholders are not always obvious or explicit. The physical health of a community may, for example, be at stake when a corporation decides to empty toxic waste near residential sites. Stakes—actual and potential—must be identified in the analysis.

There are also stakes that are present, past, and future oriented. For example, stakeholders may seek compensation over a firm's past actions, as is the case with claimants whose lawyers recently argued that certain airlines owed their clients monetary compensation after having threatened their emotional stability when pilots announced impending disaster (engine failure) that, subsequently, did not occur. Stakeholders, on the other hand, may seek future claims; that is, they may seek injunctions against firms announcing plans to drill oil or build nuclear plants in designated areas.

Stakeholders

A **stakeholder** is "any individual or group who can affect or is affected by the actions, decisions, policies, practices, or goals of the organization" (Freeman 1984, 25). The **primary stakeholders** of a firm include its owners, customers, employees, and suppliers. Also of primary importance to a firm's survival are its stockholders and board of directors. The chief executive officer (CEO) and other top-level executives can be stakeholders, but in the stakeholder analysis, they are generally considered to be actors and representatives of the firm. **Secondary stakeholders** include all other interested groups such as the media, consumers, lobbyists, courts, governments, competitors, the public, and society. In the *Exxon Valdez* oil spill, stockholders also had an ecological stake in the economic consequences of how lawsuits were settled against the company; local communities had a stake in their shoreline and wildlife; local, state, and federal courts had stakes in the legality, liability, and future rulings on this and future such incidents; local fishermen had a stake in their economic survival; Congress had stakes in serving the competing interests of oil company lobbyists as well as the public good.

Stakeholders also have stakeholders. For example, Exxon gas station operators had to face angry clients and neighbors who perceived the company as negligent and unconcerned about the environment. Identifying and managing stakeholders requires understanding the involved groups' motivations and the interests of all stakeholders. By acknowledging the stakeholders of the stakeholders, we can understand

Figure 2-1 The Importance of Various Organizational Stakeholders to Managers*

	SUPERVISORY MANAGERS	MIDDLE MANAGERS	EXECUTIVE MANAGERS
Customers	5.57	6.10	6.40
Myself	6.28	6.29	6.28
Subordinates	6.06	6.30	6.14
Employees	5.93	6.11	6.01
Boss(es)	5.72	5.92	5.82
Co-Workers	5.87	5.82	5.81
Colleagues	5.66	5.78	5.75
Managers	5.26	5.56	5.75
Owners	4.07	4.51	5.30
General Public	4.38	4.49	4.52
Stockholders	3.35	3.79	4.51
Elected Public Officials	3.81	3.54	3.79
Government Bureaucrats	3.09	2.05	2.90

*Scale of 1 to 7 (1=lowest; 7=highest).

Source: Barry Z. Posner, and Warren H. Schmidt. "Values and the American Manager: An Update." *California Management Review* 26, no. 2 (Spring 1984). Copyright 1984 by The Regents of the University of California. Reproduced with permission of The Regents.

the sources of influence and power of the major interest groups in our analysis.

Who Are the Most Important Stakeholders?

Who are the most important stakeholders for executive, middle-level, and supervisory managers in America? Figure 2-1 shows the results from a study that surveyed over 6,000 managers and asked them to rank whom they considered most important.

Supervisory managers saw themselves as most important, followed by subordinates, employees, and coworkers. Stockholders ranked near the bottom. *Middle managers*, similarly, saw themselves and subordinates as the most important stakeholders, followed by employees and customers. This group also ranked stockholders near the bottom. *Executive managers* ranked customers first and themselves second, followed by employees. The authors of the survey concluded, "The stereotype of managers as running the nation's corporations for the primary benefit of their stockholders does not seem to be borne out by the data" (Posner and Schmidt 1984, 207). It cannot be concluded from these results that managers see themselves as more important than the survival of their company or its profits. These results do suggest, however, that profit may not be the only concern of managers and that other significant stakeholders can influence profitability (Steiner and Steiner 1988).

Similarly, in a *Wall Street Journal* article, "How Do You Spell Success? Executives Dismiss Money As a Measure," a Harrison Conference Services survey reported that executives most wanted *respect* from bosses, peers, and subordinates. The article quoted executives who stated "support for a charitable foundation," "job satisfaction," "self-respect," and "satisfying stockholders" as other important indicators of success.

Again, profit is important and necessary, but perhaps is not always the only or the most important indicator of success for executives. There also seems to be a belief that money is a result—not necessarily a primary cause—of success. These findings taken together strongly suggest that a "stakeholder" approach, in addition to a "stockholder" approach, is essential for managing corporate policy and relationships.

2.3 HOW TO EXECUTE A STAKEHOLDER ANALYSIS

Assume you are the CEO working with your top managers in a firm that has just been involved in a major controversy of international proportion. The media, some consumer groups, and several major customers have called you. You want to get a handle on the situation without reverting to unnecessary "fire-fighting" management methods. A couple of your trusted staff members have advised you to adopt a planning approach quickly, while responding to immediate concerns, in order to understand the "who, what, where, when, and why" of the situation before jumping to many hasty "hows." Your senior strategic planner suggests you lead and participate in a stakeholder analysis. What is the next step?

The stakeholder analysis is a series of steps aimed at:

1. Mapping stakeholder relationships
2. Mapping stakeholder coalitions
3. Assessing the nature of each stakeholder's interest
4. Assessing the nature of each stakeholder's power
5. Constructing a matrix of stakeholder moral responsibilities
6. Developing specific strategies and tactics
7. Monitoring shifting coalitions (Frederick et al. 1988)

Figure 2-2   *Sample Questions for "Stakeholder Review"*

---

1. Who are our stakeholders currently?
2. Who are our potential stakeholders?
3. How does each stakeholder affect us?
4. How do we affect each stakeholder?
5. For each division and business, who are the stakeholders, etc.?
6. What assumptions does our current strategy make about each important stakeholder (at each level)?
7. What are the current "environmental variables" that affect us and our stakeholders [inflation, GNP, prime rate, confidence in business (from polls), corporate identity, media image, and so on]?
8. How do we measure each of these variables and their impact on us and our stakeholders?
9. How do we keep score with our stakeholders?

Source: R. Edward Freeman. *Strategic Management: A Stakeholder Approach.* Boston: Pitman, 1984, 242. Reproduced with permission of the publisher.

Each step is described in the following sections. Let us explore each one and then apply them in our continuing scenario example.

Step 1. Mapping Stakeholder Relationships   R. Edward Freeman (1984) offered questions that help begin the analysis of identifying the major stakeholders (see Figure 2-2). The first five questions, in particular, offer a quick "jump start" on the analysis. (Questions 6 through 9 may used in later steps when you assess the nature of each stakeholder's interest and priorities.)

Let us continue our example with you as CEO. While brainstorming questions 1 through 5 with those individuals whom you have selected in the firm and who are most knowledgeable, current, and close to the sources of the problems and issues at hand, you may want to draw a stakeholder map and fill in the blanks. Note that your stakeholder analysis is only as valid and reliable as the sources and process you use to obtain your information. As a first pass, using only internal staff will get the process going. As more controversial, incomplete, or questionable issues arise, you may wish to go outside your immediate core planning group to obtain additional information and perspective. A general picture of an initial stakeholder map is shown in Figure 2-3.

If you were the CEO of Exxon, your map may resemble the one in Figure 2-4, a hypothetical stakeholder map presented by a student assuming the role of David Glickman, Exxon's public relations executive.

Figure 2-3 Stakeholder Map of a Very Large Organization

Source: R. Edward Freeman. *Strategic Management: A Stakeholder Approach.* Boston: Pitman, 1984, 25. Reproduced with permission of the publisher.

Step 2. Mapping Stakeholder Coalitions After identifying and mapping the stakeholders who are directly and indirectly involved with your firm over the specific incident you are addressing, the next step is to determine and map any coalitions that have formed. Coalitions among and between stakeholders form around issues and stakes that they have—or seek to have—in common. Different interest groups and lobbyists will sometimes join forces against a "common enemy." Competitors may also join forces if they see an advantage in number. In reference to the Exxon example in Figure 2-4, it would not be unlikely to see Alaskan fishermen, consumers, and unemployed groups from the crisis form a coalition with lobbyists and political action committees (PACs). Mapping actual and potential coalitions around issues can help you, as the CEO, anticipate and design strategic responses toward these groups—before or after they form.

Step 3. Assessing the Nature of Each Stakeholder's Interest Step 3, assessing the nature of each stakeholder's interest, and Step 4, assessing the nature of each stakeholder's power, overlap to some extent. Figure 2-5 is a guide for determining the nature of each stakeholder's interest.

Figure 2-4 Exxon Valdez Stakeholder Map

Reproduced with permission of David Glickman and Professor Kathryn Rogers, Pitzer College, Claremont, California.

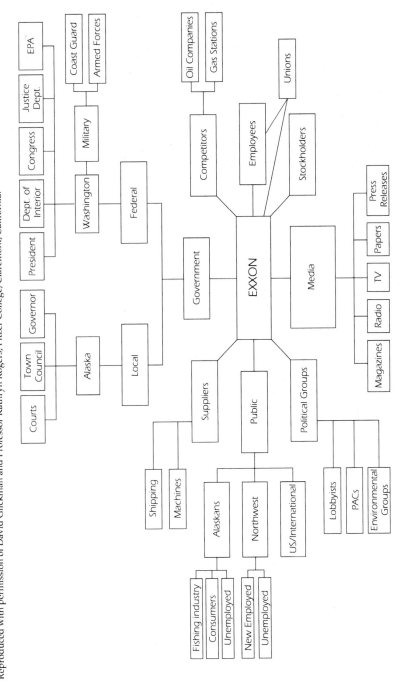

Figure 2-5   A Stakeholder Audit

	SUPPORTERS (ACTIVE)	UNCOMMITTED (NONACTIVE)	OPPOSITION (ACTIVE)
Who are the stakeholders? Currently active? Not active? Potentially active For or Against?			
Actions: What are they doing, e.g., what pressures and procedures are they using, and what actions have they taken to get what they want? What are the thresholds between their indifference and activism? What could trigger their response? What are their sensitive areas? What are they asking for; what will they ask for; what do they want— i.e., what are their objectives?			
Beliefs: What do their executives believe in? Is their knowledge of us accurate or inaccurate? What assumptions do they make about us? What assumptions about them are *implicit* to our strategy? How do they think we affect their success, and they ours? What is their power relative to us? What is our power over them?			

When identifying the "supporters" (active and uncommitted) and the "opposition" in Figure 2-5, we have already begun to assess the relative power of each stakeholder's interests.

In our example, you as Exxon CEO with your staff may determine that your supporters in the *Exxon Valdez* oil spill crisis might be some of your stockholders and employees. Your opposition, or those who may seek to further disrupt your operations and public image, might be two PACs, three media companies, and so on. By systematically completing the categories through brainstorming the actions, beliefs, cooperative potential, and stakes of your stakeholders, you force a broader, more

	SUPPORTERS (ACTIVE)	UNCOMMITTED (NONACTIVE)	OPPOSITION (ACTIVE)

How do they measure our performance, and we measure theirs?

What do we really want? Are these
objectives legitimate? Are they
satisfied? Are we satisfied? What
do they really want?

How will time and current trends
affect their satisfaction, relative
power, and activism?

Cooperative potential:

With which of our stakeholder sets
are they related or dependent?

What differences are there between
them and us, or our other stakeholders? Are these differences
fundamental or superficial?

How could they be influenced, and
by whom, at what cost?

Stakes:

What is their stake in us, and what
is our stake in them? How important are these stakes?

What is their real power in our
affairs? Is theirs an *equity* interest,
or is it economic? Do they seek
influence for some other reason?

What power do we have in their
affairs?

Source: Kenneth Hatten and Mary Louise Hatten. *Effective Strategic Management.* Englewood Cliffs,
N.J.: Prentice Hall, © 1988, 116. Reproduced with permission of Prentice Hall.

objective picture of the situation, the players, and your firm's potential
and actual role in the situation.

Step 4. Assessing the Nature of Each Stakeholder's Power   This part of
the analysis asks, "What's in it for whom? Who stands to win, lose, or
draw over certain stakes?" Three types of power stakeholders can use
are (1) voting power, (2) political power, and (3) economic power
(Freeman 1984). For example, owners and stockholders can vote their
choices to affect the firm's decisions in the *Exxon Valdez* situation.
Federal, state, and local governments can exercise their political power

Figure 2-6 *Stakeholder Analysis*

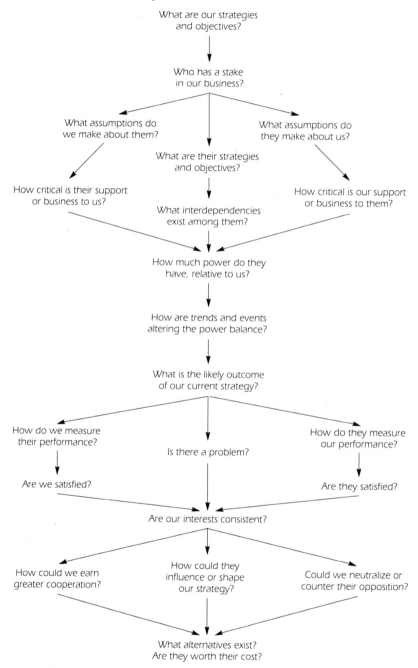

Source: Kenneth Hatten and Mary Louise Hatten. *Effective Strategic Management.* Englewood Cliffs, N.J.: Prentice Hall, © 1988, 114. Reproduced with permission of Prentice Hall.

by increasing regulations over shipping firms to avert future oil spills. Consumers can exercise their economic power by boycotting Exxon's products. What other sources of stakeholder power exist?

Figure 2-6 provides a series of short questions that assist in identifying and assessing the power of different groups' stakes. (Note that some of the questions in Figure 2-6 may repeat or overlap earlier probes.)

This part of the analysis forces you to attempt to identify your so-called allies' and opponents' strategies regarding their issues toward your firm. It also assists you in questioning your potential strategies toward each stakeholder and asks you to identify the groups with whom you wish to cooperate, neutralize, or counter over particular issues and claims. For example, in the *Exxon Valdez* incident, you may discover that a powerful lobbyist group that is organizing a lawsuit against Exxon could be neutralized if you met with their leaders, learned about their grievances, and negotiated demands; negative press could possibly be averted if you faced the issues directly with two particular stakeholders. Again, this step asks you to assess the nature of each stakeholder's power. This information will enable you to decide later how, when, and who from Exxon should respond to these stakeholders.

Step 5. Constructing a Matrix of Stakeholder Moral Responsibilities
After mapping stakeholder relationships and coalitions and assessing the nature of each stakeholder's interest and power, the next step is to determine what responsibilities and moral obligations your company has to each stakeholder. Carroll (1989, 72) constructed a matrix of stakeholder responsibilities. It is a simple depiction to visualize and to draw. Visualize a graph with two axes. The stakeholders (owners, customers, employees, community, public, activist groups, and others) are listed down the left-hand column, and the nature of your firm's responsibilities (that is, economic, legal, ethical, and voluntary) to each stakeholder is placed across the top, as shown in Figure 2-7. For example, as Exxon's CEO, you may see the firm's *economic responsibility* to the owners as preventing as many costly lawsuits as possible. *Legally,* you want to protect the owners from corporate as well as personal liability and damage. This would entail proactively negotiating disputes outside the courts, if possible, in an equitable way to all. *Ethically,* you could see Exxon advising its owners to show their responsibility by paying to help clean up the shoreline, by establishing policies to prevent another such catastrophe from occurring, by helping compensate Alaskan fishermen who lost work, and so on. Chapter 3 explains ethical principles and guidelines that can assist in this type of decision making. *Voluntarily,* for example, you may

Figure 2-7 Stakeholder Moral Responsibility Matrix

Nature of Focal Company Responsibilities

	Legal	Economic	Ethical	Voluntary
Owners				
Customers				
Employees				
Community Interest Groups				
Public (Citizens at Large)				

Stakeholders (left axis label)

also advise Exxon's owners to show responsibility by publicly announcing their plans and roles in resolving the crisis equitably and by offering services and remuneration to affected local communities. This process continues until you have completed matching the economic, legal, ethical, and voluntary responsibilities you have and can develop strategies toward each stakeholder in the situation.

Step 6. Developing Specific Strategies and Tactics   Using your results from the preceding step, you can now proceed to outline the specific strategies and tactics you wish to use with each stakeholder. (These strategies are based on Freeman [1984] and Carroll [1989].)

First, you will consider whether to approach each stakeholder directly or indirectly. Second, you need to decide whether to take the offensive or defensive. Third, you will determine whether to accommodate, negotiate, manipulate, resist, avoid, or do nothing. Finally, you will decide what combination of strategies you should employ with each stakeholder. Again, while developing specific strategies, it is important to keep the following points in mind: (1) Your goal is to create a win–win set of outcomes, if possible. However, this may mean economic costs to your firm if, in fact, members of your firm were responsible to certain groups for harm caused by or as a consequence of their actions. (2) Ask "What is our business? Who are our customers? What are our responsibilities to the stakeholders, to the public and to the firm?" Keep your mission and responsibilities in mind as you move forward. (3) Consider what the probable consequences of your actions will be. For whom? At what costs? Over what time period? Ask "What does a win–win situation look like for us?" (4) Keep in mind that the *means* you use are as important as the *ends* you seek, that is, how you approach and treat each stakeholder can be as important as what you do with and to them. Specific strategies can now be articulated and assigned to corporate staff for review and implementation. Remember, social responsibility is a key variable, as important as the economics and politics of a decision, since social responsibility links to costs and benefits in other areas as well. At this point you can ask to what extent your strategies are just and fair, and you can consider the welfare of the stakeholders affected by your decision. We will discuss ethical principles in more detail in Chapter 3.

In actual experience, executives use a range of strategies, especially in crisis situations over time, to respond to external threats and stakeholders. Their strategies often are short-sighted and begin in a defensive or reactive mode. In observing and using a stakeholder analysis, it is important to question why executives respond to their stakeholders as they do, especially in threatening situations (for example, the silicon gel breast implant incidents that Dow Corning faced). Again, following the questions and methods in this chapter systematically helps you understand why key stakeholders respond as they do in critical incidents.

Step 7. Monitoring Shifting Coalitions   Because time and events can change the stakes and stakeholders, you will want to monitor the evolution of the issues as they are affected by media exposure, politics, economics, legal actions, and public reaction. Creating and updating a "time line" can be helpful. One method is simply to draw a horizontal line on a paper, starting at the beginning of the situation, crisis or incident, and place points from left to right with abbreviations below or above the line that identify the time (month, day, year, or combination), the major event that occurred, and the key player(s). A vertical time line is illustrated in Figure 2-8, which is a chronology of events in the Savings and Loan (S & L) crisis. In this illustration, the year is listed on the left-hand column and the corresponding key events on the right. Time lines can help you track decisions to maintain perspective and decide prospective strategies.

Figure 2-8 Time Line of the S&L Crisis, 1980–1990

YEAR	S&L FAILURES	KEY EVENTS
1980	11	Volcker's Fed drives interest rates up to battle inflation, beginning three-year squeeze that left many S&Ls insolvent.
1981	28	Federal Home Loan Bank Board invents regulatory accounting, turning huge losses into "capital," delaying day of reckoning for many years.
1982	63	Congress passes Garn–St. Germain Act, partly deregulating thrifts; several state legislatures totally deregulate the industry.
1983	36	Taggart named California S&L Commissioner.
1984	22	Knapp ousted at American Savings.
1985	31	Energy bust begins, unmasking bad investments by Texas S&Ls; Empire Savings of Mesquite becomes first big failure from reckless lending.
1986	46	Congress fails to adopt Reagan administration plan to raise $15 billion to pay for closing of insolvent S&Ls.
1987	47	Congress adopts watered-down plan to raise $10 billion, but limits spending and protects certain insolvent S&Ls.
1988	205	Bank Board sells many failed thrifts by issuing loans to acquirers; estimated costs: $39 billion. Northeast bust begins.
1989	328	Congress passes sweeping rescue and reregulation legislation, raising $50 billion for more closings.
1990	181	Estimated cost of 1988 deals rises to roughly $70 billion.
TOTAL	998	Estimated total losses: $200 billion.

NOTE: Failures include all liquidations, assisted mergers, and conservatorships.

Source: *The Wall Street Journal*, November 2, 1990, A4. © 1990 Dow Jones & Company, Inc. All rights reserved. Reproduced with permission of the publisher.

Summary of Stakeholder Analysis

You have now completed the basic stakeholder analysis and should be able to proceed with strategy implementation in more realistic, thoughtful, interactive, and responsible ways.

Figure 2-9   Functional Area Manager Stakeholder

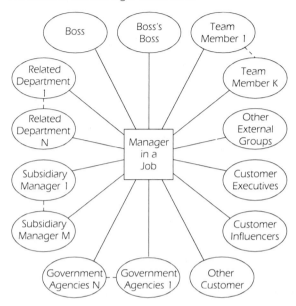

Source: R. Edward Freeman. *Strategic Management: A Stakeholder Approach.* Boston: Pitman, 1984, 218. Reproduced with permission of the publisher.

The stakeholder analysis provides a rational, systematic basis for understanding economic, political, social, and moral issues involved in complex relationships between an organization and its constituents. It helps to guide and structure strategic planning sessions and to decide how to meet the moral obligations of all stakeholders. The extent to which the resultant strategies and outcomes are moral and effective for a firm and its stakeholders depends on many factors, including the values of its leaders, the power, legitimacy, the uses of available resources, and the exigencies of the changing environment.

2.4 MORAL RESPONSIBILITIES OF FUNCTIONAL AREA MANAGERS

One goal of a stakeholder analysis is to force organizational managers to articulate the moral responsibility of their company's and their own professional obligations to their different constituencies. It also focuses the enterprise's attention and moral decision-making process on external events. The stakeholder approach applies internally as well—especially to individual managers in traditional functional areas. These managers "must be seen as the conduit through which they can reach other external stakeholders. (They may also be an impediment, but even so, in many organizations they remain the major available channels open to stakeholders.)" (The material in this section is based on Freeman [1984].)

Because our concern is to focus on managing moral responsibility in organizational stakeholder relationships, we will briefly outline some of the general responsibilities of selected functional managerial area managers in order to illustrate moral dilemmas that can arise in their work.

Figure 2-9 illustrates a general functional area manager's stakeholders. The particular functional area can be written in while reading the descriptions discussed below. Note that the same procedures, steps 1 through 7 presented in the stakeholder analysis section on pages 34–43, can also be used for this level of analysis.

Traditional functional areas include marketing, research and development (R&D), manufacturing, public relations, and human resource management (HRM). There are several other line and staff functions such as finance, information systems, planning, and legal that we will not cover here. We will discuss the basic moral dimensions of each of the five functional areas. Even though functional areas are often blurred in emerging network organizational structures and self-designing teams, many of the responsibilities of these managerial areas remain intact. Understanding these managerial roles from a stakeholder perspective helps clarify the pressures and moral responsibilities of the positions.

Marketing and Sales Managers as Stakeholders

With increasing frequency, marketing and sales managers constantly interact, directly or indirectly, with customers. Because customers have been recognized as an integral part of most businesses, these managers must create and maintain customer interest and loyalty and be concerned with consumer safety and welfare regarding the use of products while, at the same time, increasing revenue and obtaining new accounts. Many marketing and sales professionals are also responsible for determining and managing the firm's advertising, as well as the truthfulness (and legality) of the data and information they issue to the public about products and services. They must also interact with many of the other functional areas, as well as with advertising agencies, customers, and consumer groups. Moral dilemmas can arise for marketing managers who may be requested to promote unsafe products or implement advertising campaigns that are untrue or not in the consumer's best interests.

Marketing managers at Nestlé, the Swiss conglomerate, were forced to battle criticisms of advertising and selling infant formula in Third World countries. The criticisms centered on the company's persuading women to bottle feed, instead of breast feed, their infants. Because of impure water, poor health conditions, and illiteracy, women in these countries used the formula improperly. Executives at Nestlé never imagined the international controversy this would cause.

A major moral dilemma for marketing managers is having to choose a profitable decision over a socially responsible one (Abratt and Sacks 1988). The stakeholder analysis for marketing managers is helpful in these morally questionable situations in terms of (1) mapping who the major parties are (or may become) in moral dilemmas, (2) identifying what strategies stakeholders can (or will) use to protect their interests and rights, (3) determining what obligations the marketing manager and the company have toward each stakeholder, and (4) deciding the extent to which the firm's profit interests are legitimate and moral in this situation.

R&D Engineering Managers as Stakeholders

R&D managers and engineers are responsible for the safety and reliability of product design. Faulty products can mean public outcry, which can result in increased public attention, unwanted media exposure, and possible (perhaps justifiable) lawsuits. R&D managers must work and communicate effectively and conscientiously with professionals in manufacturing, marketing, and information systems; senior managers; contractors; and government representatives, to name a few stakeholders. As studies and reports on the *Challenger* space shuttle disaster illustrate, engineers and managers at NASA and the cooperating company, Thiokol, had different priorities, perceptions, and technical judgments regarding the "go, no-go" decision of that space launch. Lack of individual role responsibility, critical judgment and the expression of critical judgment contributed to the miscommunication and resulting disaster (Werhane 1991).

Moral dilemmas can arise for R&D engineers whose technical judgment and risk assessments conflict with administrative managers seeking profit and time-to-market deadlines. R&D managers can benefit, in the same ways just discussed for marketing personnel, from doing a stakeholder analysis in situations like the *Challenger* launch—before such situations occur.

Public Relations Managers as Stakeholders

Public relations (PR) managers must constantly interact with outside groups and corporate executives, especially in an age in which media and external relations and company exposure play such vital roles. PR managers are responsible for transmitting, receiving, and interpreting information on employees, products, services, and the company. The firm's public credibility and image are at issue with the way PR professionals manage stakeholders, since PR people often must negotiate the boundaries between corporate loyalty and credibility from external groups who often use different criteria for measuring success and responsibility than do corporate executives, especially during crises. Moral dilemmas can arise when PR managers must defend or protect company actions or policies that have questionable or known harmful effects on the public or certain stakeholders. A stakeholder analysis can prepare and inform PR managers of the situation, the stakes, and the strategies they must address.

Manufacturing Managers and Engineers as Stakeholders

Manufacturing managers and engineers are responsible for product safety, quality, and control. R&D professionals design products, and manufacturers produce them. Manufacturers also share in the safety and quality of products after the products leave the factory. Manufacturing managers must communicate with R&D professionals, corporate executives, marketing professionals, customers, and environmental groups, to name a few of their stakeholders. As the case of the *Challenger* space shuttle suggested, technical engineering manufacturers' perceptions and risk assessments of what constitutes a safe product must be weighed against societal responsibility and safety interests. Often, the moral dilemma facing the manufacturing engineer is whether and how to voice opposing judgments on a product's safety to administrators concerned less with technical safety and more with profit.

Human Resource Managers as Stakeholders

Human resource managers (HRMs) are on the front line of helping other managers recruit, hire, fire, promote, evaluate, reward, discipline, transfer, and counsel employees. Human resource managers negotiate union settlements and assist the government in regulating Equal Employment Opportunity Commission (EEOC) standards. Human resource management professionals must translate employee rights and laws into practice. They also research, write, update, and maintain company policies on employee affairs. They face constant ethical pressures and uncertainties over issues about invasion of privacy and violations of employees' individual and constitutional rights. HRM professionals' stakeholders include but are not limited to employees, other managers and bosses, unions, community groups, government employees, lobbyists, and competitors.

Moral dilemmas can arise when affirmative action policies are threatened in favor of corporate decisions to hide biases or protect profits. HRM professionals also straddle the often fine line between the individual rights of employees and corporate self-interests, especially in incidents where layoffs, reductions in force (RIFs), and other hiring or firing decisions are involved. As industries restructure, merge, downsize, and expand internationally, the HRM's work becomes even more complicated. Human rights versus corporate profit will always be a tightrope these professionals must walk in making decisions.

Functional area managers, then, are confronted with balancing operational, profit goals with corporate moral obligations toward stakeholders. These pressures are considered "part of the job." Unfortunately, clear corporate directions to resolve dilemmas involving conflicts over individuals' rights and corporate economic interests generally are not available. Using a stakeholder analysis is a step toward clarifying the issues, stakes, and parties involved in resolving potential or actual ethical dilemmas. Chapter 3 presents moral decision-making principles and criteria that can assist individuals and managerial role holders in thinking through responsible actions.

Functional Management Stakeholder Analysis and Moral Responsibility

Why use the stakeholder analysis with individual functional area managers, and why involve functional managers in using a stakeholder analysis? First, by thinking in terms of stakeholders, managers can acknowledge and begin to change their perceptual biases, blind spots, and activities regarding how they actually see and perform their roles and moral responsibilities toward external and internal groups that affect the firm's and their unit's operations. Second, by seeing how different managers in a firm handle their complex stakeholder relationships, individual managers can begin to create value and realize corporate moral and legal obligations toward stakeholders. Third, the basis for increasing the quality of cross-functional communication and integration can be developed. The process and results of the stakeholder analysis can provide a platform for opening communication channels to discuss stressful, unrealistic, or immoral expectations, problems, and pressures that often lead to illegal and unethical activities, such as creating faulty products, price-fixing, cheating, and lying. Finally, by identifying specific stakeholders' responsibilities, functional area managers can begin to see common patterns of pressures, resources, and ethical issues *across the firm.* An enterprise's moral identity and mission can be identified or reinforced. Moreover, managers can begin to think and operate with moral responsibility as they perform their work. These advantages create opportunities for corporate executives to develop and implement meaningful enterprise ethical codes, policies and procedures that set and maintain a moral corporate climate and culture.

2.5 **EXECUTING A STAKEHOLDER ANALYSIS AS AN OBSERVER**

We have discussed how to execute a stakeholder analysis from the perspectives of a corporate executive and an individual manager. As an observer or stakeholder outside or inside a company, or as a student who is executing a stakeholder analysis, this technique provides useful information and perspective toward understanding strategic political, economic, and moral relationships. The procedures and steps outlined in Section 2.2 are used by observers as well as by corporate members.

Questions and issues* that surface when executing a stakeholder analysis as an observer or student include the following:

1. Does the company have to be the center or focus of the analysis?
2. How detailed do the maps and analysis have to be?
3. What issues are the most important for each stakeholder and who determines this in a stakeholder analysis?

*These issues are based primarily on my experiences of teaching the stakeholder analysis and business ethics over several years to MBA students at Bentley College in Waltham, Massachusetts.

4. How objective or reliable can the analysis be if the primary responsibilities are not directly involved or questioned?

5. Can an analysis be done before or during an event?

6. What difference or value, especially regarding the use of ethics, can a stakeholder analysis add?

In response to the first question, "Does the company have to be the focus of the analysis?" the stakeholder analysis does focus primary and secondary strategic relationships around the CEO, the firm's executives, or a key manager. An individual employee stakeholder can also be the focus of an analysis if, at a microlevel, issues relating to employee rights or responsibilities in the workplace are at issue. Usually, it is a corporation or organization whose planned or unintentional acts command the attention of external groups and the public. It is, therefore, the corporation and its key executives whose actions with other stakeholders must be understood. This is especially the case when influential or comprehensive decisions must be made that affect the lives and welfare of many people, as in the *Exxon Valdez* example. This does not mean that other stakeholders, such as functional area managers, are less important or that we as observers cannot also refocus attention around any one of their positions and strategies. This can also be done.

The second question, "How detailed do the maps and analysis have to be?" can be addressed as follows: (1) Include only as much detail as is necessary to capture the essence of understanding the "who, what, where, when, why, and how" of stakeholder relations being studied and the primary issues at hand; (2) KIS: If we "keep it simple," the analysis will move along and not get bogged down in too much detail. There is no absolute rule about how detailed the analysis should be. This is a judgment call. A key concern is to have accurate, relevant, and timely information on the topic at hand; the abbreviation of this information on the maps is a tactical matter. Also, factors like time, effort, and monetary costs constrain our ability to have all available information on a stakeholder. Good judgment is needed.

Third, "What issues are the most important for each stakeholder, and who determines this in a stakeholder analysis?" A response to this question is also a matter of judgment. Results from issue identification are as valid and reliable as the methods used to collect the data and the collectors' responsibility and conscientiousness in determining the most pertinent issues. Also, having more than one competent and knowledgeable person involved and giving feedback in this process will result in a more objective approach and conclusions. If possible, circulate your issue list to those who can help you identify key issues. Use discretion, depending on the nature of your topic and the individuals with whom you are dealing.

Fourth, "How objective or reliable can the analysis be if the primary individuals or groups are not directly involved or questioned?" Obtaining information, impressions and perspectives from the major stakeholders and players is the primary objective in executing the analysis. However, this is not always possible. As is often the case with pollsters and political consultants in campaigns, stakeholders' strategies and tactics have to be sought from other sources. Your task must therefore involve as thorough and comprehensive an indirect investigation as possible. Again, your results and inferences are as valid and reliable as your methods, expertise, and conscientiousness. The closer you get to the primary sources, the more reliable your information should be.

Fifth, "Can an analysis be done before or during an event?" Yes. Your information in these instances is more tentative and variable. Your analysis becomes more of a monitoring or prediction report than a completed profile. However, this is more often the case in a stakeholder analysis than not. Corporate executives, strategic planners, and PR managers are also usually involved in a critical event before they turn to mapping it. They are not historians. This is one purpose of a stakeholder analysis. It is a type of field action research used for making strategic decisions and determining moral responsibility.

Sixth, "What difference or value, especially regarding the use of ethics, can a stakeholder analysis add?" Having an informed, comprehensive understanding of a corporation's strategic relationships to its stakeholders in a critical incident or event is better than having little or no information at all. Having a very biased or unreliable picture may also not be helpful. Again, the purpose of the stakeholder analysis as presented here is to gain a realistic understanding of strategic social responsibility relationships, options, and actions of a firm toward its constituents so that corporate leaders can act morally in their policy decisions. A stakeholder analysis provides a gathering of diverse perspectives and information pertaining to an event. One party's ethical judgments are not taken as absolute in such an analysis.

Also, using these methods helps the participants to (1) separate and discriminate among legal, political, economic, and moral issues and consequences of stakeholder actions and policies; (2) learn to use informed, ethical judgment in determining and managing moral obligations to stakeholders; (3) learn to separate facts from inferences; and (4) learn to evaluate the power, legitimacy, and motivations of organizational stake-holders' positions and strategies.

2.6 STAKEHOLDER ANALYSIS AND ETHICAL REASONING

Because the stakeholder analysis is an analytical method, there are no prescribed ethical principles or responsibility rules "built in." Ethical reasoning in the stakeholder analysis asks, "What is equitable, just, fair, and good for those who affect and are affected by business decisions?" Also, "Who are the weaker stakeholders in terms of power and influence? Who can, will, and should assist weaker stakeholders in making their voices and participation in the decisional process and outcomes heard?" Finally, the stakeholder analysis requires the focal or principal stake-holders to define and fulfill their ethical obligations to the affected constituencies.

Chapter 3 explains major ethical principles that can be used to examine individual motivation in resolving an ethical dilemma. While Chapter 3 focuses on the micro- or individual level of ethical reasoning, the logic underlying the ethical principles discussed can also be extended to a more macro- or policy level, as we will explain in that chapter.

SUMMARY

Organizations and businesses in this century have increased in complexity and power. Because of their numerous economic and noneconomic transactions with different groups in the environment, a method is required to understand an organization's moral obligations and relationships to its constituencies.

The stakeholder approach provides an analytical method for determining how various constituencies affect and are affected by business activities. The stakeholder model also provides a means for assessing the power, legitimacy, and moral responsibility of managers' strategies in terms of how they meet the needs and obligations of various stakeholder groups.

A stakeholder analysis is also a strategic management tool that allows firms to map and manage relationships with constituents in any given or projected situation. An individual or group is said to have a "stake" in a corporation if it possesses an interest, share, or claim in the outcome of that corporation's policies, procedures, or actions. A "stakeholder" is defined as an individual or group who can affect or be affected by the actions, policies, practices, or goals of the organization.

Recent studies have indicated that profits and stockholder approval may not be the most important driving forces behind management objectives. Job enrichment, concern for employees, and personal well-being are also important objectives.

The implementation of a stakeholder analysis involves a series of steps designed to help a corporation understand the complex economic, political, and moral factors involved in its obligations toward different constituencies.

The moral dimensions of traditional managerial functional area roles (marketing, research and development, manufacturing, public relations, and human resource management) are discussed from a stakeholder perspective. The stakeholder approach can assist functional area managers in resolving difficulties resulting from conflicts over individual rights and corporate economic objectives. This approach can assist managers to think through and chart morally responsible decisions in their work and toward the corporation and its stakeholders.

The use of the stakeholder analysis by an observer or third party is also presented as a means for understanding social responsibility issues between a firm and its constituents. Finally, ethical reasoning is discussed as it relates to the stakeholder approach.

Questions

1. Describe the stakeholder approach and method.

2. Define the term stakeholder. Give examples of primary and secondary stakeholders.

3. What changes have occurred since the industrial age that have facilitated the need for a stakeholder approach?

4. What are some of the types of power stakeholders can use to support their positions? Briefly explain these.

5. From the survey cited in the chapter, who do supervisory managers see as the most important stakeholders? Middle managers? Executive managers?

6. What are the traditional functional areas of management? Who are the principal stakeholders with whom each one deals? Could teams use a stakeholder approach in their project or business environment? Explain.

7. What are the reasons for encouraging functional area managers to use the stakeholder approach? Would these reasons apply to teams?

8. Identify six common questions that arise when executing a stakeholder analysis. Identify your questions regarding your use of this method.

Exercises

1. Describe a situation in which you were a stakeholder. What were the issues? What were your stakes? What was the outcome? Who won, who lost, and why?

2. Recollect your personal work history. Who was your manager's most important stakeholder(s)? Why? Did you agree or disagree?

3. Briefly invent your own corporation. What is the industry? Your environments? Your product or service? Trace through the steps of a stakeholder analysis and map out a stakeholder relationship. Describe the nature of your firm's responsibilities to each stakeholder.

4. Describe each of the steps used in a stakeholder analysis and apply this framework to an incident in the news or press (such as the *Exxon Valdez* oil spill).

5. Choose one of the traditional functional areas of management. Describe a dilemma involving this function from the news or a recent article. Discuss how a stakeholder model could assist in developing a resolution in your example.

References and Suggested Readings

Abratt, Russell, and D. Sacks. "The Marketing Challenge: Towards Being Profitable and Socially Responsible." *Journal of Business Ethics* 7 (1988): 497–507.

Bowie, Norman. "New Directions in Corporate Social Responsibility." *Business Horizons* (July/August 1991): 56–65.

Bowie, Norman, and Ronald Duska. *Business Ethics*. 2d ed. Englewood Cliffs, N.J.: Prentice-Hall, 1991.

Carroll, Archie. *Business and Society: Ethics and Stakeholder Management*. 1st and 3d eds. Ohio: South-Western Publishing Co., 1989 and 1993.

———. "The Pyramid of Corporate Social Responsibility: Toward the Moral Management of Organizational Stakeholders." *Business Horizons* (July/August 1991): 39–48.

Dumanoski, Diane. "One Year Later—The Lessons of Valdez." *The Boston Globe*, April 2, 1990, 29.

Evan, William, and R. Freeman. "A Stakeholder Theory of the Modern Corporation: Kantian Capitalism." *In Ethical Theory and Business*. 3d ed. Edited by Tom L. Beauchamp and Norman E. Bowie. Englewood Cliffs, N.J.: Prentice-Hall, 1988.

Frederick, William, et al. *Business and Society: Corporate Strategy, Public Policy, Ethics*. 6th ed. New York: McGraw-Hill, 1988.

Freeman, R. Edward. *Strategic Management: A Stakeholder Approach*. Boston: Pitman, 1984.

Hatten, Kenneth, and M. L. Hatten. *Effective Strategic Management Analysis and Action*. Englewood Cliffs, N.J.: Prentice-Hall, 1988.

Herkert, Joseph. "Management's Hat Trick: Misuse of 'Engineering Judgment' in the *Challenger* Incident." *Journal of Business Ethics* 10 (1991): 617–620.

Posner, Barry, and Warren Schmidt. "Values and the American Manager: An Update." *California Management Review* (Spring 1984).

Rawkins, Robert. "U.S. Indicts Exxon in Oil Spill." *The Miami Herald,* February 28, 1990.

Steiner, George A., and John F. Steiner. *Business, Government, and Society, A Managerial Perspective,* 5th and 6th eds. New York: Random House, 1988 and 1991.

The Wall Street Journal. "How Do You Spell Success?" October 30, 1990, A1.

Weiss, Joseph. *The Management of Change: Administrative Logics and Actions.* New York: Praeger, 1986.

Werhane, Patricia. "Engineers and Management: The Challenge of the *Challenger* Incident." *Journal of Business Ethics* 10 (1991): 605–616.

3

Ethical Principles and Decision-Making Guidelines

Ralph Simms, a newly graduated MBA, was hired by a prestigious U.S.-based multinational firm and sent, with minimal training, to open negotiations with a high-ranking Middle Eastern government official. Simms's assignment was to "do whatever it takes to win the contract; it's worth millions to us." The contract would enable Simms's firm to select and manage technology companies that would install a multi-million-dollar computer system for that government. While in the country, Simms was told by the representative government official that Simms's firm had "an excellent chance to get the contract" if the official's nephew, who owned and operated a computer company in that country, could be assured "a good piece of the action." The official told Simms this would remain a confidential matter and closed by saying, "That's how we do business here; take it or leave it." Simms called his superior in Chicago and informed him of what had happened. Simms was told, "Take it! But use *your best judgment* on how to handle the details."

Complex ethical dilemmas in business situations usually involve tough choices that must be made among conflicting and competing interests. Should Ralph Simms move to close the lucrative deal or not? Is he being offered a bribe? Is the official's request legal? Is it ethical? Is this a setup? Would Ralph be held individually responsible if something went wrong? Who is going to protect him should legal complications arise? How is Ralph supposed to negotiate such a deal? (He wasn't taught that in a management class.) What does Ralph stand to win and lose if he does or does not accept the official's offer? Finally, what *should* Ralph do to act morally responsible in this situation? What is the right action to take? These are the kinds of questions and issues that we will address in this chapter. There may be no obvious or easy answers, but there are principles and guidelines that can help you identify and think through issues that underlie ethical dilemmas. The aim here is to present ethical principles and guidelines that can help you evaluate—as shown in Figure 3-1—your own and others' moral responsibilities in resolving ethical dilemmas.

The stakeholder analysis in Chapter 2 illustrated how to map and plan social responsibility strategies between corporate managers and external stakeholders. This chapter introduces and summarizes fundamental ethical principles and decision rules to use when making difficult moral decisions in complex business transactions. We intentionally do not offer exhaustive explanations of ethical principles or the philosophical reasoning underlying these principles. That is beyond the scope of the book and can be found in our citations and other philo-

Figure 3-1 Intended Effects of Business Ethics Education on Stakeholder Belief Systems and Decisions

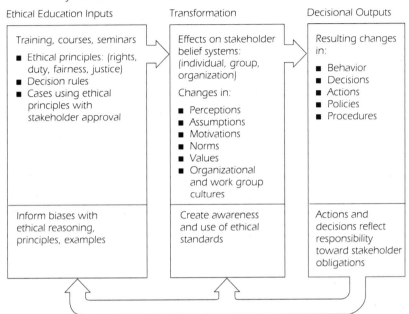

sophical works. Our aim however, is to simplify and briefly present a summary of major ethical principles and guidelines that can be applied in a stakeholder analysis framework, that is, a decisional context that involves business settings. We begin this section by presenting ethical reasoning at the individual level. The ethical reasoning processes, principles, and decision rules are also applicable at the corporate policy and group levels.

3.1 DECISION CRITERIA IN ETHICAL REASONING

A first step in addressing ethical dilemmas is to identify the problem(s) and related issues. This is particularly necessary in a stakeholder approach, since the problems and issues depend on who the stakeholders are and what their stakes entail. Before discussing specific ethical principles, we begin by offering important decision criteria in ethical reasoning. How would you, as you read these, apply the criteria to Ralph Simms's situation?

Laura Nash (1981, 78–90) presented 12 questions to help clarify ethical problems:*

1. Have you defined the problem accurately?

2. How would you define the problem if you stood on the other side of the fence?

3. How did this situation occur in the first place?

4. To whom and to what do you give your loyalty as a person and as a member of the corporation?

5. What is your intention in making this decision?

6. How does this intention compare with the probable results?

7. Whom could your decision or action injure?

8. Can you discuss the problem with the affected parties before you make your decision?

9. Are you confident that your decision will be as valid over a long period of time as it seems now?

10. Could you disclose without qualm your decision or action to your boss, your chief executive officer (CEO), the board of directors, your family, or society as a whole?

11. What is the symbolic potential of your action if understood? If misunderstood?

12. Under what conditions would you allow exceptions to your stand?

Nash states that these 12 questions can help individuals openly discuss and articulate responsibilities needed to solve ethical problems. She notes that sharing these questions can facilitate group discussions, build cohesiveness and consensus around shared points, serve as an information source, uncover ethical inconsistencies in a company's values, help a CEO see how senior managers think, and increase the nature and range of choices. She also notes that the discussion process is cathartic.

To return briefly to the opening case, if Ralph Simms considered the first point presented above, he might, for example, define the problem he faces from different levels or perspectives (as Chapter 1 illustrated). At the *organizational level,* his firm stands to win a sizable contract if he accepts the government official's conditions. His firm's image and reputation could also be jeopardized in the United States if indeed this deal

*Laura Nash. "Ethics Without the Sermon." *Harvard Business Review* (November/December 1981): 88. Copyright ©1981 by the President and Fellows of Harvard College. All rights reserved. Reproduced with permission of the Harvard Business Review.

turned out to be a scandal, if a controversy arose among competitors, or if the media covered the events in a critical way. At the *societal level* the issues are complicated. In this Middle Eastern country, this type of bargaining might be acceptable. In the United States, however, Ralph could have problems with the Foreign Corrupt Practices Act. Is this a bribe? And is Ralph acting officially on behalf of his company or as an individual? At the *individual level*, Ralph must decide if his values and conscience can tolerate the actions and consequences this deal involves. He must also consider the economic, political, social, and moral costs and benefits he will incur from his company if he decides to accept or reject this assignment. Ralph must also decide to whom his loyalty belongs in this situation, as a person and as an employee. Whom could his decision potentially injure? As you can see, these questions can serve to help Ralph clarify his goal in making a decision and the prices he is willing or not willing to pay.

Manuel Velasquez (1988, 32–43) also offered criteria that can be used in ethical reasoning and that help systematize and structure our arguments:

1. Moral reasoning must be logical. Assumptions and premises, both factual and inferred, used to make judgments should be known and made explicit.

2. Factual evidence cited to support a person's judgment should be accurate, relevant, and complete.

3. Ethical standards used in a person's reasoning should be consistent. When inconsistencies between one's ethical standards in an argument or decision are discovered, one or more of the standards must be modified.

If Ralph Simms, from our opening case, were to use Velasquez's criteria, Simms would articulate the assumptions underlying his decision. If Simms, for example, chose to accept the government official's offer, he might say that he assumed it was not a bribe; that even if it were a bribe, he assumes he will not get caught; and that even if he or his company did get caught, he would be willing to incur any penalty individually—including loss of his job. Moreover, Ralph would want to obtain as many facts as he could regarding both U.S. laws and the Middle Eastern country's laws on such negotiating practices as the one he will accept. He will also gather information from his employer and check the accuracy of the information against his decision. Finally, Ralph will be consistent in his standards. If he chooses to accept the foreign official's conditions, he must be willing to accept additional contingencies consistent with those conditions. He would not, for example, midway through helping the official's nephew obtain part of the contract, suddenly decide that these actions were wrong and "unethical" and then back out. Ralph must think through these contingencies before he makes a decision.

Finally, a simple but powerful question can be used throughout your decision-making process in solving ethical dilemmas: "What is my motivation for choosing a course of action?" By examining individual motives and separating these from known motivations of others, clarity and perspective are gained. Ralph, for example, may ask, "Why did I agree to negotiate with the official on his terms? Was it for money? To keep my job? To impress my boss? For adventure?" Ralph may also ask whether his stated motivation from the outset will carry his commitments through the entire contracting process.

Moral Responsibility

A major aim of ethical reasoning is to gain a clearer and sharper logical focus on problems in order to act in morally responsible ways. Velasquez (1988) stated that individuals are morally responsible for their actions and the harmful effects of their actions when (1) a person knowingly and freely so acted or when the person caused the act to happen when that act was morally wrong or hurtful to others, and (2) when a person knowingly and freely *failed* to act or prevent a harmful act that, also, was morally wrong for a person to have failed to do or prevent from happening. Although there is no universal definition of what constitutes a morally wrong act in absolute terms, we suggest that an act and the consequences of an act are morally wrong if physical or emotional harm or damage is done to another as a result of the act committed. Again, the degree of harm and the other conditions mentioned above must also be considered.

Two conditions that eliminate a person's moral responsibility for causing injury or harm are *ignorance* and *inability* (Velasquez 1988). A person, however, who intentionally prevents himself or herself from understanding or knowing that a harmful action will occur is still responsible. Also, a person who negligently fails to inform himself or herself about a potentially harmful matter may still be responsible for the resultant action. There are, of course, mitigating circumstances that can excuse or lessen a person's moral responsibility in a situation. Velasquez (1988) mentions such circumstances as (1) the seriousness or lack of seriousness of a wrongful act, (2) circumstances that show a person is uncertain about his or her knowledge of a wrongdoing, (3) circumstances that cause a person difficulty in avoiding doing an act, and (4) circumstances that affect the degree to which a person caused or helped cause a harmful injury. As we know from court trials, proving intent or motive for an alleged illegal act is not an easy matter. Similarly, showing the extent to which a person is morally irresponsible for complicated harmful actions can also be difficult to determine. For example, was the captain of the *Exxon Valdez* morally responsible individually for the resultant harm done to the Alaskan coastline and the local economies? Are the Savings and Loan officers individually morally responsible for the billions their institutional investment failures cost taxpayers? What principles and standards can we, as well as judges and juries, use to establish moral responsibility for ourselves and others?

In the following sections, we explain and discuss five fundamental ethical principles that can be used in our ethical reasoning for choosing particular alternatives and justifying difficult decisions and actions. The principles include (1) relativism, (2) utilitarianism, (3) universalism, (4) rights, and (5) justice. After discussing these principles, we will present four social responsibility modes and four individual styles of ethical reasoning. Finally, some "quick ethical tests" are presented that you may also use to clarify ethical dilemmas. We admit at the outset of this discussion that we do not go into great depth in presenting philosophical detail. The sources we cite provide a fuller discussion for those interested.

No single principle may be sufficient in helping you or a manager make tough ethical decisions. Our intent is to inform and develop your repertoire of ethical concepts so that you may have a range from which to choose and think through moral problems. The aim here is to present some major ethical principles and examples of ethical reasoning in order to increase your awareness of ethical knowledge and guidelines so that your resultant decisions, actions, and policies reflect fairness, justice, and responsibility toward those whom you serve as well as your own interests. While reading this section, we suggest you think of different levels of stakeholders and situations in which stakeholders such as individuals, students, managers, owners, suppliers, competitors, government regulators, and interest groups might apply these principles in their actions.

3.2 ETHICAL RELATIVISM

Ethical relativism holds that there are no single, universal standards or rules that can be used to guide or evaluate the morality of an act. What is right for you may be wrong for me. This view argues that each person has and sets his or her own moral standards by which their actions are judged. Only the individual's self-interests and values are relevant for judging his or her behavior. This form of relativism is referred to as **naive relativism**.

If Ralph Simms in the opening case were to adopt the principle of ethical relativism in his decision making, he might, for example, choose to accept the government official's offer in order to promote his own standing in his firm. He might reason that his self-interests would best be served by making any deal that would push his career ahead. On the other hand, Simms could also use ethical relativism to justify his rejection of the offer. Simms might say that any possible form of such questionable negotiation is against his beliefs. The point behind this principle is that individual standards are the basis of moral authority.

The logic of ethical relativism also extends to cultures. **Cultural relativism**, as the position is called, argues, "When in Rome, do as the Romans do." What is morally right for one society or culture may be wrong for another. Moral standards vary from one culture's customs, belief systems, and value structure to another. Cultural relativists would argue that firms and business professionals doing business in a country are obliged to follow that country's laws and moral codes. A criterion that relativists would use in justifying their actions is, "Are my beliefs, moral standards, and customs satisfied with this action or outcome?"

The benefits of ethical and cultural relativism are that these principles recognize the distinctiveness of individual and social values, customs, and moral standards. These views take seriously the conscientiousness and unique belief systems of different individuals and societies. Different social norms and mores are seen in cultural context.

There are also several problems with ethical and cultural relativism. First, these views consist of an underlying laziness (Steiner and Steiner 1988). Individuals who justify their morality only from their own personal beliefs without taking into consideration other ethical principles may use the logic of relativism as an excuse for not having or developing moral standards that can be argued and tested against other claims, opinions, and standards. Second, this view contradicts everyday experience. Moral reasoning is developed from conversation, interaction, and argument. What I believe or perceive as "facts" in a situation may or may not be accurate. How can I validate or disprove my ethical reasoning and moral judgments if I do not communicate, share, and remain open to change my own standards? Third, ethical relativists can become absolutists. That is, individuals who claim their moral standards are right—regardless of whether they are right or wrong—can be closed to outside influence and accept only their beliefs as true. Also, what if my beliefs conflict with yours? Who is right then? Who decides and on what grounds? In practice, ethical relativism does not effectively or efficiently solve complicated conflicts in which many parties are involved. There must be a tolerance for accepting doubt and permitting our observations and beliefs to be informed. Finally, cultural relativism suffers from the same problems as those listed above. While it is important to observe and respect the values and moral customs of different cultures, especially since business professionals are increasingly operating across national boundaries, we must still not be lazy or blindly absolute or divorce ourselves from rigorous moral reasoning or laws aimed at protecting individual rights, justice, and fairness. As Freeman and Gilbert (1988, 36) ask, "Must American managers in Saudi Arabia treat women as the Saudis treat them? Must American managers in South Africa treat blacks as the white South Africans treat them? Must white South Africans treat blacks in the U.S. as U.S. managers treat them? Must Saudis in the U.S. treat women as U.S. managers treat them?" They continue, "It makes sense to question whether or not the norms of the Nazi society were in fact morally correct" (p. 39). Using rigorous ethical reasoning in solving moral dilemmas is important across cultures. This does not imply that flexibility, sensitivity, and awareness of individual and cultural moral differences are not necessary; they are. It does mean that upholding principles of rights, justice, freedom, and fairness in some situations may conflict with the other person's or culture's belief systems and standards. Depending on the actions and decisions taken from one's moral stands, a price may have to be paid for maintaining one's moral, and sometimes legal, standards. Often, negotiations, agreements, and understanding can be reached without overt conflict when different ethical principles or cultural standards clash. Other times, a price may have to be paid to uphold one's moral integrity.

Ethical Relativism and Stakeholder Analysis

When considering the principles of relativism in conducting a stakeholder analysis, ask the following questions:

1. What are the major moral beliefs and principles at issue for each stakeholder affected by this decision?

2. What are my moral beliefs and principles in this decision?

3. To what extent will my ethical principles clash if a particular course of action is taken? Why?

4. How can conflicting moral beliefs and principles be avoided or negotiated in seeking a desirable outcome?

3.3 **UTILITARIANISM**

Jeremy Bentham (1748–1832) and John Stuart Mill (1806–1873) are acknowledged as founders of the concept of **utilitarianism**. While there are various interpretations of the concept, basically the utilitarian view holds that an action is judged as right, good, or wrong depending on its consequences. The ends of an action justify the means taken to reach those ends. As a consequentialist principle, the moral authority that drives utilitarianism is the calculated consequences of an action, regardless of other principles that determine the means or motivations for taking the action. Utilitarianism also includes the following tenets: (from Carroll 1989; Mill 1957; Velasquez 1988):

1. An action is morally right if it produces the greatest good for the greatest number of people affected by it.

2. An action is morally right if the net benefits over costs are greatest for all affected, as compared to the net benefits of all other possible choices considered.

3. An action is morally right if its immediate and future direct and indirect benefits are greatest for each individual, and if these benefits outweigh the costs of those considered for other alternatives.

Utilitarian concepts are widely practiced by government policy makers, economists, and business professionals. Utilitarianism is a useful principle in conducting a stakeholder analysis, since it forces decision makers to (1) consider collective as well as particular interests, (2) formulate different alternatives based on the greatest good for all parties involved in a decision, and (3) estimate costs and benefits of alternatives for different groups affected (Delong 1981).

In the opening scenario of the chapter, Ralph Simms would use utilitarian principles in his decision making by identifying each of the stakeholders and groups who would be affected by his decision. He would then calculate the costs and benefits of his decision as it would affect each group. Finally, he would decide a course of action based on the greatest good for the greatest number. For example, after identifying all the stakeholders in his decision, including his own interests, Simms may estimate that rejecting the official's offer would produce the greatest good for the people of the country where the contract would be negotiated since obtaining bids from the most technically qualified companies would best serve the interest of those receiving the services.

Problems with utilitarianism include the following:

1. There is no agreement about what the "good" to be maximized for all concerned in different situations is. Is it truth, health, peace, profits, pleasure, cost reductions, national security? (See Hoffman and Moore 1990.) Who decides what is good for whom? Whose interests are primary in the decisions?

2. Utilitarianism does not judge the rightness or wrongness of actions in and of themselves but rather in their consequences. What if some actions are wrong in themselves? Should decision makers proceed to take that action based only on its consequences?

3. How are costs and benefits of such nonmonetary stakes as health, safety, and public welfare measured? Should a monetary or dollar value be assigned to nonmarketed benefits and costs such as safety, health, and the environment? (See Kelman 1981.) What if actual or even potential harmful effects of an action cannot be measured in the short term but are believed to have potentially long-term, say 20- or 30-year, lagged effects? Should that action be chosen?

4. Utilitarianism as a principle does not consider the individual. It is the collective, the aggregate, for whom the greatest good is estimated. Are there instances when individuals and individual interests should be valued in a decision?

5. The principles of justice and rights are ignored in utilitarianism. The principle of justice is concerned with the *distribution* of good, not the amount of total good in a decision. The principle of rights is concerned with individual entitlements, regardless of collective calculated benefits. Utilitarianism does not focus on this problem.

Even given these problems of utilitarianism, the principle is still valuable under the following conditions: when resources are lacking or scarce, when priorities are in conflict, when there is no clear choice of fulfilling everyone's needs and goals, and when large or diverse collectives and groups are involved in a zero sum decision, that is, when there are a fixed and limited number of resources to be distributed (Delong 1981; Velasquez 1988, 116).

Utilitarianism and Stakeholder Analysis

Because you will use utilitarian principles when conducting a stakeholder analysis, the following points should be considered:

1. Define how costs and benefits will be measured in selecting one course of action over another. Include social as well as economic and monetary costs and benefits; include long-term and short-term costs and benefits.

2. Define what information you will need and use to determine costs and benefits in making comparisons.

3. Identify procedures and policies you will use to explain and justify your cost/benefit analysis.

4. State your assumptions in defining and justifying your analysis and conclusions.

5. Ask what moral obligations you have toward each of your stakeholders, after the costs and benefits have been estimated for particular strategies.

3.4 UNIVERSALISM

Immanuel Kant (1724–1804) is considered one of the leading founders of the principle of **universalism**. Also referred to as "deontological ethics," the principle of universalism holds that the means justify the ends of an action, not the consequences. Universalism, therefore, is also referred to as a **nonconsequentialist** ethic.

Kant's principle of the **categorical imperative**, unlike utilitarianism, places the moral authority for taking an action on an individual's *duty* toward other individuals and humanity.

The categorical imperative consists of two parts.* The first part states that *a person should choose to act if and only if she or he would be willing to have every person on earth, in that same situation, act exactly that way.* This principle is absolute and allows for no qualifications across situations or circumstances. The second part of the categorical imperative states that in an ethical dilemma, *a person should act in a way that respects and treats all others involved as ends as well as means to an end.*

Kant's categorical imperative forces decision makers to take into account their duty to act responsibly and respectfully toward all indi-

---

*The following discussion is based on material from Hoffman and Moore 1990; Kant 1964; Steiner and Steiner 1988; and Velasquez 1988.

viduals in a situation. Individual human welfare is a primary stake in any decision. Decision makers must also consider formulating their justifications and reasons as principles to be applied to everyone.

In Ralph Simms's example, if he followed principles of universalism, he might ask, "If I accept the government official's offer, could I justify that anyone anywhere acts the same way?" If he answers in the negative, he should not accept the offer.

The weaknesses of universalism and of Kant's categorical imperative include the following: First, these principles are imprecise and lack practical utility. It is difficult to think of all humanity each time one must make a decision in an ethical dilemma. Second, it is difficult to resolve conflicts of interest when using a criterion that states that all individuals must be treated equally. There are degrees of differences in different stakeholders' interests and relative power in certain situations. However, Kant would remind us that it is the human being and his or her humanity that must be considered above the stakes, power bases, or consequences of our actions. Still, it is often impractical not to consider these other elements in an dilemma. Finally, what if a decision maker's duties conflict in an ethical dilemma? The categorical imperative does not allow for prioritizing one's duties. A primary purpose of the stakeholder analysis is to prioritize conflicting duties—duties toward competitors, customers, employees, suppliers, owners, the media, and the public. It is, again, difficult to take absolute positions when limited resources and time and conflicting values are factors in ethical dilemmas.

Universalism and Stakeholder Analysis

The logic underlying universalism and the categorical imperative can be helpful in applying a stakeholder analysis. Even though we may not be able to employ Kant's principles absolutely, we can consider the following uses of his ethics:

1. Identify individuals as well as aggregates and their welfare and risks in considering policy decisions and outcomes.

2. Identify the needs of individuals involved in a decision, the choices they have, and the information they need to protect their own welfare.

3. Identify any manipulation, force, coercion, or deceit that might be harmfully used against individuals involved in a decision.

4. Identify duties of respecting and responding to individuals affected by particular decisions before adopting policies and actions that affect individual lives.

5. Ask if the desired action or policy would be acceptable to these individuals involved if they were informed of the policy intentions. Under what conditions would they accept the decision?

6. Ask if the designated action or policy would acceptably be repeated as a principle by different individuals in a similar situation. If not, why? And would the designated action continue to be employed?

3.5 RIGHTS

The moral authority that drives the ethics of **rights** is that of entitlement. Individual rights mean entitlements and unquestioned claims. Every American is guaranteed in the Declaration of Independence the rights of life, liberty, and the pursuit of happiness. The U.S. Constitution holds that each citizen is guaranteed certain fundamental rights. These rights are founded on a legal basis in the U.S. system of legislation and justice. The principle of rights is one of the most powerful concepts enabling and protecting individual freedom, dignity, and choice. This principle is the cornerstone of American democracy.

Moral rights are based on legal rights and on the principle of duties. My moral right implies that you have certain duties toward aiding—or at least not obstructing—my rights. Moral rights are also based and viewed from an *individual* perspective, not a societal or group point of view. Individual freedom, welfare, safety, health, and happiness are the essential core values of moral rights. Chapter 6 deals with the rights of employees and employers in the workplace.

Rights can also override utilitarian principles. Many times, violations of rights are solved by the criterion of "Whose rights have precedence in a given situation?" Lawsuits are won and lost on the principle of individual rights not being upheld or protected.

Ralph Simms might, in our earlier example, ask what his rights are in this situation. If he believes that his constitutional and moral rights would be violated by accepting the offer or from his firm's pressuring him to accept the offer, he would consider refusing to negotiate on the foreign official's terms.

The limitations of the principle of rights include the following:

1. The entitlement justification of individual rights can be used by certain individuals and groups to disguise and manipulate selfish, unjust political claims and interests (see Steiner and Steiner 1988).

2. Protection of rights can exaggerate certain entitlements in society at the expense of others. Fairness and equity issues may be raised when rights of certain individuals and groups take precedence over the rights of others in similar situations. Issues of reverse discrimination have, for example, resulted from this reasoning.

3. There is also the question of the limit of rights. To what extent should industrial and government practices that may benefit the entire society but threaten certain individual or group rights be permitted to occur?

Rights and Stakeholder Analysis

Using the principle of rights in a stakeholder analysis is particularly useful when conflicting legal and/or moral rights of individuals occur or when individual and group rights may be violated if certain courses of action are pursued. The following guidelines can be observed in using this principle (Velasquez 1988):

1. Identify the individuals and their rights that may be violated by a particular policy or course of action.

2. Determine the legal and moral basis of these individuals' rights. Does the decision violate these rights?

3. Determine to what extent the action to be taken has moral justification from utilitarian principles if individual rights may be violated. National crises and emergencies may warrant overriding certain individual rights for the public good.

3.6 **JUSTICE**

The principle of **justice** deals with fairness and equality. Here the moral authority that decides what is right and wrong concerns the fair and equitable distribution of opportunity and hardship to all. The principle of justice is also concerned with punishment for wrong done to the undeserving. John Rawls (1971), a contemporary philosopher, offered two principles of fairness that are widely recognized as representative of the principle of justice:

1. Each person has an equal right to the most extensive basic liberties compatible with a similar liberty for others.

2. Social and economic inequalities are arranged so that they are both (a) reasonably expected to be to everyone's advantage and (b) attached to positions and offices open to all.

The first principle states that all individuals should be treated equally. The second principle states that justice is served when all persons have equal opportunity and advantage through their positions and offices to society's opportunities and burdens. Equal opportunity or access to opportunity does not guarantee equal distribution of wealth. Society's disadvantaged may not be justly treated, some critics claim, whenever only equal opportunity is offered. The principle of justice also addresses the unfair distribution of wealth and opportunity and the infliction of harm.

Richard DeGeorge (1986, 76) discusses four types of justice. **Compensatory justice** concerns compensating someone for a past harm or injustice. For example, affirmative action programs, discussed in Chapter 6, are justified in part as compensation for decades of injustice and injury that minorities have suffered (Velasquez 1988, 332). **Retributive justice** concerns serving punishment to someone who has inflicted harm on another. A criterion for applying this justice principle is, "Does the punishment fit the crime?" **Distributive justice** refers to the fair distribution of benefits and burdens. Have certain stakeholders received an unfair share of costs associated with a policy or action? Have others unfairly profited from a policy? **Procedural justice** designates fair decision practices, procedures, and agreements among parties. This criterion asks, "Have the rules and processes that govern the distribution of rewards and punishments, benefits and costs been fair?" These types of justice are part of the larger principle of justice; how they are formulated and applied varies with societies and governmental systems.

Following the principle of justice, Ralph Simms, in our example, might ask whether accepting the government official's offer would provide an equitable distribution of goods and services to the recipients of the new technology system that would be implemented in that country. Also, would self-respect for individuals involved be served by this decision? If Simms determined that justice would not be served by enabling his company to be awarded the contract without a fair bidding process, he might well recommend that his firm reject the offer.

The obvious practical problems in using the principle of justice include the following: Outside the jurisdiction of the state and its legal judicial systems where ethical dilemmas are solved by procedure and law, who decides who is right and who is wrong? Who has the moral authority to punish whom? Can opportunity and burden be fairly distributed to all when it is not in the interest of those in power to do so?

Even with these obvious shortcomings, the principle of justice adds an essential and unique contribution to the other ethical principles discussed above. Beyond the utilitarian's calculation of moral responsibility based on consequences, beyond the universalist's absolute duty to treat everyone as a means and not an end, and beyond the principle of rights, which values unquestionable claims, the principle of justice forces us to question how fairly benefits and costs are distributed to everyone, regardless of power, position, wealth, and station in life.

Justice and Stakeholder Analysis

In a stakeholder analysis, the principle of justice can be applied through these questions:

1. How equitable will the distribution of benefits and costs, pleasure and pain, reward and punishment be among stakeholders if we pursue a particular course of action? Would all stakeholders' self-respect be acknowledged?

2. How clearly have procedures been defined and communicated for distributing the costs and benefits of a course of action or policy? How fair are these procedures to all affected?

3. What provisions can we make to compensate those who will be unfairly affected by the costs of the decision? What provisions can be made to redistribute benefits from those who have been unfairly or overly compensated by the decision?

Figure 3-2 summarizes the ethical principles we have presented. This figure can be used as a reference for applying these principles individually and in a stakeholder analysis with groups.

Immoral, Amoral, or Moral Management?

It is also possible for owners, managers, and individual stakeholders to relate to their constituencies from at least three broad orientations: immorally, amorally, and morally (Carroll 1991). *Immoral treatment* of constituencies signifies a minimal or unethical approach: laying off employees without fair notice or compensation; offering upper-level management undeserved salary increases and perks; giving "golden

Figure 3-2 Summary of Five Ethical Decision-Making Principles and
Stakeholder Analysis

BELIEF SYSTEMS	SOURCE OF MORAL ACTIVITY	STAKEHOLDER ANALYSIS ISSUES
1. ETHICAL RELATIVISM (SELF-INTEREST)	Moral authority is determined by individual or cultural self-interests, customs, and religious principles. An act is morally right if it serves one's self-interests and needs.	1. What are the moral beliefs and principles of the individual(s)? 2. If a particular action or policy is chosen, to what extent will ethical principles clash? 3. In seeking a mutualy desirable outcome, how can conflicting moral beliefs and principles be avoided or negotiated?
2. UTILITARIANISM (CALCULATION OF COSTS AND BENEFITS)	Moral authority is determined by the consequences produced by an act: An act is morally right if the net benefits over costs are greatest for the majority. Also, the greatest good for the greatest number will be produced by this act.	1. Consider collective as well as particular interests. 2. Formulate different alternatives based on the greatest good for all parties involved. 3. Estimate costs and benefits of alternatives for different groups affected.
3. UNIVERSALISM (DUTY)	Moral authority is determined by the extent to which the intention of an act treats all persons with respect. Includes the requirement that everyone should act this way in the same circumstances.	1. Identify individuals whose needs and welfare are at risk with a given policy or decision. 2. Identify use or misuse of manipulation, force, coercion, or deceit that may be harmful to individuals. 3. Identify duties to individuals affected by the decision. 4. Determine if the desired action or policy is acceptable to individuals if the decision is implemented.
4. RIGHTS (INDIVIDUAL ENTITLEMENT)	Moral authority is determined by individual rights guaranteed to all in their pursuit of freedom of speech, choice, happiness, and self-respect.	1. Identify individuals and their rights that may be violated by a particular action. 2. Determine the legal and moral basis of these individual rights. 3. Determine the moral justification from utilitarian principles if individuals' rights are violated.
5. JUSTICE (FAIRNESS AND EQUITY)	Moral authority is determined by the extent to which opportunity, wealth, and burden are fairly distributed among all.	1. If a particular action is chosen, how equally will costs and benefits on stakeholders be distributed? 2. How clear and fair are the procedures for distributing costs and benefits of the decision? 3. How can those who are unfairly affected by the action be compensated?

parachutes" (attractive payments or settlement contracts between a firm and high-ranking executives) when a change in company ownership or control is negotiated (such payments are often done at the expense of shareholders' dividends and often without their knowledge or consent). Managing immorally means intentionally going against ethical principles of justice and fair and equitable treatment of other stakeholders.

Amoral management happens when owners, supervisors, and managers negligently or unintentionally treat shareholders, outside stakeholders, and employees without concern or care for the consequences of their policies or actions. No deliberate or willful wrong may be intended, but also no thought is given to moral behavior or outcomes. Minimalist actions are taken in setting policies that are solely or singularly profit oriented, production centered, or short term. Employees and other stakeholders are viewed as instruments in executing the economic interests of the firm. Strategies, control systems, leadership style, and interactions in organizations will also reflect an amoral, minimalist approach toward stakeholders. Nevertheless, the consequences of unintentional, amoral actions are real for the persons affected. Harm can be done.

Moral management of owners, upper-level executives, and supervisors places value on equitable, fair, and just concern and treatment of shareholders, employees, customers, and other stakeholder interests. Ethics codes are established, communicated, and included in training; employee rights are built into visible policies that are enforced; employees and other stakeholders are treated with respect and trust. Corporate strategy, control and incentive systems, leadership style, and interactions will also reflect morally managed organizations. Moral management is the preferred mode of acting toward stakeholders, since respect, justice, and fairness are considered in the decisions.

It is helpful to use these three orientations while observing managers, owners, employees, and coworkers. Have you observed policies, procedures, and decisions in organizations that are amoral? In the next section, we summarize a view of four social responsibility modes and roles that business executives have historically characterized and presently view as moral decision makers. The model presented in this section complements the five ethical principles offered above by offering a more macro-orientation for describing individual ethical orientations to business decisions. You may be interested in using the following framework to characterize your own moral and responsibility roles, those of your boss and colleagues, and even those of contemporary international figures in government or business.

3.7 **FOUR SOCIAL RESPONSIBILITY ROLES AND MODES**

What social obligations do businesses and their executives have toward their stockholders and society? The traditional view that the responsibility of corporate owners and managers was to serve only or primarily their stockholders' wealth and interests has been challenged and modified—but not abandoned—since the turn of this century. The debate continues over whether businesses' and managers' roles include other social stakeholders as well as economic stockholders. Because of changing demographic and educational characteristics in the workplace and the advent of laws, policies, and procedures that recognize greater awareness of employee and other stakeholder rights, distinctions have been made over the responsibility of the business to its employees and to the larger society.

Anthony Buono and Lawrence Nichols (1990) offer four ethical interpretations of the social role of business in society. Figure 3-3 illustrates these roles. The four social responsibility modes reflect the roles of business toward stockholders and a wider audience of stakeholders.

Figure 3-3 illustrates two distinct social responsibility orientations of businesses and managers toward society: the "stockholder model" (the responsibility of the corporation is primarily to its economic stockholders) and the "stakeholder model" (the responsibility of the corporation is also to its social stakeholders outside the corporation). The two sets of motives underlying these two orientations are "self-interest" and "moral duty." We will discuss (1) stockholder, self-interest and (2) stockholder, moral duty orientations first, followed by (3) stakeholder, self-interest and (4) stakeholder, moral duty orientations. The first two orientations under the stockholder orientation are "productivism" and "philanthropy."

Productivists view social responsibility of the corporation in terms of rational self-interest and the direct fulfillment of stockholder interests. Productivists believe the major—and some would say only—mission of business is to obtain profit. The free market is the best guarantee of moral corporate conduct in this view. Supply-side economists, as productivists for example, argue that the private sector is the vehicle for social improvement. Tax reduction and economic incentives that boost private industry are policies that productivists advocate as socially responsible. Ronald Reagan's "trickle down" policies of social benefits from private-sector wealth are a recent example of this view. The economist Milton Friedman is an example of a productivist.

Philanthropists who also have a stockholder view of the corporation, hold that social responsibility is justified in terms of moral duty toward

Figure 3-3   *Four Social Responsibility Modes and Roles*

ORIENTATIONS

		Stockholder Model	Stakeholder Model
MOTIVES	Self-interest	1 Productivism	2 Progressivism
	Moral Duty	3 Philanthropy	4 Ethical Idealism

Source: Anthony F. Buono and Lawrence T. Nichols. "Stockholders and Stakeholder Interpretations of Business' Social Role." In *Business Ethics: Readings and Cases in Corporate Morality*, 2d ed., edited by W. Michael Hoffman and Jennifer Moore. New York: McGraw-Hill, 1990, 172. Reproduced with permission of Anthony F. Buono.

helping less advantaged members of society through organized, tax deductible charity and stewardship. Proponents of this view believe the primary social role of the corporation is still through profit. However, moral duty drives their motives instead of self-interest solely, as is the case with productivists. Philanthropists believe that corporate profits are the primary mission of firms. But advocates of this view are stewards and believe that those who have wealth ought to share some of it with the less advantaged in society. As stockholder stewards, philanthropists share profits primarily through tax deductions. Levi Strauss in the mid-1880s was one such philanthropist. Can you think of other contemporary philanthropists?

The other dominant orientation is the "stakeholder model." **Progressivism** and **ethical idealism** are the two social responsibility modes in this perspective. Progressivists believe that corporate behavior is justified from a motive of self-interest, but they also hold that corporations should take a broader view of responsibility toward social change. Enlightened self-interest is a value that characterizes progressivists. Rheinhold Niebuhr, the famous Christian theologian, was a modern example of a progressivist who argued for the involvement of the church in politics to bring about reasoned, orderly reform. He also worked with unions and other groups to improve conditions and wages of workers. Progressivists support such policies as affirmative action programs, environmental protection, employee stock option programs (ESOPs), and energy conservation.

Finally, ethical idealists believe that social responsibility is justified when corporate behavior directly supports stakeholder interests from moral duty motives. Ethical idealists, like Ralph Nader, hold that, to be fully responsible, corporate activity should help transform business into an institution in which workers can realize their full human potential. Employee ownership, cooperatives, and community-based and community-owned service industries are examples of this type of corporate transformation that ethical idealists have advocated. The boundaries between business and society are fluid for ethical idealists. Corporate profits are to be shared for humanitarian purposes, to help bring about a more humane society. There is, of course, a spectrum for each of these four responsibility modes. There is, for example, a variety of ethical idealists whose advocates profess different visions and programs regarding the obligations of business to society. Some are more radical than others in orientation. For example, there are ethical idealists who call for the transformation of society in order to redistribute wealth.

Which orientation best characterizes your beliefs of business responsibility to society at this time: productivism, philanthropism, progressivism, or ethical idealism? Which view do you believe businesses should assume? Why?

3.8 INDIVIDUAL ETHICAL DECISION-MAKING STYLES

In addition to the four social responsibility modes presented above, Stanley Krolick (1987) developed a survey that interprets individual primary and secondary ethical decision-making styles. The four styles are (1) individualism, (2) altruism, (3) pragmatism, and (4) idealism. Although these four styles are not exhaustive, we summarize them here to complement the social responsibility modes and the ethical principles discussed above. Caution must be taken in using any of these schemes in order not to label or stereotype oneself or others. These categories are, at best, guides for further reflection, discussion, and study.

Individualists are driven by natural reason, personal survival, and preservation. The self is the source and justification of all actions and decisions. Krolick (1987) states that individualists believe "If I don't take care of my own needs, I will never be able to address the concerns of others." The moral authority of individualists is their own reasoning process based on self-interests. Individualism is related to the principle of naive ethical relativism and to productivism, discussed earlier.

Altruists are concerned primarily with other people. Altruists will relinquish their own personal security for the good of others. They would, as an extreme, like to save the future of the human race. The moral authority and motivation of altruists is to produce the greatest good for the largest number of people. Unlike utilitarians, altruists would not diligently calculate and measure costs and benefits. Providing benefits is their major concern. Altruists justify their actions by upholding the integrity of the community. They enter relationships from a desire to contribute to the common good and to humankind. Altruists are akin to universalists and philanthropists in earlier discussions.

Pragmatists are concerned primarily with the situation at hand, not with the self or the other. The basis of moral authority and motivation of the pragmatist is with the perceived needs of the moment and the potential consequences of a decision in a specific context. The needs of the moment dictate the importance of self-interest, concern for others, rules, and values. Facts and situational information are justifications for the pragmatist's actions. Pragmatists may abandon significant principles and values in order to produce certain results. Pragmatists are closest to utilitarians in our earlier scheme. While this style seems the most objective and appealing, Krolick (1987) cautions that the pragmatist's shifting ethics may make this person's orientation difficult and unpredictable to work with or under in a business environment.

Idealists are driven by principles, rules, regulations, and values. Reason, relationship, or desired consequences of action will not substitute for the idealist's adherence to principles. Duties for the idealist are absolute. The moral authority and motivation for idealists is commitment to principle and consistency. Values and rules of conduct are the justifications idealists use to explain their actions. Seen as people of high morals, idealists can also be rigid and inflexible. Krolick (1987, 18) notes that "this absolute adherence to principles may blind the Idealist to the potential consequences of a decision for oneself, others, or the situation." This style is related to the social responsibility mode of ethical idealism and to the principle of universalism, which were discussed above.

Which style best characterizes your ethical orientation? The orientation of your colleagues? Your boss?

Communicating and Negotiating Across Ethical Styles

Krolick (1987) states that when working or communicating with each style, one must also observe *the other person's ethical style*. The first step is to "concede that the other person's values and priorities have their own validity in their own terms and try to keep those values in mind to facilitate the process of reaching an agreement" (p. 20). Toward that end, Krolick proposes these guidelines when communicating, negotiating, or working with one of the following ethical orientations:

- *Individualist*—point out the benefits to the other person's own self-interest.

- *Altruist*—focus on the benefits for the various constituencies involved.

- *Pragmatist*—emphasize the facts and potential consequences of action.

- *Idealist*—concentrate on the principles or duties at stake.

Learning to recognize and communicate with other ethical styles and the willingness to be flexible in accommodating your ethical style to others, without sacrificing your own, is an important skill in working effectively with others in organizations.

3.9 **QUICK ETHICAL TESTS**

In addition to the ethical principles and social responsibility modes presented above, there are other shorter "ethical tests" one may use before making decisions. Many of these quick rules are based on or reflect the principles discussed in this chapter.

These are practical, quick guides and "checkpoints" that, if observed, could change the actions you would automatically take in ethical dilemmas.

The Center for Business Ethics at Bentley College articulated six simple questions for the "practical philosopher." (These questions are duplicated in Bowditch and Buono 1990.) These are used in training programs. Before making a decision or acting ask:

1. Is it right?
2. Is it fair?
3. Who gets hurt?
4. Would you be comfortable if the details of your decision were reported on the front page of your local newspaper?
5. What would you tell your child to do?
6. How does it smell? (How does it feel?)

Other quick ethical tests, some of which are classical, include the following (which are based on guidelines found in Steiner and Steiner [1988] and rephrased in Carroll [1989]):

- *The Golden Rule:* "Do unto others as you would have them do unto you." This includes not knowingly doing harm to others.

- *The Intuition Ethic:* We know apart from reason what is right. We have a moral sense about what is right and wrong. We should follow our "gut feeling" about what is right.

- *The Means–Ends Ethic:* We may choose unscrupulous but efficient means to reach an end if the ends are really worthwhile and significant. Be sure the ends are not the means.

- *The Test of Common Sense:* "Does the action I am getting ready to take really make sense?" Think before acting.

- *The Test of One's Best Self:* "Is this action or decision I'm getting ready to take compatible with my concept of myself at my best?"

- *The Test of Ventilation:* Do not isolate yourself with your dilemma. Get others' feedback before acting or deciding.

- *The Test of the Purified Idea:* "Am I thinking this action or decision is right just because someone with appropriate authority or knowledge says it is right?" An action may not be right because someone in a position of power or authority states that an action is right. You may still be held responsible for taking the action.

Use these principles and guidelines in examining the motivations of stakeholders' strategies, policies, and actions. Why do stakeholders act and talk as they do? What principles drive these actions?

Concluding Comments

Individual stakeholders have a wide range of ethical principles, orientations, and "quick tests" to draw on before taking action or solving an ethical dilemma. Specifically, in a given business situation in which we have mapped stakeholders and their stakes (from Chapter 2), this chapter can assist our analysis of the moral dimension of the stakeholder approach by helping us identify what Freeman and Gilbert (1988, 109) call the "ground rules" or "implicit morality" of institutional members:

> Think of the implicit morality of an institution as the internal rules which must be followed if the institution is to be a good one of its kind. The rules are often implicit, because the explicit rules of an institution may well be the reason that the institution functions rather badly. . . . Another way to think of the implicit morality of an institution is as the internal logica of the institution. Once this internal logica is clearly understood, we can evaluate its required behaviors against external standards. (p. 109)

In the following chapter, we present the conceptual basis of the organization as stakeholder and examine the moral dimensions of a corporation's strategy, leadership, culture, and issues of corporate self-regulation.

SUMMARY

Complex ethical dilemmas in business situations involve making tough choices among conflicting and competing interests. This chapter presents twelve questions and three decision criteria that can assist individuals in determining the most suitable course of action. These principles can also be applied at the group and corporate levels of analysis.

Individuals can gain a clearer perspective of their own motivations and actions by distinguishing them from the motivations of others. This perspective can be useful in guiding your own decision-making process, and understanding the ethical reasoning and decision criteria from this chapter can also enable you to reason more critically when examining other stakeholders' ethical reasoning.

A primary goal of ethical reasoning is to help individuals act in morally responsible ways. Ignorance and bias are two conditions that blind a person's moral awareness. Five principles of ethical reasoning are presented to expose the reader to different methods of ethical decision making. The five methods include (1) ethical relativism (consisting of naive relativism and cultural relativism), (2) utilitarianism, (3) universalism, (4) rights, and (5) justice. Each principle is discussed in terms of the utility and drawbacks associated with it. Guidelines for thinking through and applying each principle in a stakeholder analysis are provided. These principles are not mechanical recipes for selecting a course of action. They are "filters" or screens to be used in clarifying dilemmas.

Four social responsibility roles or orientations of business are presented. Productivism and philanthropy are two roles influenced by stockholder concerns. Progressivism and ethical idealism are driven by stockholder concerns but are also influenced by external stakeholders.

Individuals also have different ethical decision-making styles. Four different but not exclusive styles include individualism, altruism, pragmatism, and idealism. It is important to understand another person's ethical decision-making style when engaging in professional or other types of communication and negotiation. These styles are a starting point for reflecting and identifying our (and others') predominant decision-making characteristics. Styles can change.

The final section of this chapter offers quick "ethical tests" that can be used to provide insight into your decision-making process and actions. These methods and principles of ethical reasoning can enable individuals to better understand moral issues as well as their own motivations and intentions.

Questions

1. What is a first step in addressing ethical dilemmas?

2. What are three criteria that can be used in ethical reasoning to help systematize and structure our thinking and arguments?

3. What single focal question is often most powerful in solving ethical dilemmas?

4. What are two conditions that eliminate a person's moral responsibility for causing injury or harm?

5. Briefly explain five fundamental ethical principles that can be used in ethical reasoning.

6. What are some of the problems associated with cultural relativism? The benefits?

7. Why is utilitarianism useful in conducting a stakeholder analysis? What are some of the problems we may find in using this principle?

8. Briefly explain the categorical imperative. What does it force you, as a decision maker, to do when choosing an action in a moral dilemma?

9. Explain the difference between the principles of rights and justice. What are some of the strengths of each principle? What are some of the weaknesses?

10. What are the four social responsibility modes? How can these be used?

11. Briefly explain each of the individual ethical decision-making styles. Which style do you consider most closely characterizes your own?

12. Which of the ethical "quick tests" do you prefer for yourself? Why?

Exercises

1. Write an example from your experience of a serious ethical dilemma. Use the 12 questions developed by Laura Nash, presented in the chapter, to offer a resolution to the problem, even if your resolution is different the second time. Did you use any of the questions in your original experience? Would any of these questions have helped you? How? What would you have done differently? Why?

2. Identify a real-life example of an instance when you thought ignorance absolved a person, group, or organization from moral responsibility. Then identify an example when a person, group or organization simply failed to become fully informed about a moral situation. Under what conditions do you think individuals are morally responsible for the effects of their actions? Why?

3. Which of the four social responsibility modes of business in the chapter do you most identify with? Why? Identify a company that reflects this orientation. Explain why you believe the company is an example of the mode you have chosen. Would you want to work for this company? Would you want to be part of the management team? Explain.

4. Select a company in the news/press that has acted morally and one that has acted immorally. Using this chapter, characterize the "ethics" of each company or of its spokespersons or executives.

References and Suggested Readings

Bowditch, James, and Anthony Buono. *A Primer on Organizational Behavior.* 2d ed. New York: John Wiley and Sons, 1990.

Buono, Anthony F., and Lawrence T. Nichols. "Stockholder and Stakeholder Interpretations of Business' Social Role." In *Business Ethics: Readings and Cases in Corporate Morality.* 2d ed. Edited by W. Michael Hoffman and Jennifer Moore. New York: McGraw-Hill, 1990.

Carroll, Archie. *Business and Society: Ethics and Stakeholder Management.* 1st and 2d eds. Cincinnati: South-Western Publishing Co., 1989 and 1993.

———. "The Pyramid of Corporate Social Responsibility: Toward the Moral Management of Organizational Stakeholders." *Business Horizons* (July/August 1991): 38–48.

DeGeorge, Richard T. *Business Ethics,* 2d and 3d eds. New York: Macmillan, 1986 and 1990.

Delong, James V. et al. "Defending Cost-Benefit Analysis: Replies to Steven Kelman" *AEI Journal on Government and Society* (March/April 1981): 39–43.

Freeman, R. Edward, and Daniel Gilbert, Jr. *Corporate Strategy and the Search for Ethics.* Englewood Cliffs, N.J.: Prentice-Hall, 1988.

Hoffman, W. Michael, and Jennifer Moore, *Business Ethics: Readings and Cases in Corporate Morality.* 2d ed. New York: McGraw-Hill, 1990.

Jackall, Robert. *Moral Mazes: The World of Corporate Managers.* New York: Oxford University Press, 1988.

Kant, Immanuel. *Groundwork of the Metaphysics of Morals,* translated by H. J. Paton. New York: Harper & Row, 1964.

Keeley, Michael. *A Social-Contract Theory of Organizations.* Notre Dame, Ind.: University of Notre Dame Press, 1988.

Kelman, Steven. "Cost-Benefit Analysis, An Ethical Critique." *AEI Journal on Government and Society* (January/February 1981): 33–40.

Krolick, Stanley. *Ethical Decision-Making Style: Survey and Interpretive Notes.* Beverly, Mass: Addison-Wesley Training Systems, 1987.

Mill, John Stuart. *Utilitarianism.* Indianapolis: Bobbs-Merrill, 1957.

Nash, Laura. "Ethics Without the Sermon." *Harvard Business Review* (November/December 1981): 88.

Rawls, John. *A Theory of Justice.* Cambridge, Mass.: Harvard University Press, 1971.

Steiner, George A., and John F. Steiner, *Business, Government, and Society: A Managerial Perspective.* 5th and 6th eds. New York: Random House, 1988 and 1991.

Toffler, Barbara Ley. *Tough Choices: Managers Talk Ethics.* New York: John Wiley & Sons, 1986.

Velasquez, Manuel G. *Business Ethics: Concepts and Cases.* 2d and 3d eds. Englewood Cliffs, N.J.: Prentice-Hall, 1988 and 1992.

Walton, Clarence. *The Moral Manager.* Cambridge, Mass.: Ballinger, 1988.

4

The Corporation as Stakeholder

Moral Dimensions of Strategy,
Structure, Leadership,
Culture, and Self-Regulation

Asbestosis, mesothelioma, and lung cancer, all life-threatening diseases, share a common cause: microscopically inhaled particles of asbestos over an extended period of time.

The link between these diseases and enough inhaled asbestos particles is a medical fact. Manville Corporation is a multinational mining and forest product manufacturer and has been a leading commercial producer of asbestos. As of March 1977, 271 asbestos-related damage suits were filed against the firm by workers. The victims claimed the company did not warn them of the life-threatening dangers of asbestos. Since 1968, Manville has paid over $50 million in such claims. And since the 1950s, the Manville Corporation has faced hundreds of lawsuits from workers: The estimate is over $1 billion. By 1982, Manville faced over 500 new asbestos lawsuits filed each month. Consequently, in August 1982, Manville filed for Chapter 11 bankruptcy in order to reorganize and remain solvent in the face of the asbestos-related lawsuits; the firm was losing over half the cases that reached trial. The reorganization was approved, and Manville set up a $2.5 billion trust fund to pay asbestos claimants. Shareholders surrendered half their value in stock, and it was also agreed that projected earnings over 25 years would be reduced to support the trust.

The extent of Manville's social responsibility toward its workers, litigants, the communities it serves, and society has, at best, been mixed. Manville, since 1972, has been active and cooperative with the U.S. Department of Labor and the AFL/CIO in developing standards to protect asbestos workers. However, Dr. Kenneth Smith—the medical director of one of the firm's plants in Canada—refused on court record in the 1970s to inform Manville workers that they had asbestosis. Lawsuits ensued.

There is also the complication and confusion of evolving and changing legislation on asbestos. The Supreme Court, as stakeholder, has not taken a stand on who is liable in these situations: Are insurance firms liable when workers are initially exposed to asbestos and later develop cancer, or are they liable 20 years later? Also, right-to-know laws are not definitive in state legislatures. Does that leave Manville and other corporations liable for government's legal indecision?

Was Manville acting responsibly by using bankruptcy as a strategy for not paying for its fair share of damages? Or, was bankruptcy a reasonable and responsible corporate response to this situation? Of the 16,500 personal-injury plaintiffs, 2,000 have died since the reorganization in 1982. Manville still faces court battles and the prospect of not remaining solvent. One chairman and CEO have resigned, and the company has quit the asbestos business. One estimate is that lawyers stand to gain over $1 billion in fees from settlements paid by Manville's trust. Who is winning and who is losing? What ethical principles have Manville's executives used to do business? Does Manville deserve to go bankrupt, or have its corporate leaders done the best they could in this situation?

(For sources supporting this section, see Buchholz [1989]; Dahl [1985]; Lanza et al. [1935]; Rotbart [1984]; Sharplin [1988]; and Shaw [1991].)

4.1 DOES A CORPORATION HAVE A CONSCIENCE?

The Manville case raises important questions about the nature and responsibility of corporations as stakeholders in complex legal and moral dilemmas: For example, "Are corporations such as Manville rational, impersonal institutions? Are corporations collectives of politically and economically driven groups? Does a corporation have a conscience? Is a corporation morally responsible to society? If so, to what extent?" These questions are part of an ongoing debate that underscores the following problematic issues: (1) If a corporation does not have a conscience and is primarily an impersonal profit-making institution, what responsibilities does it have to its stakeholders, such as consumers, employees, and government, and to society? What rules, and who, should govern and control its activities, which have moral implications for its stakeholders, if it cannot or will not do so? (2) If a corporation is more than a profit-making institutional stakeholder, what is the source and basis of its moral responsibility? To whom is it responsible beyond its economic obligations? How should it implement its moral and social responsibilities to its stakeholders?

We begin our discussion by presenting and evaluating two contrasting views of the nature of corporations and their social responsibility: (1) The first view holds that the corporation does not have a conscience and is an impersonal institution—a stakeholder committed only to its stockholders; (2) the second view holds that corporations are analogous to individuals—the corporation has a conscience and acts as a moral agent in its stakeholder relationships. We then present a third perspective of the corporation as economic and social stakeholder. This perspective attempts to reconcile the earlier contrasting views. Following this view, we discuss the internal organization of corporations as stakeholders and the influence of strategy, structure, and culture on social responsibility. Finally, we conclude the chapter by identifying issues regarding the self-regulation of corporations and shareholders.

First View: Corporations Do Not Have a Conscience

No one disputes the fact that most corporations like Manville are in business to make profits for owners and shareholders. A key question is whether corporations can and should be morally responsible to stakeholders other than their shareholders. The "corporation as impersonal, profit-making institution" view (the productivist view from Chapter 3) holds that the primary, and some would agree the only, obligation of businesses is to make profits, not to act morally responsible. This view is important to the domain of business ethics, since the definition of corporations as impersonal entities suggests that moral blame and liability cannot be attributed to an institution. This is a utilitarian-based view that assumes that corporations provide the greatest (in terms of material wealth) good for the largest number in society.

Adam Smith (1723–1790) was an early proponent of this view. He held that individual "self-interest" motivated and promoted the economic well-being of society and that the "invisible hand" guided and promoted the general welfare of society. Businesses, according to this view, are seen as amoral (not immoral) institutions that promote the self-interests and economic motives of owners. Social responsibility does require rules and rule enforcement. This is the responsibility of the state, not of businesses.

Thomas Hobbes's and John Locke's philosophies also reflected this logic. According to their view, the major stakeholders whom corporations should be concerned about are owners, shareholders, and those groups that promote profit-making capabilities. Society benefits when businesses make a profit. The production role of business is emphasized over the distribution and responsibility roles.

Recent advocates of this view include the economist Milton Friedman; Theodore Levitt, a Harvard professor; and John Kenneth Galbraith, a noted economist. Friedman (1970) has been widely quoted as stating that "there is one and only one social responsibility of business—to use its resources and engage in activities designed to increase its profits as long as it stays within the rules of the game, which is to say, engages in open and free competition without deception and fraud." Friedman believes that the free-market system defines the "rules of the game" and that it is adequate to help firms meet their primary responsibility of earning profit for owners and shareholders. Friedman advocates that corporations are not in business to help society. He has argued that managers who pursue "social responsibility" activities at work are not using stockholders' money as intended; they are "taxing" shareholders, since they are acting as publicly elected officials instead of private employees (Hoffman and Moore 1990).

Similarly, Theodore Levitt (1958; also quoted in Shaw 1991) has stated that "business has only two responsibilities—to obey the elementary canons of face-to-face civility (honesty, good faith, and so on) and to seek material gain."

According to this view of corporations, sources of moral responsibility lie outside the firm. The "invisible hand," the "hand of the government," and other means of moral control must monitor and discipline corporate behavior. John Kenneth Galbraith (1956)—also an advocate for the view of the corporation as an impersonal institution—argues for government control over corporate moral behavior, and not for increased corporate social responsibility.

Some contemporary philosophers also reflect the view that corporations are not persons and do not have intentions. Persons inside corporations are believed to be socially responsible, however. For example, Manuel Velasquez (1982) argued that corporations should not be seen as persons for two reasons: First, individual wrongdoers will not be sought and punished if the "corporation" can be held responsible for wrongful acts. Consequently, corporate immoral acts will not be deterred. Second, understanding corporations as intentional persons will cause us to view them as "larger-than human" persons "whose ends and well-being are more important than those of its members." Consequently, the corporation's members may "legitimately be sacrificed to the corporation's interests and the good of the individual may be subordinated to the corporation's good" (quoted in Des Jardins and McCall 1990). Therefore, it is the people in the corporation, not the corporation itself, who must be held accountable for illegal and immoral acts. Velasquez argues that although corporations have social and moral obligations, businesses as institutions do not have intentions or act as persons.

In the opening case, Manville was held legally liable as a corporation for its workers who contracted cancer while working with asbestos. What would the advocates of the "corporations as impersonal, profit-making institutions" view argue here: Was Manville as a corporation morally responsible for harm done to the employees who became cancer victims? Who in the corporation over the past several decades should be held legally and morally responsible for the asbestos-related cases?

We should be aware of the following criticism regarding this still popular view. First, understanding organizations as impersonal institutions without intention strengthens the myth we discussed in Chapter 1: That is, corporations and their actions are amoral. To argue that corporations as institutions have no moral basis on which to be held accountable is to suggest that corporate managers have free reign to commit sizable resources to activities that may be harmful to the consuming public. For example, if Manville could not as a corporation be held morally responsible by stakeholders such as the media, interest groups, government, citizens, and employees, then managers might be less restrained in subjecting its workers to dangerous asbestos manufacturing processes. Second, to view corporations as impersonal institutions without intention could provide protection for powerful owners and top managers at the expense of lower-level employees who could be made scapegoats for illegal activities. Third, corporations are human as well as economic institutions. As such, why should these legally state-registered institutions not be held liable and responsible for the welfare of communities in which they do business and for their employees who make their existence possible? Fourth, competitive economic production and profit alone do not necessarily produce the greatest good for the largest number (see Bowie and Duska 1990). Without cooperation from local, state, and federal governments and the public, many businesses could not cover their maintenance or "external costs," that is, the costs incurred by businesses but paid by society (such as the side effects of air and water pollution that we must bear). Related to this criticism is the fact that not all businesses survive according to the "survival of the fittest" in the free market. Some businesses are regulated and supported by the government, that is, by the public's tax dollars. Utilities are an example. The "invisible hand" is not so invisible in these and other cases, as the Chrysler Corporation has shown. Without a government loan in 1979, Chrysler probably would not have survived.

Second View: Corporations Have a Conscience

The opposing view holds that corporations are analogous to individuals. As such, corporations have consciences, not literally but as moral agents acting on behalf of the firm's ownership and shareholders. Corporate behavior can, therefore, be evaluated according to ethical standards as individual behavior is. Corporations act with intentionality and should, therefore, be held morally accountable for their actions. Also inherent in this view is the notion that firms not only are legally and morally liable for their actions but also should perform socially responsible acts; they should be "good citizens."

Kenneth Goodpaster and John Matthews (1982; see also Hoffman and Moore 1990), for example, argue that because corporations are credited with having goals, economic values, and strategies, they should also have a conscience. These authors do not believe that corporations should literally be equated with individuals but that understanding organizations as persons provides a framework superior to the first view presented above for analyzing corporate responsibility. If corporations do not have intentionality, these authors argue, how can they be held morally accountable as collectives?

Peter French (1977; see also Hoffman and Moore 1990) also argued that corporations act intentionally and should be held morally accountable for their actions. French argued that corporations act through their **"corporate internal decision (CID) structure,"** which is composed of a corporate flowchart and a corporate policy. Corporate decisions embody the decisional structure of the flowchart and the intentionality of a firm's policy. French links and associates corporate decisions with the notion of an individual through the CID. The CID "incorporates" actions of individuals as a collective.

French (quoted in Hoffman and Moore 1990) wrote, "The CID Structure licenses redescriptions of events as corporate and attributions of corporate intentionality while it does not obscure the private acts of executives, directors, etc." According to French, corporate decisions are not identical with decisions of individuals within the firm. Still, decisions that are passed through the CID represent the firm as an individual collective.

Like the first view, this perspective of the corporation also has limitations. It is intuitively difficult to equate collective command structural and policy decisions only with individuals. Large corporations, in particular, are shifting collectives and coalitions with diverse opinions and decisions—even though presidents and top managers make and enforce decisions that represent the corporation. But, is Manville analogous to an individual? Should Manville's decisions regarding asbestos victims' claims over several decades be the liability of the corporation or of those decision makers who authorized the work policies and orders? Or does the liability belong both to individuals in the corporation and to the corporation?

The view of the corporation as an individual and moral agent does place intentionality and social responsibility back inside the corporation; however, as the criticisms above suggest, this view is anthropomorphic and does not take into consideration the political complexity of internal operations and diverse interests inside contemporary corporations. A third view of the nature and role of corporations regarding social responsibility is presented below. This view, which we support in this book, attempts to reconcile many of the problems from the first two views.

4.2 THE CORPORATION AS SOCIAL AND ECONOMIC STAKEHOLDER

The third view of the corporation as a social and economic stakeholder in the community is based on a pragmatic assessment of the nature of the relationships between firms and the constituencies they serve. In this section, we will discuss the moral basis of the relationship between corporations and the groups with which they interact.

The stakeholder perspective (see Evan and Freeman 1988) essentially views the for-profit corporation as a legal entity and collective of individuals and groups. The CEO and top-level managers are hired to maximize profits for the owners and shareholders. However, to accomplish this, corporations must also respond to a variety of stakeholders' (employees, customers, suppliers, government agencies) needs, rights, and legitimate demands. From this perspective, the corporation has primary obligations to the economic mandates of its owners; however, to survive and succeed, it must also respond to legal, social, political, and environmental claims from a host of stakeholders inside and outside its boundaries.

Corporations are, then, socially and morally responsible to their constituencies to the extent that they maintain responsible relationships with their stakeholders and respond to their legitimate rights and claims according to ethical standards of fairness and justice, as well as utilitarian costs and benefits analyses. The stakeholder view supports no specific moral principle of right and wrong but enables corporations and their stakeholders to adopt moral principles and guidelines according to the stakes and moral constraints in different situations. The point is that corporations are obligated and constrained to respect the rights and legitimate interests of their constituencies in order to do business well.

In contrast to the second view presented above, corporations are not like individuals, since firms outlive individuals and plan into future generations. Consequently, interests of corporations are not identical to individual interests. Therefore, to understand corporations as having consciences is not an apt metaphor; however, the view that corporations must act socially and morally—as well as legally and economically— toward their stakeholders is an essential part of the stakeholder theory.

The Social Contract

The stakeholder view of the corporation is also based on the concept of a **social contract**. Developed by early political philosophers, a social contract

> is a set of rules and assumptions about behavior patterns among the various elements of society. Much of the social contract is embedded in the customs of society. For example, in integrating minorities into the workforce, society has come to expect companies to do more than the law requires. . . . Some of the "contract provisions" result from practices between parties.

Like a legal contract, the social contract often involves a quid pro quo (something for something) exchange. *(Gordon, Mondy, Sharplin, and Premeaux 1990)*

The social contract between a corporation and its stakeholders is often based on implicit as well as explicit agreements. For example, it is argued that

The success of many businesses is directly related to the public's confidence in those businesses. A loss of public confidence can be detrimental to the firm and to its investors. One way to retain and to reinforce public confidence is by acting in an ethical manner, a manner that shows a concern for the investing public and the customers of the firm. *(Torabzadeh et al. 1989)*

Patricia Werhane (1989) illustrated the noneconomic basis that binds corporations to their stakeholders in the following argument against insider trading:

My contention has been that the principal ethical arguments against insider trading do not, by themselves, suffice to show that the practice is unethical and should be illegal. The strongest arguments are those that turn on the notion of a fiduciary duty to act in the interest of shareholders, or on the idea of inside information as company "property." But in both arguments, the impermissibility of insider trading depends on a contractual understanding among the company, its shareholders and its employees. *(Werhane 1989, 177)*

Werhane continued by arguing that "fiduciary relationships" are based on "trust and dependence" in which one stakeholder or party acts on behalf of the interest of another. Such relationships, she states, are essential in doing business in a complex society.

Laura Nash's (1990, 101) use of the concept of the **covenantal ethic** is also related to the concept of social contract (or covenant) and lies at the heart of a stakeholder approach. The covenantal ethic focuses on the importance of social as well as economic relationships among businesses, customers, and stakeholders. Nash states that relationships and social contracts (or covenants) between corporate managers and customers are oriented and are not "buyer *or* seller beware" but "seller must care." Nash states,

A manager's understanding of problems will not be in terms of concrete products, specific cost reductions, or even balance sheets (though obviously these will be secondary results and scorecards), but in terms of the quality of the relationships that are inevitably created by any business activity. *(Nash 1990, 104)*

Nash speaks of the quality of a covenantal context as an "enabling relationship" that adds value and is based on the mutual benefit of buyer and seller. Without trusting relationships, long-term economic business transactions do not succeed.

The stakeholder perspective as based on social contracts and a covenantal ethic argues that corporations have social and moral—as well as legal, political, economic, and environmental—obligations to perform toward their constituencies in order to maintain and benefit from mutually sustaining relationships. For example, CEOs, upper-level managers, and boards of directors have a primary moral obligation of accurately and honestly informing shareholders on an ongoing basis of the company's economic status and progress. Acting socially responsible toward their communities, host countries, and society is an important noneconomic obligation for companies. Corporations have social and moral obligations of providing a safe and healthy work environment for their employees. Firms must also offer fair and equitable wages for work performed. Corporations also have a moral obligation to accurately inform consumers about their services and the contents of their products and to provide safe services and products.

Pragmatic Principles for Corporate and Stakeholder Relationships

Norman Bowie and Ronald Duska (1990, 34–37) argue at a more general level that corporations' obligations—in addition to making a profit—include acting justly; causing no avoidable, unjustifiable harm; and preventing harm where there is a need and proximity and in situations where there are no others to intervene. These writers also argue that corporations realistically should be moral according to the criteria of "ought-implies-can" and according to a "moral minimum" standard. "Ought-implies-can" means that companies are not required to produce the most safe products if the cost will stop consumers from buying them; consumers also weigh price against safety concerns. Why expect or require firms to produce the safest product that will not sell? Companies ought to do what they can do.

The "moral minimum" standard holds that firms should not produce products or services or engage in activities that inflict avoidable harm on others. At a minimum, corporations should design, manufacture, distribute, and sell safe products that will sell, according to this standard.

Moral Basis and Social Power of Corporations as Stakeholders

Keith Davis (1975) reasoned that the social responsibility of corporations is based on social power and that "if business has the power, then a just relationship demands that business also bear responsibility for its actions in these areas." Davis termed this view the "iron law of responsibility." He stated, "[I]n the long run, those who do not use power in a manner in which society considers responsible will tend to lose it." Davis discussed five broad guidelines or obligations that business professionals should follow to be socially responsible: (1) Business has a social role of "trustee for society's resources." Since society entrusts business to use its resources, business must wisely serve the interests of all stakeholders of the firm, not just owners, consumers, or labor. (2) "Business shall operate as a two-way open system with open receipt of inputs from society and open disclosure of its operations to the public." (3) "Social costs as well as benefits of an activity, product, or service shall be thoroughly calculated and considered in order to decide whether to proceed with it." Technical and economic criteria must be supplemented with the social effects of activities, goods, or services before a company proceeds. (4) "The social costs of each activity, product, or service shall be priced into it so that the consumer (user) pays for the effects of his consumption on society." (5) "Business institutions as citizens have responsibilities for social involvement in areas of their competence where major social needs exist." These five guidelines provide a foundation for creating and reviewing the moral basis of corporate stakeholder relationships.

Limitations of the Stakeholder View

The stakeholder view of corporations is increasingly becoming a useful perspective for understanding a firm's social and moral responsibilities to its constituencies. But this view also has critics. Some argue that this view is mainly economically based and focuses on maximizing profit (Buchholz 1991; Donaldson 1989). It is also argued that this view has no solid theoretical grounding for corporate social responsiveness. For example, Rogene Buchholz (1991) stated that "[T]he stakeholder model is a useful tool to analyze and describe the various relationships a corporation has to its main constituents in society, but it is by no means a serious theoretical attempt to provide a new paradigm that would even begin to replace the economic paradigm."

While it is true that the stakeholder view of corporations does not dictate an absolute set of ethical standards that firms should follow in doing business, it is realistic and practical and permits researchers and organizational members to apply a range of ethical principles to specific situations. From an ethical point of view, the stakeholder perspective also constrains corporations to act for the benefit of their constituencies, both economically and according to justice, fairness, and utilitarian guidelines. Finally, we note that Archie Carroll (1991, 43) includes philanthropic responsibilities (along with economic, legal, and ethical responsibilities) in the stakeholder perspective: "[O]ne would not encounter many business executives today who exclude philanthropic programs from their firms' range of activities. It seems the role of corporate citizenship is one that business has no significant problem embracing." Given the strengths and shortcomings of the stakeholder view of corporate moral responsibility, we argue that it is the most practical, least absolutist conceptual framework with which to examine corporate social responsibility in ethical dilemmas. It focuses on relationships and obligations of the corporation to its constituencies within the marketplace.

In the next section, we focus attention inside the corporation as stakeholder and discuss how strategy, structure, leadership, and culture influence moral responsibility.

4.3 CORPORATE STRATEGY AND MORAL RESPONSIBILITY

"Structure follows strategy" is an accepted organizational principle in management literature. A corporation's structure, according to managerial contingency theory, should match and "fit" its strategy if the organization is to function coherently and competitively. Corporate culture and moral responsibility also follow and are influenced by strategy. In this section, we discuss the relationship among corporate strategy, structure, leadership, and moral responsibility. How do strategy and structure influence and affect the moral behavior of employees? Corporate leaders are responsible for directing the formulation and articulation of strategy.

Figure 4-1 illustrates the related nature of strategy to other organizational dimensions. For purposes of ethical analysis, Figure 4-1 provides a model for discussing the organizational and conceptual relatedness among strategy, structure, culture, professionals, and control systems. We are particularly interested here in the effects of these interactions on

Figure 4-1 Related Nature of Corporate Strategy, Organizational Dimensions, and Moral Responsibilities

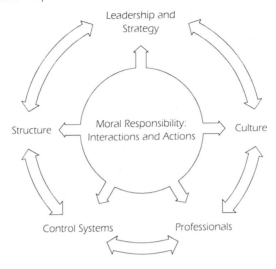

the morality of the actions and behavior of corporate employees. We argue in this section that intended and enacted strategy influences the legality and morality of corporate activities in the following ways: (1) Strategy sets the overall management direction of business activities. Enterprise strategy can, for example, emphasize revenue growth over customer satisfaction or product quality. It can emphasize technical concern over professional development. Or, corporatewide strategy can include and direct a firm's activities to social issues, employee rights, and other stakeholder obligations. (2) Strategy directs the emphasis of activities that top management values and rewards. In this sense, strategy reflects management's statement of what is important ethically. (3) Strategy sets the "tone and tenor" of business activities and transactions. Strategies that overemphasize profits may set a tone for business activity that ignores customer concern and safety or innovative ideas. Furthermore, organizational reward and control systems often reflect the emphasis and tone of the larger strategic direction. Emphasis on profits at the expense of employee development usually is reflected in rigid and unrealistic incentive and revenue quota systems. Enterprise strategy, then, sets and affects expectations, ways of doing business, rewards, and motivations as well as performance. Strategy influences the types of control systems that govern business activities and the pressures that lead to moral or immoral behavior.

Four Levels of Strategy

In Chapter 2, we explained how a stakeholder analysis is used as a strategic method for mapping a firm's social responsibility toward external stakeholders. Here we offer a general overview of what strategy is, and we focus on how strategy directs and influences a corporation's moral responsibility inside and outside the firm.

Corporations formulate at least four levels of strategies: enterprise, corporate, business and functional (Hofer and Schendel 1979; quoted in Carroll 1989; see also Thompson and Strictland 1980). The **enterprise strategy** is the broadest level. It identifies the corporation's role in society, defines how the firm will be perceived by stakeholders, represents its principles and values, and shows what the firm stands for (Freeman 1984). The **corporate strategy** identifies the firm's goals, objectives, and business areas through which policies and plans are based. **Business strategy** translates the corporate strategy into more detailed goals and objectives for specific business activities. **Functional strategy** takes business strategy into even more detail at the marketing, research and development, production, sales, and other functional areas of the business.

At the enterprise level of strategy, the CEO and upper-level managers state their social responsibility and stakeholder commitments. Corporate strategy should also reflect ethical considerations. For example, Freeman and Gilbert (1988) stated that "[t]o understand why corporations choose to do what they do, we must understand the values at work in the actions of multiple stakeholders. Understanding corporate strategy means understanding the competing value claims of multiple stakeholders." Extending this logic, Freeman and Gilbert stated two axioms for corporate strategy: (1) "Corporate strategy must reflect an understanding of the values of organizational members and stakeholders," and (2) "[c]orporate strategy must reflect an understanding of the ethical nature of strategic choice." According to Freeman and Gilbert, the rights of individuals and human goals should be primary in corporate strategy.

Johnson & Johnson's now exemplary credo, in Figure 4-2, illustrates a corporation's values statement that underlies its enterprise and corporate strategies. Here the values of the corporation's members and the responsibilities of the corporation to its stakeholders are clearly laid out. Another well recognized values statement that drives both enterprise and corporate strategies is the "Beliefs of Borg-Warner" from the Borg-Warner Corporation, presented in Figure 4-3.

Figure 4-2 Johnson & Johnson Credo

OUR CREDO

We believe our first responsibility is to the doctors, nurses and patients, to mothers and fathers and all others who use our product and services. In meeting their needs everything we do must be of high quality.
We must constantly strive to reduce our costs in order to maintain reasonable prices.
Customers' orders must be serviced promptly and accurately.
Our suppliers and distributors must have an opportunity to make a fair profit.

We are responsible to our employees, the men and women who work with us throughout the world.
Everyone must be considered as an individual. We must respect their dignity and recognize their merit.
They must have a sense of security in their jobs.
Compensation must be fair and adequate, and working conditions clean, orderly and safe.
We must be mindful of ways to help our employees fulfill their family responsibilities.
Employees must feel free to make suggestions and complaints.
There must be equal opportunity for employment, development and advancement for those qualified.
We must provide competent management, and their actions must be just and ethical.

We are responsible to the communities in which we work and to the world community as well.
We must be good citizens—support good works and charities and bear our fair share of taxes.
We must encourage civic improvements and better health and education.
We must maintain in good order the property we are privileged to use, protecting the environment and natural resources.

Our final responsibility is to our stockholders.
Business must make a sound profit.
We must experiment with new ideas.
Research must be carried on, innovation programs developed and mistakes paid for.
New equipment must be purchased, new facilities provided and new products launched.
Reserves must be created to provide for adverse times.
When we operate according to these principles, the stockholders should realize a fair return.

Source: Reprinted with permission of Johnson & Johnson.

Figure 4-3 *The Beliefs of Borg Warner: To Reach Beyond the Minimal*

Any business is a member of a social system, entitled to the rights and bound by the responsibilities of that membership. Its freedom to pursue economic goals is constrained by law and channeled by the forces of a free market. But these demands are minimal, requiring only that a business provide wanted goods and services, compete fairly, and cause no obvious harm. For some companies, that is enough. It is not enough for Borg-Warner. We impose upon ourselves an obligation to reach beyond the minimal. We do so convinced that by making a larger contribution to the society that sustains us, we best assure not only its future vitality, but our own.

This is what we believe.

We believe in the dignity of the individual.

However large and complex a business may be, its work is still done by dealing with people. Each person involved is a unique human being, with pride, needs, values, and innate personal worth. For Borg-Warner to succeed, we must operate in a climate of openness and trust, in which each of us freely grants others the same respect, cooperation, and decency we seek for ourselves.

We believe in our responsibility to the common good.

Because Borg-Warner is both an economic and social force, our responsibilities to the public are large. The spur of competition and the sanctions of the law give strong guidance to our behavior, but alone do not inspire our best. For that we must heed the voice of our natural concern for others. Our challenge is to supply goods and services that are of superior value to those who use them; to create jobs that provide meaning for those who do them; to honor and enhance human life; and to offer our talents and our wealth to help improve the world we share.

These are broad strategic value and social responsibility directives that serve as a basis for elaborating specific goals, objectives, policies, and plans of business and functional areas in human resource management, research and development, financial planning, sales, and other managerial areas. Socially responsive personnel policies serve as a basis and platform for setting and operationalizing performance and evaluation standards, affirmative action hiring, layoffs, and outplacement policies. Noneconomic financial objectives that promote customer service and treatment can be identified. Sales strategies that seek to inform and protect customers from false information can be implemented. Product specifications, labels, and warranties that have public interests and safety in mind can be operationalized. Without written ethical principles in enterprise strategy statements, companies are less likely to

We believe in the endless quest for excellence.

Though we may be better today than we were yesterday, we are not as good as we must become. Borg-Warner chooses to be a leader—in serving our customers, advancing our technologies, and rewarding all who invest in us their time, money and trust. None of us can settle for doing less than our best, and we can never stop trying to surpass what already has been achieved.

We believe in continuous renewal.

A corporation endures and prospers only by moving forward. The past has given us the present to build on. But to follow our visions to the future, we must see the difference between traditions that give us continuity and strength, and conventions that no longer serve us—and have that courage to act on that knowledge. Most can adapt after change has occurred; we must be among the few who anticipate change, shape it to our purpose, and act as its agents.

We believe in the commonwealth of Borg-Warner and its people.

Borg-Warner is both a federation of businesses and a community of people. Our goal is to preserve the freedom each of us needs to find personal satisfaction while building the strength that comes from unity. True unity is more than a melding of self-interests; it results when values and ideals also are shared. Some of ours are spelled out in these statements of belief. Others include faith in our political, economic, and spiritual heritage; pride in our work and our company; the knowledge that loyalty must flow in many directions; and a conviction that power is strongest when shared. We look to the unifying force of these beliefs as a source of energy to brighten the future of our company and all who depend on it.

Source: Reprinted with permission of the Borg-Warner Corporation.

include moral imperatives in their business strategies, plans, operations and interactions.

The corporate value statements of Johnson & Johnson and Borg-Warner (in Figures 4-2 and 4-3) reflect exceptional companies with executive officers who believe in directing their firms in ethical ways. Experience shows that enterprise and corporate strategies of companies that emphasize inflexible or unrealistic profit and revenue quotas are more likely to result in illegal and immoral activities, as these companies pursue singularly defined economic mandates. The Heinz Corporation (Goodpaster 1981) illustrated such an example in the late 1970s. Although that company had an ethics code, it was not reflected in the corporate strategy or in the structure, culture, and control systems of the firm's operations. Unethical and questionable legal activities followed: lying on employees' and divisions' performance quotas, revising and cheating on quarterly sales figures to meet fixed unrealistic profit quotas, and expensing prepayments that should have been capitalized. These immoral activities followed the strategic directive of the firm in that period: predictable, sustained earnings. Are there other firms you can identify whose enterprise and corporate strategies omit noneconomic value orientations toward stakeholders and whose business practices proved detrimental to customers, suppliers, employees, and society?

Strategy Implementation and Evaluation

Implementing and managing strategic social and moral responsibility directives are difficult tasks since these activities are harder to assess and measure than economic ones. Here we outline Hofer and Schendel's (1979) six-step strategic management process and suggest ways moral and social responsibility can be implemented with the strategic implementation of a corporation's goals and objectives.

The strategic management process includes the steps of (1) formulating goals, (2) formulating strategies, (3) implementing strategies, (4) controlling strategies, (5) evaluating strategies; and (6) analyzing the environment.

Many of these steps overlap and loop back; implementing and managing strategy is, in practice, not an absolutely linear process. Controlling and evaluating strategies are interactive processes. Analyzing the environment often requires reformulating goals and strategies. We focus here on how moral and social responsibility, not economic or political, issues can be part of the strategy implementation and evaluation process.

In practice, as we stated earlier, economic, political, technological, and environmental goals, strategies, and issues often evolve into social and moral problems and dilemmas for corporations, especially in emergencies and crises—as the *Exxon Valdez* and Manville Corporation cases showed.

At the goal formulation stage, moral and social responsibility priorities and issues must be identified or sanctioned by the CEO, as we stated earlier. The goals reflect the CEO's and the firm's values. Such priorities might include enhancing the physical environment, protecting consumers, and building safe products. Value statements, such as those from Borg-Warner and Johnson & Johnson, illustrate the basis for formulating corporate goals.

The strategy formulation stage identifies the competitive analysis of the firm's strengths and weaknesses in terms of managerial, financial, and social issues. With regard to social issues, a moral perspective should be articulated at this stage and reflect a concern for the visibility, vulnerability, and obligations of social issues in a firm's strategies. During this stage, managers not only must estimate the firm's risks and opportunities in pursuing specific goals but also must spell out the firm's obligations to relevant stakeholders (that is, to suppliers, to consumers and customers, to competitors, to the government, to communities, and to society) vis-à-vis each goal. For example, the Johnson & Johnson credo states that customers' orders must be serviced promptly and accurately.

During the third stage, implementing the strategy, managers and employees from the entire organization are usually involved in different ways. Social and moral responsibilities play a role in strategy implementation in ensuring that the procedures and means of putting strategy and resources into action are just, fair, and equitable, and that the corporation is morally fulfilling its fiduciary responsibilities to its stakeholders. For example, the Johnson & Johnson credo specifically articulate a directive to reduce costs to maintain reasonable prices.

During the fourth stage, strategy evaluation, and the fifth stage, strategy control, corporate managers set standards to measure intended against actual performance of their actions. During these stages, managers also assess the moral and social, as well as the economic, results with their stated performance criteria. During the strategy control stage, corrective action should be taken if results are not in line with stated goals and objectives. During both of these stages, the "social audit" can be used for checking, evaluating, and correcting unethical activities.

Social Audits

The **social audit** concept (see Baver and Fenn [1933]; Carrol and Beiler [1975]; Corson and Steiner [1974]; and Estes [1976]) was developed in the 1970s as a way for corporations to keep track of their social responsibility performance. Measuring a firm's performance against its social goals or issues is the aim. Carroll listed (1989) minority employment, pollution/environment, working conditions, consumerism issues, and philanthropic contributions as social issues that are included in social audits. Internal personnel, consultants, task forces, and board-level committees have been employed to oversee and perform social audits.

The problems with the use of the social audit have largely been in the measurement techniques used. Traditional accounting techniques have not proved adequate (Sturdivant and Vernon-Wortzel 1990). Currently, different companies use several approaches to keep score of their social performance. Still, the use of a social audit sends a message to the firm's stakeholders: "We take our moral responsibility to our stakeholders seriously."

Finally, during the sixth stage of the strategic implementation process, the environmental analysis, managers scan, monitor, identify, and forecast issues and trends in the (1) technological, (2) political, (3) economic, and (4) social environments to determine the effects of targeted issues on the organization—before the issues and trends occur (Fahey 1987; Fleming 1978–85). John Naisbitt's books entitled *Megatrends* and Alan Toffler's book *Future Shock* are attempts to scan, monitor, and predict environmental issues and the possible effects they may have on organizations and individuals. There are also many research "thinktanks"— opinion and survey organizations (such as the Yankelovich Group and the Roper Organization) that perform environmental analyses.

From a stakeholder perspective, a firm would be interested in identifying environmental issues that might affect its stakeholder obligations and relationships. Obtaining accurate information from the environment can assist managers in estimating the stakes associated with an issue's occurrence and potential costs. Strategies can then be formulated to address the issues. From a social and moral perspective, managers would be concerned about fulfilling their stakeholder obligations through their strategies. Predictions about changes in the work force in the year 2000, for example, suggest that responsible corporations must be prepared to equitably and justly manage the needs of aging employees and dual-career families, and to increase female entrants and foreign and minority workers. Flex-time, health programs, and flexible management styles must be implemented to manage this changing work force responsibly. Managers must be trained to understand and implement employee programs that address diversity in the work force. The strategic issues management process is discussed in more detail in Chapter 5.

Corporate Structure and Moral Responsibility

After strategies are defined, the appropriate organizational structure should be designed and enacted to accommodate the implementation of strategies. In this section, we discuss the relationship of structure and moral responsibility.

Most larger corporations are hierarchically governed and structured. Figure 4-4 illustrates a typical larger corporation's hierarchical gover-

Figure 4-4 Hierarchically Governed Structure

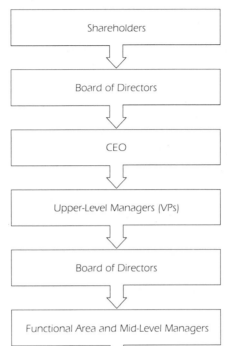

nance system. The hierarchy extends from shareholders to the board of directors, to the CEO, to the upper-level vice presidents, and then to the functional area managers, with the employees reporting to the managers. Although shareholders are not part of the internal corporation, we include them here, since their interests should be considered in the structuring and policy-setting decisions of the firm.

Corporations can be structured at lower levels below the CEO in a number of ways, and larger ones usually include several of the ones listed here: by function, product line, geography, and matrix (that is, by function and special project or program). Corporations can also be organized by different arrangements: For example, by divisions, by branch offices, or by "strategic business units" (SBUs)—which can perform as independent profit centers. Divisional structures can be either centralized or decentralized, depending on the nature of the business, the strategy, and environmental threats and opportunities. We turn our discussion to a more general level of analysis, that is, centralized versus decentralized structure, since little is known or has been formally studied regarding ethical behavior and the specific arrangements discussed above.

A survey of 443 industrial sales people that was reported in the *Wall Street Journal* found that structure does affect ethical behavior. Specifically, highly supervised employees in bureaucratic firms were more likely to act ethically than employees in entrepreneurial, laissez-faire firms. The article noted, "There is evidence people think through the risk of getting caught" in firms with more supervised structures.

Another notable study (Cullen, Victor, and Stephens 1989) reported that a subunit's location in the organizational structure affects its ethical climate

> At [a] savings and loan association and also at [a] manufacturing plant, the employees at the home offices reported less emphasis on laws, codes, and rules than did the employees at the branch offices. Perhaps control by formal mechanisms becomes more necessary when direct supervision by top management is not feasible.

Decentralization appears to permit, or encourage, more unethical behavior among employees than more supervised, controlled structures.

A recent account of Citicorp bank's credit card processing division illustrates the relationship among organizational structure, competitive pressures, and immoral and illegal behavior (Lipin 1991). The bank fired the president and 11 senior executives of that division because they had fraudulently overstated revenue by $23 million over 2 years. The illegal inflating of revenue by division employees may reflect the problem that employee bonuses were tied to unrealistic revenue targets. Citicorp is centralizing its organizational functions. "Some insiders as well as observers believe the decentralized structure left the bank susceptible to potential abuse by employees." Regarding this example, a Merrill Lynch banking analyst is quoted: "But as they go through a management centralization and tighten control of independently run businesses, people will look with scrutiny to see whether there are other control problems" (Lipin 1991, A3). Pressures from upper-level managers who overemphasize unrealistic, bottom-line quarterly revenue objectives, and who give unclear policies and procedures to guide ethical decision making in business transactions, may contribute to immoral behavior in more decentralized structures.

There is also evidence that shows that middle- and lower-level managers, in particular, feel pressured to compromise their personal moral standards to meet corporate expectations (Carroll 1975; Posner and Schmidt 1984). Cases and anecdotal studies suggest that managers in larger firms may compromise their personal ethics to corporate expectations for several reasons: (1) Decentralized structures with little or no coordination to central policy and procedures encourage a climate for immoral activities when pressures for profit making increase; (2) unrealistic, short-term, bottom-line profit quotas add pressure on employees to commit unethical actions; (3) overemphasis on numbers-driven, financial incentives encourages shortcuts around responsible decisions; and (4) amoral organizational and work unit cultures can create an environment that condones illegal and immoral actions. Certainly more studies are needed in this area before definite conclusions can be made. The discussion above is intended to open the topic for debate and elaboration.

Professionals, Control Systems, and Moral Responsibility

Enterprise and corporate strategies can also influence the professionals and managers hired and retained in corporations, as well as the types of structures and control systems that are implemented. For purposes of our discussion on the moral dimensions of strategy, structure, people, and corporate systems, we repeat our argument: Corporations that support strategies overemphasizing short-term, numbers-driven profits at the expense of concern for employees, shareholder interest, and customer service generally can actively or through negligence protect and even promote those who engage in amoral or immoral behavior. These corporations also tend to have lax accounting and cost-control systems and probably will not have ethics codes—or if such do exist, they will not be properly communicated or enforced.

The Heinz Corporation case cited earlier, which detailed that firm's operations between 1972 and 1980, illustrated many of these questionable legal and immoral practices. Heinz, which was driven by a strategy that emphasized predictable earnings, had a decentralized divisional structure that was tied to a fixed-profit quota system that pressured employees to meet divisional revenue projections or face no divisional or individual merit increases. Later audits showed a financial control system and ethics code that were ineffective. Several managers were illegally and immorally padding their revenues and lying to meet corporate expectations. One upper-level manager was promoted; no employees involved in the immoral and legally questionable activities were fired. The operations at Heinz during this period raised these questions: What type of corporate culture existed to permit these activities? Where was the board of directors during these happenings? Where was corporate moral and operations leadership during this period? Did the decentralized divisional structure encourage immoral activities? Again, as Figure 4-1 indicates, strategy does drive and influence organizational structure, culture, people, and control systems—in either moral, amoral, or immoral ways.

4.4 CORPORATE LEADERSHIP, CULTURE, AND MORAL RESPONSIBILITY

"The glue that holds the high-ethics firm together is not culture, goals, superordinate goals, participating employee stock ownership, or leadership. It is purpose" (from Pastin [1986]; quoted in Hoffman and Moore [1990, 627]).

Purpose in corporations is *espoused* through the values and principles of the founders and CEOs; purpose is *enacted* through the policies, procedures, examples, and behaviors of the leaders and their followers. Leadership, as we argued earlier, influences strategy, culture, control and reward systems, and even the nature and tone of interactions in the corporation. In this section, we discuss leadership styles through which corporate executives and managers influence the moral, amoral, or immoral culture and direction of the firm. We begin this discussion with the following generalizations about the nature of corporate leadership: (1) Without followers, leaders cannot lead. Leadership is, to some extent, a function of followership. In fact, many employees at lower levels embody the conscience of the corporation through their own actions. (2) Related to the first observation is the fact that leadership is often dispersed and shared in corporations. This is—and must be—the case with regard to the moral environment and behavior of the firm. One person, even the CEO, cannot be the only moral example in the corporation. While the top-level leader sets the moral tone and example, the followers must share moral leadership in order for a moral environment to thrive. (3) There is no one or best style of moral leadership or management. In the discussion below, we present two models of moral leadership. The first is a continuum, and the second is profiled as leadership in three "acts." Both models are intended to show how moral leadership in organizations can be evaluated.

Moral Leadership Styles

For the purpose of discussing the nature of ethics and leadership, moral leadership in organizations and the ethical systems on which they are based can be viewed along a continuum: (Hitt 1990, 138–174):

LESS ETHICAL			MORE ETHICAL
Manipulator (end-justifies-means ethic)	Bureaucratic administrator (rule ethic)	Professional manager (social contract ethic)	Transforming leader (personal-istic ethic)

The *manipulator* leadership style is based on a Machiavellian ethic (Machiavelli 1966) that views leadership amorally. That is, the end result justifies the means taken to reach an aim. Power is the driving force behind a manipulator's motives. This is an egotistically and essentially economically motivated moral leadership style. It lacks trust and relationship-building interests and qualities. It is oriented toward the short term. While the motives underlying this style may be amoral, the consequences could prove immoral for those affected. Have you ever worked under someone who used this style?

The *bureaucratic administrator* is a rule-based moral leadership style. Based on the theories of famed German sociologist Max Weber (Gerth and Mills, 1946), the bureaucratic administrator acts on rational principles embodied in an ideal organizational bureaucracy: that is, fixed rules that explain the purpose and functions of the organization; a hierarchy that shows the chain-of-command control structure; well-defined job descriptions; professional managers who communicate and enforce the rules; and technically qualified employees who are promoted by expertise and rewarded by rank and tenure. The driving force behind this style is *efficiency* (that is, "doing things right"; functioning in the least wasteful manner) more so than effectiveness (that is, producing the intended result or aim; "doing the right things").

Although this leadership style has an admirable aim of basing decisions only on objective, rational criteria, the moral problem with it lies in the "sin of omission." That is, a leader may follow all the rules exactly but hurt someone unintentionally—again, amorally—by not attending to legitimate human needs because the option to do so was not prescribed or included in the rules. A professional bus driver, for example, has orders not to stop between two cities for any reason. A bystander may have been accidentally and fatally shot by a hunter. The driver sees and recognizes the victim but refuses to stop because of the rules. The bystander dies. Is the bus driver's failure to stop morally justified because he followed the rules? Rules cannot address all problems and needs in what we know are imperfect and political organizations. The well-intentioned bureaucratic administrator may try to act amorally, but his or her efforts could result in immoral and irresponsible consequences to others. Do you recognize this moral leadership style? Have you ever worked for someone who used this style?

The *professional manager* aims at effectiveness, "doing things right." This style is grounded in Peter Drucker's (1978) principles and view of managers as professionals, who have the expertise and tools for getting work accomplished effectively through others. Based on a social contract ethic, this management style relies—like the previous two styles—on amoral techniques and assumptions for getting work done. For example, professional career managers use rational objectives and their training to accomplish the organization's work. It is the organization's corporate culture and the social contract—that is, implicit and explicit agree-ments—made between managers and organizational executives that set the ground rules and ethics that guide and govern the manager's behav-ior. Social contracts are not always ethically justifiable.

A major ethical problem with this leadership style lies in the real possibility that the collective corporate culture and dominant governing group may think and act amorally or immorally. "Groupthink" (that is, consensus-dominated decision making based on uncritical, biased think-ing) may occur (Janis 1972). The collective may lead itself astray. Professional managers by training and expertise are still prone to uneth-ical behavior. Do you recognize professional managers or leaders who act amorally or immorally as "professionals"?

Finally, the *transforming leadership style*, based on James MacGregor Burns's (1978) theory (see also Hitt 1990), is grounded on a personal-istic ethic. The transformational leader bases his or her effectiveness on relationships with followers. This style also focuses on the charisma, energy, and excitement the leader brings to relationships. The transformational leader is involved in the growth and self-actual-ization of others and views others according to their potential. This type of leader identifies and elevates the values and motives of others. This leader empowers, coaches, and helps promote other leaders. This leadership style is moral in that "it raises the level of human conduct and aspirations of both leaders and led, and thus has a transforming effect on both" (Hitt 1990).

William Hitt (1990, 170) moved the continuum of moral leadership discussed above one step beyond the transformational leader to what he termed an "encompassing approach to leadership," or "the effective leader–manager." The encompassing leader learns from the shortcomings of each of the previously discussed four leadership styles and uses the strengths of all. For example, manipulative leadership does value the effective use of power. However, the deception and dysfunctional uses of power of this style should be avoided. The bureaucratic administrator values the effective use of rules, roles, and responsibilities; however, these should not become ends rather than means. The professional manager values results; however, human concerns should be valued more highly than physical and fiscal resources and results. The transformational leader values human empowerment; however, even this characteristic is not the complete job of management.

We would add that leaders and managers as individual and organizational stakeholders must critically observe their obligations to all stakeholders, including their own conscience, according to the ethical criteria of rights, justice, and duty—as well as to a utilitarian logic. It is essential for those who must select or hire organizational executives and managers, who must also lead, to know the person's values and moral leadership style.

Act I, II, and III Moral Leaders

A more dynamic model of moral leadership is illustrated in Figure 4-5.* This model illustrates the interdependence among leaders from industry to industry and from organization to organization and even between historical generations of leaders. Also, this model shows that not all leaders begin as well-known public figures. Citizens and community leaders become leaders.

Leaders and leadership styles are depicted here as Act I, Act II, or Act III profiles. This conceptual discussion is based on Professor Thomas Cronin's (Colorado College) view of leadership. The emphasis here is on the roles and responsibilities leaders assume relative to an issue, policy, or law. The model is also dynamic because leaders can move from one style to another, and also because the evolution and relationship between leadership and issues (organizational or societal) can be studied and explained over time and within or outside of institutions.

Act I leaders originate and frame issues. They are usually outside of formal organizations and are on the frontier of change—whether it is

*The concept of Act I, II, and III leaders is based on and expanded from a lecture given by Dr. Thomas Cronin at Bentley College in 1991. Joseph W. Weiss (Bentley College) holds the copyright for this revised model.

Figure 4-5 Moral Dimensions of Leadership Roles and Policy

Leadership Style and Ethical Motivation	Leadership and Policy-making Roles
ACT III (utilitarian and egotism)	Enforcing and representing policies and laws (institutionalizing; symbolizing)
ACT II (duty, fairness, future good)	Consolidating and enacting issues into policy, law (negotiating; legislating)
ACT I (justice, duty)	Originating and framing issues (mobilizing, coalition building)

Source: Copyright © Joseph Weiss. Waltham, Mass.: Bentley College, 1992.

organizational or societal. These leaders are the prophets, the grass-roots movers and shakers. They are the framers of issues and sometimes the protesters who make previously invisible issues visible. They usually lead by personal example, experience, and charismatic motivation. Martin Luther King, Jr., started as an Act I leader in the civil rights movement. Ralph Nader started as a grass-roots consumer advocate. The leaders of the MADD (Mothers Against Drunk Driving) and SADD (Students Against Drunk Driving) movements are Act I leaders.

Act I leaders often act from a moral sense of duty and justice. They have personally experienced or observed a sense of injustice or no justice from the judicial system and move to create awareness and responsiveness to harm done to themselves, to their relatives, or to a disadvantaged group whom they represent. It should also be noted that Act I leaders can and do become Act II and even Act III leaders, as did Martin Luther King, Jr., and Ralph Nader. Who are other Act I leaders you can identify?

Act II leaders move issues that have been formed by Act I leaders into policy and law. This leadership style requires negotiating, coalition building, politicking, and legislating. These leaders can be either part of formal organizations or adjunct to them. Act II leaders must use formal and informal power effectively to mobilize issues into system policy and laws. Act II leaders are morally motivated from a sense of duty and fairness. They act to consolidate issues into lasting forms of policy and law. They understand their moral obligation to others and other generations. They also have a moral sense of historical mission.

Lyndon Johnson was a preeminent Act II leader. He legislated more bills into law (especially civil rights) than any president before or since. He attempted to legislate and enact his vision of "the Great Society." Lee Iacocca can also be considered an Act II leader. His presidency at Chrysler helped that firm avoid bankruptcy and return to competitiveness based on quality and service. Can you think of other Act II leaders, nationally, internationally, or locally?

Act III leaders enforce and promote laws, policies, and issues that have been forged by Act I and Act II leaders. These leaders institutionalize and then symbolize the significance and continuation of issues, policies, and laws. Act III leaders also use charisma and personal example as well as powerful contacts and networks to enforce and perpetuate the viability of policies and laws. Many times, Act III leaders act from a utilitarian and even egotistical ethic. They weigh the benefits of adopting and promoting policies and laws for others and for themselves and their own best self-interests. For example, Ronald Reagan, referred to as "the Great Communicator," could be considered an Act III leader. As a figurehead, he symbolized traditional American values here and abroad. With a significantly increasing national deficit, loss of industrial competitiveness internationally, and eroding civil rights momentum among minorities, President Reagan continued to successfully symbolize a stable, powerful, proud, and enthusiastic national figure of patriotism and confidence among nations and the American electorate. Jesse Jackson is an Act III leader. He successfully symbolizes and represents antidrug and crime policies and promotes hope and ideals. Who are other Act III leaders you can name in industry or government, or from your work experience?

Act I, II, and III leaders are motivated by a wide range of ethical principles. We have argued that Act I leaders are often morally motivated by a personal and communal sense of duty and justice. Act II leaders are moved by a sense of duty and fairness and by a need to affect the future good of generations to come. Act III leaders are influenced by utilitarian and personal self-interest ethics.

We emphasize the relationship between corporate culture and moral leadership. Corporate culture is directly influenced by organizational leaders whose examples, strategies, and styles influence the organization's culture. Corporate culture, as we discuss in the following section, has become a popular and important topic in the discussion of business ethics, since culture embodies and transmits moral ideals as well as amoral and immoral practices. Still, it is important to note that leadership has a significant impact on culture in firms.

Corporate Culture and Moral Responsibility

Purpose, as embodied in corporate culture, is the glue that holds organizations together. Corporate culture is the shared values and meanings that members hold in common and that are articulated and practiced by an organization's leaders. Organizational and corporate cultures are both visible and invisible, formal and informal. They can be studied by observation, by listening and interacting with people in the culture, and in the following other ways: (1) by studying the physical setting; (2) by reading what the company says about its own culture; (3) by observing and testing how the company greets strangers; (4) by watching how people spend time; (5) by understanding career path progressions; (6) by noting length of tenure in jobs, especially with middle managers; and (7) by observing anecdotes and stories (Deal and Kennedy 1982).

Corporate culture is related to ethics through (1) the values and leadership styles that the leaders espouse and practice; (2) the heroes and heroines that the company rewards and holds up as models; (3) the rites, rituals, and symbols that organizations value; and (4) the way organizational executives and members communicate among themselves and with their stakeholders.

Corporate Values

The Johnson & Johnson credo (as shown in Figure 4-2) and the beliefs of Borg-Warner (Figure 4-3) are illustrations of exemplary statements of corporate values. Both businesses are also successful in the marketplace. In addition, Bill Hewlett and Dave Packard of the very successful Hewlett-Packard (HP) company have what is termed "the HP Way." Bill Hewlett stated HP's driving values this way:

> I feel that in general terms it is the policies and actions that flow from the belief that men and women want to do a good job, a creative job, and that if they are provided the proper environment, they will do so. But that's only part of it. Closely coupled with this is the HP tradition of treating each individual with consideration and respect, and recognizing personal achievements. (*Based on Deal and Kennedy 1982*)

Another example of corporate values that are used to define corporate culture and drive operations is found in the Boeing Corporation of Seattle. The origins of Boeing's values were articulated by its former CEO William Allen (Keogh 1988):

- Be considerate of my associates' views.
- Don't talk too much. . .let others talk.

- Don't be afraid to admit that you don't know.
- Don't get immersed in detail.
- Make contacts with other people in industry.
- Try to improve feeling around Seattle toward the company.
- Make a sincere effort to understand labor's viewpoint.
- Be definite; don't vacillate.
- Act—get things done—move forward.

Strong Corporate Culture Traits

HP, Boeing, Johnson & Johnson, and the Borg-Warner firm (later bought by General Electric) all exemplify what Deal and Kennedy (1982, 9–12) termed "strong cultures": That is (1) they have a widely shared philosophy; (2) they value the importance of people; (3) they have heroes (presidents and products) that symbolize the success of the company; and (4) they celebrate rituals, which provide opportunities for caring and sharing, for developing a spirit of "oneness" and "weness."

What are the values of the company you work for or the institution in which you are a student or member? Do the leaders and culture embody these values in their actions and policies? Are the values written down? Do others know the values? Do the values reflect a concern and obligation for the organization's stakeholders? Do the values reflect a utilitarian, justice, duty, or egotistical ethic? Are the values taken at face value only, or are they practiced and implemented by other employees?

Cultures in Trouble

Organizations that stress competition, profit, and economic or introverted self-interests over stakeholder obligations and that have no morally active direction often have cultures that are in trouble. Signs of cultures in trouble or weak cultures include the following (from Keogh 1988):

- An inward focus
- A short-term focus
- Morale and motivation problems
- Emotional outbursts
- Fragmentation and inconsistency (in dress, speech, physical settings, work habits)

- Clashes between subcultures

- Ingrown subcultures

- Dominance of subculture values over shared company values

- No clear values or beliefs about how to succeed in business

- A lot of beliefs with no priorities about which are important

- Different beliefs in different parts of the company

- Destructive or disruptive cultural heroes rather than builders of common understanding about what is important

- Disorganized or disruptive daily rituals

Heroes and heroines in corporations set the moral tone and direction by their present or even remembered examples.

They are the role models; they define what is successful and attainable; they symbolize the company to outsiders and insiders; they preserve the valued qualities of the firm, set standards of excellence, and motivate people (Keogh 1988). Jack Welch from General Electric, Lee Iacocca at Chrysler, Tom Watson from IBM, Ken Olson at Digital Equipment Corporation, and others have left their mark on corporations as active, concerned, and socially responsive and involved leaders. Jimmy Carter, an unpopular president during his term, now has higher popularity ratings than when he was in office and will probably be remembered as a highly ethical president and person. President Carter still works on housing and inner-city projects to assist the poor and economically disadvantaged. Who are the heroes and heroines in your organization? By what qualities and characteristics are they remembered? Are they moral, immoral, or amoral leaders?

Finally, rituals and communication in companies help define corporate culture and the moral nature of the culture (Keogh 1988, 64–67). Corporately sanctioned rituals that bring people together, that foster an openness, and that promote cross-functional and integrated hierarchical levels of communication can lead to a lowering of stress and encourage moral behavior. Social gatherings, picnics, recognition ceremonies, and other company outings in which corporate leaders are present and in which sharing of values, stories, problems, accomplishments, and aspirations takes place also can lead to cultures that value people and the company's aims. Companies that reinforce secrecy, hidden agendas, and physical settings that isolate executives from managers and employees and that emphasize status over human concern often reflect cultures that are in trouble. Troubled corporate and organizational cultures can breed and encourage unethical activities. How would you characterize the rituals and communication patterns in your organization or institution? Do these promote moral, immoral, or amoral behavior?

High-Ethics Firms and Cultures

We conclude this section with a description of Mark Pastin's (1986) characterization of four principles of "high-ethics" firms. We would argue that high-ethics firms have high-ethics cultures. As Pastin noted, his principles are not meant to foster a Pollyannaish optimism about ethics and businesses; rather, he sought to "foster a realistic raising of our sights." He studied 25 "high-ethics, high-profit" firms, which include Motorola, 3M, Cadbury Schweppes, Arco, Hilby Wilson, Northern Chemical, and Apple, to name a few. Here are the four principles of high-ethics firms and cultures (Pastin 1986; quoted in Hoffman and Moore 1990):

Principle 1: High-ethics firms are at ease interacting with diverse internal and external stakeholder groups. The ground rules of these firms make the good of these stakeholder groups part of the firm's own good.

Principle 2: High-ethics firms are obsessed with fairness. Their ground rules emphasize that the other person's interests count as much as their own.

Principle 3: In high-ethics firms, responsibility is individual rather than collective, with individuals assuming personal responsibility for actions of the firm. These firms' ground rules mandate that individuals are responsible to themselves.

Principle 4: The high-ethics firm sees its activities in terms of a purpose. This purpose is a way of operating that members of the firm value. And purpose ties the firm to its environment.

In the last section of this chapter, we present the corporation as moral self-regulator. The discussion presented above on the internal role of leadership, strategy, structure, and culture in relation to ethics took us inside the corporation as stakeholder. Next, we turn to the role of shareholders, boards of directors, CEOs, and other mechanisms to discuss who regulates the moral activities of firms.

4.5 THE CORPORATION AS MORAL REGULATOR

Can corporations regulate and govern their own legal and moral behavior? To whom are corporations accountable? Answers to these questions reflect an ongoing debate both in the corporate world and in business ethics circles. Those who argue that corporations can and should regulate themselves, that they are accountable only to their boards of directors (who represent their shareholders), and who entrust their governance to their CEOs, and leaders view the nature of the corporation as private property. (Representatives of this view include Geneen [1984] and Shapiro [1979]. Excerpts from these works are in Hoffman and Moore [1990].) As such, proponents of this position argue that it is the responsibility of corporate boards and upper-level managers to police and govern their own operations.

The major opposing view to this position holds that corporations are more than private property; they are public institutions, since they are part of a democratically governed and constitutionally ruled society (Nader, Green, and Seligman 1976; excerpted in Hoffman and Moore 1990). As such, corporations should have outside members who represent a wider range of stakeholder interests on their boards of directors. Corporations should also be more open to outside review in order to represent the interests of consumers, employees, and the public. Proponents of this view also argue that corporations are unable to govern their operations. Boards of directors often are inept, uninformed, and powerless to govern the corporation. Boards become "rubber stamps" (Carroll 1989) for CEOs who, in many cases, also chair their own boards. The resulting situation is that CEOs often become their own and only bosses. Before turning to some mediating recommendations between these two views, we extend our discussion of this debate to examine the consequences of what is happening to corporations that are poorly governed or misrepresented.

Corporate Restructuring, Mergers, Acquisitions, and Takeovers

The debate that surrounds the sweeping activity in the 1980s and into the 1990s of corporate restructuring, mergers, acquisitions and **takeovers** centers around the two different views of the corporation outlined above: (1) The corporation is private property in a free-market system. As such, it deserves to be bought, dismembered, and sold if it does not earn a profit and remain competitive. (2) The opposing view argues that the corporation is part of the larger public society and economy. Insider trading, greed, and corruption of powerful business interests do not represent the concerns of shareholders or of the economy. Therefore, corporations need representation from society and even protection by it sometimes to truly be competitive.

Those who believe that unlimited takeovers, mergers, and acquisitions are a normal part of a competitive free-market system, and that takeovers usually signal poor management by professionals who did not maximize value, argue that lower than expected stock prices reflect failing management practices (Jensen 1984). Carl Icahn, a proponent of this view, has stated (Reich 1989), "Most of the approximately 2,000 takeovers and leveraged buyouts since 1981 have been characterized by a redeployment of assets to create greater competitive and economic gains." He continued:

> A most interesting. . . fact about takeovers is that in all bids for control—hostile or friendly—a price much higher than current market value is paid for the company. This is generally referred to as a "premium for control." But generally, what the acquirer is really saying when he or she pays this premium is that the company is actually worth more if the ability to remove top management exists.

This view argues that if corporations cannot govern themselves, they deserve to be sold and/or restructured. This is a form of effective governance, according to this view.

Robert Reich (1989) a former teacher at Harvard's John F. Kennedy School of Government and Secretary of the Department of Labor under President Clinton, argues the opposing view. He stated, "The record of the 1970s and 80s is dismally clear on this point. There is little evidence to suggest that mergers have on the average enhanced the profitability or productivity of merging enterprises." Reich argues that the American economy has suffered as a result of the massive corporate restructuring, buyouts, and takeovers. He noted that average wages, adjusted for inflation, have stagnated, and that corporate profits have not rebounded to 1973 peak levels, as indicated by the Dow Jones industrial average. Reich offers as one major example the 1985 merger of R. J. Reynolds tobacco company with Nabisco, the giant food-processing firm. At the time, that merger was seen as a brilliant strategy. Reynolds would diversify into foods. Three years afterward, the merged enterprise was breaking up; investment bankers were offering billions for the opportunity to dismember the businesses and sell them.

Reich cites four reasons why leveraged buyouts, mergers, and large-scale takeovers done mainly or solely for quick-fix profit motives do not always succeed: (1) myopia, (2) wasted talent, (3) debt, and (4) distrust. First, the myopic, short-term perspective does not enable firms to develop new technologies. Profit pressures inhibit real technological growth. Second, "asset rearranging" by "paper entrepreneurs" wastes the energy of talented scientists and managers. The short-term profit perspective does not grow business and technological talent. Third, corporate takeovers and buyouts require financial borrowing and leveraging— namely, debt. The average American firm paid 16 cents of every dollar on pretax earnings in interest on its debt 25 years ago. This figure was 33 cents in the 1970s. The Brookings Institute predicted that if the level of debt that existed in the 1980s prevails, 1 in 10 American firms will go bankrupt in the coming decades. Finally, Reich argued that an economy based on asset rearranging plays one group's gain against another's loss. "Without trust," he states, "people won't dedicate themselves to common goals. They will turn their energies instead to defending their own inter- est. In a corporation, this means declining productivity."

Of course not all leveraged buyouts, mergers, and acquisitions are executed from motives of greed or from conspiracies among inside traders, financiers, board members, and upper-level managers. The ram- pant and uncontrolled growth of these sweeping transactions in the 1980s and the stock market crash in 1987 caused considerable concern among business professionals, economists, and business ethicists over the legitimate use of buying and selling companies as a competitive strat- egy. These large-scale and numerous transactions not only have national economic repercussions but raised the question, as discussed earlier, "Who governs the corporation?" While the debate over buying and sell- ing corporations as a competitive strategy continues, concern over increasing the moral power and capability of effective internal gover- nance bodies and systems also remains a vital interest of many business owners, professionals, and ethicists. In the remaining parts of this sec- tion, we summarize other questionable governance problems before dis- cussing methods for increasing the effectiveness of corporate governance at the shareholder, board of directors, and employee levels.

Other Questionable Governance Problems in Corporations

In publicly held corporations, according to the stakeholder theory, as dis- cussed at the beginning of this chapter, boards of directors and CEOs are obliged to fairly and justly govern the firm by promoting the inter- ests of their shareholders and stakeholders. This has not been the case in many companies, especially in the 1980s. The buying and selling frenzy of corporations for quick profits, as discussed earlier, has increased a host of other questionable legal and moral corporate activi- ties, which raise the question of how to improve responsible corporate governance. (This section is based on Carroll [1989]; DeGeorge [1990]; Hoffman and Moore [1990]; and Prokesch [1988].) For example, **insider**

trading (that is, one individual in a firm accessing vital information to use for personal monetary advancement) has led to scenarios as portrayed in the 1987 film *Wall Street*. Individuals use inside professionals to learn if a firm will sell to another company at a certain price per share above current stock price. That person then buys shares at present market value and later sells for profit at a higher price. This type of scandal usually involves cooperation from high-level managers in a firm. Dennis Levine and Ivan Boesky represent the insider trading scandals par excellence in the 1980s. Insider trading is illegal.

Two other questionable legal and moral corporate practices that are related to hostile takeovers and quick for-profit restructuring are "golden parachutes" and "greenmail."

Golden parachutes are deals contracted between a firm and its high-level executives to protect and compensate the executives should the corporation be sold, merged, or restructured. Golden parachutes were designed to reward executives for their loyalty, to prevent top officers from leaving before a restructuring was complete, and to inhibit corporate raiders because of the high cost of releasing a firm's executives. Over half the country's largest companies have golden parachutes, up from 35% in 1987 (Lublin 1991). Experience has shown that golden parachutes represent deals that corporate executives usually make for themselves without shareholder knowledge or approval. Informed and angered stockholders have and continue to sue boards of directors for permitting this practice—RCA had allotted golden parachutes to executives for upward of $62 million.

The United Shareholders' Association, an activist group, introduced proxy resolutions at over a dozen firms in 1990 to kill golden parachutes without shareholder approval. Thirty-two percent of stockholders voting approved this step (Lublin 1991). The Federal Deposit Insurance Corporation and federal banking regulators are also introducing rules to stop golden parachutes.

Greenmail, the buying back of shares by firms from corporate **raiders** at increased market prices, is another practice that was spurred by the takeover buying frenzy in the 1980s. As portrayed in the Broadway play and 1991 film *Other People's Money*, a corporate raider buys a percentage of stock in a company. The raider then threatens a hostile takeover of that firm. The firm's executives are threatened and leveraged to repurchase the stock from the raider at a higher price. The raider walks away with a quick profit. The company has to use assets or operating funds or borrow to buy back the shares. The forced nature of the threatened takeover raises ethical questions about this practice as a legitimate means to correct poor management. Also, the likelihood of insider cooperation in providing information and assistance raises the question of collusion and adequate governance of the firm.

How can governance be improved in corporations to address these and other immoral practices? In the remaining parts of this chapter, we will discuss recommendations and methods that have been proposed and used in many companies. In the following section, enhanced roles of boards of directors and shareholders are presented. Also, corporate codes of ethics, ombudsmen, and peer review programs are discussed as means to improve moral conduct in corporations.

Expanded Roles of Corporate Boards and Shareholders

Harold Geneen (1990), a former ITT CEO, stated, "Among the boards of directors of Fortune 500 companies, I estimate that 95% are not fully doing what they are legally, morally, and ethically supposed to do. And they couldn't even if they wanted to" (p. 226). Corporate boards of directors are supposed to:

- Establish and monitor procedures that assure that operating executives are informed of and obey applicable federal, state, and local laws

- Approve or veto all important executive management business proposals such as corporate by-laws, mergers, or dividend decisions

- Hire and dismiss the chief executive officer and be able to disapprove the hiring and firing of the principal executives of the corporation

- Report to the public and the shareholders how well the corporation has obeyed the law and protected the shareholders' investment (Nader, quoted in Hoffman and Moore 1990, 213)

Reasons why boards of directors do not execute these responsibilities are well known: CEOs often chair the boards, thereby controlling their own agendas. Because board members are not well staffed and do not have the time, money, or interest to monitor companies, they relinquish control to CEOs and high-level managers.

Ralph Nader, the famed consumer advocate, has recommended restructuring boards to (1) hire full-time professional, salaried directors with staffs to carry out a board's functions; (2) integrate the homogeneity of the board by electing nine corporate directors to limited terms, each with different oversight responsibilities (for example, finances, shareholder rights, employee concerns); (3) make the share-holder electoral process more democratic. Stockholders who own 0.1 percent of common voting stock, or 100 or more individuals—not including a current corporate executive—could nominate three persons as directors to the board. (4) Also, having corporations become "feder-ally chartered" (presently corporations are required to register only in a state) would make firms more accountable and would open to public disclosure more of their activities (Nader, quoted in Hoffman and Moore 1990, 214–219).

Nader's proposals which are viewed as more extreme recommenda-tions, move a corporation closer to governance by society than by its pri-vately controlled board. Nevertheless, these suggestions are a starting point for corporate board changes. However, without shareholder inter-est and commitment, and without the necessary corporate leadership to initiate and follow through on these types of recommendations, boards of directors will probably remain "rubber stamps" of company execu-tives who control the directions, operations, and legal and moral behav-ior of firms.

Activist Roles of Shareholders in Corporate Governance

Since the 1970s, shareholders have been taking a more activist role in becoming involved in strategic corporate activities and proposals. Because of corporate abuses involving large-scale restructuring, takeovers, golden parachutes, greenmail, and other legally and morally questionable activities, two groups in particular have formed to exert influence on boards: the Council of Institutional Investors (CII) and the United Shareholders' Association (USA). These groups are exerting their power by influencing corporate agendas on social, economic, and political investing at board meetings; by suing corporations; and by introducing proxy shareholder resolutions on such issues as stopping golden parachutes and "poison pill" proposals (that is, perks and money guaranteed to be paid to executives if a takeover occurs; the aim is to discourage a takeover by making it too costly). The point here is that shareholders are aligning their interest into visible, powerful groups in order to exert their legitimate and rightful governing influ-ence as a major stakeholder over CEOs and CEO-dominated boards of directors. Because of the political and dispersed nature of power in large corporations, it is often, not always, necessary for shareholders to use the legal system, as well as organized activist voting roles, to make their voices and votes heard by corporate managers.

Corporate Self-Governance

Many corporations do attempt to govern their activities conscientiously by using ethics codes, ombudsmen, and peer review programs and mechanisms. At an operational level, corporate leaders in most large firms establish personnel policies and ethical codes of conduct to instruct and guide employee behavior. Major purposes of **ethics codes** include the following: (1) state corporate leaders' dominant values and beliefs that are the foundation of the corporate culture; (2) define the moral identity of the company inside and outside the firm; (3) set the moral tone of the work environment; (4) provide a more stable, permanent set of guidelines for right and wrong actions; (5) control erratic and auto-cratic power or whims of employees (Bowie and Duska 1990); (6) serve business interests (since unethical practices invite outside government, law enforcement, and media intervention); (7) provide an instructional and motivational basis for training ethical guidelines and for integrating ethics into operational policies, procedures, and problems; (8) constitute a legitimate source of support for professionals who face improper demands and intrusions on their skills or well-being; (9) offer a basis for adjudicating disputes among professionals inside and between those inside and outside the firm; and (10) provide an added means of social-izing professionals, not only in specialized knowledge but also in beliefs and practices the company values and rejects (Brooks 1989).

A 1986 survey of U.S. corporate ethics codes found that the most important topics to include were (1) general statements of ethics and phi-losophy; (2) conflicts of interest; (3) compliance with applicable laws; (4) political contributions; (5) payments to government officials/political parties; (6) inside information; (7) gifts, favors, entertainment; (8) false entries in books and records; and (9) customer/supplier relations (Frankel 1989). Notable firms go further in detailing corporate obliga-tions. For example, as exhibited earlier, Johnson & Johnson's credo and Borg-Warner's codes include and define their obligations to various stakeholders. Also, Boeing, General Mills, GTE, HP, McDonnell Douglas, Xerox, Norton, Chemical Bank, and Champion International, to name a few firms, have exemplary ethics codes and corporate value statements.

The problems with corporate ethics codes in general are as follows: (1) Most are too vague to be meaningful; that is, the codes do not inform employees about how to prioritize among conflicting interest of distrib-utors, customers, and the company. What does being a "good citizen" really mean in practice? (2) Codes do not set priorities among beliefs, values, and norms. Should profit always supersede concern for customers or employees (Frankel 1989)? (3) Codes are not enforced in firms, and (4) codes are not communicated throughout most firms.

Ethics codes are a necessary but not sufficient means of assisting professionals in managing moral conduct in companies. Often a crisis or scandal that makes national media coverage is required to awaken executives to the need for enforced ethical codes of conduct. Certainly the Clarence Thomas hearings jolted and sensitized organizations in the United States to the problems surrounding sexual harassment in the workplace. Still, as stated in Chapter 1, companies increasingly continue to adopt ethics codes and to include ethics in their training programs.

Ombudsman and Peer Review Programs.   Other processes corporations use to prevent and manage immoral activities in the workplace are ombudsman and peer review programs. The **ombudsman** approach provides employees with a means of having their grievances heard, reviewed, and solved. Originating in Sweden, this concept was first tried at Xerox in 1972 and then at General Electric and Boeing (see Carroll [1989]). Ombudsmen are third parties inside the corporation to whom employees can take their grievances. At Xerox, employees are encouraged to solve their problems through the chain of command before seeking the ombudsman. However, if that process fails, the employee can go to the ombudsman, who acts as an intermediary. The ombudsman, with the employee's approval, can go to the employee's manager to discuss the grievance. The ombudsman can continue through each managerial layer, including the president, if the problem is not satisfactorily solved for the employee. Ombudsmen have no power themselves to solve disputes or override managers' decisions.

Complaints usually center on salary disputes, job performance appraisals, layoffs, employee benefits, and job mobility in the firm. At General Electric, ombudsmen report that they handle 150 cases a year.

A problem with the ombudsman approach is that managers may feel that their authority is threatened. Employees who seek out ombudsmen might also worry about their managers retaliating against them from fear or spite. Confidentiality also has to be observed on the part of the ombudsmen.

The program has met with success at Xerox, General Electric, and Boeing. These three companies adopted job-posting procedures as a result of the program; Boeing introduced flexible work hours. The program also reflects the effectiveness of management policies and styles. Moreover, pressures are released and addressed, thus preventing unethical and illegal behavior.

The **peer review panel** is another program that over 100 larger companies have used to enable employees to express and solve grievances and complaints, thus relieving stress and pressures that could lead to immoral activities. (This section is based on Carroll [1989] and Rubenstein [1986].) Employees use the chain of command initially whenever a problem exists. If the supervisors or executives do not solve the problem, the employee can request a peer review panel to hear and help decide a solution. Two randomly selected workers in the same job and classification are chosen along with an executive from another work unit. The selection must be reviewed against company policy. Peer review panels work when top management supports such due process procedures and when these mechanisms are perceived as long-term, permanent programs.

Privately held and operated corporations must govern their own operations. In reality, government agencies, laws, regulations, and to some extent competitive forces in the free-market system act to constrain corporate illegality and immoral activities. The debate over to what extent outside professionals and bodies should control private companies' activities will continue. At one end of the spectrum of control is the issue of paternalism (that is, private firms do not want "Big Brother" to dictate their actions). At the other end of the spectrum is the issue of monopoly (that is, without some outside control, corporations will misuse their power and usurp stakeholders' rights and best interests).

Ethics Offices. **Ethics offices** provide another method for handling moral questions and concerns in the workplace. Over 15% of the nation's companies that employ 50,000 or more people have established ethics offices over the last 5 years (Frankel 1989). Several of the larger corporations include Nynex, Pacific Bell, Texas Instruments, General Dynamics, and Dow Corning. Most companies have organized ethics offices to respond to public scandals, to potentially harmful misconduct, and to competitors' pleas.

Ethics offices serve several purposes. Telephone hotlines are the first step toward opening lines of communication in the organization. Professional staffs consisting of between 2 and 6 full-time people, with as many as 20 part-time employees, handle personal grievances and complaints, coordinate problems across other functional and staff areas, and create, update, and help enforce ethics codes. At General Dynamics, for example, over 30,000 contacts with ethics officers since 1985 resulted in 1,419 sanctions, 165 terminations, 58 cases requesting financial reimbursement, 26 demotions, and 10 referrals to lawyers for civil lawsuits or to public prosecutors for criminal proceedings.

Some critics of this program have doubts as to whether "full-time" ethics offices are really necessary. They cite examples such as IBM and Johnson & Johnson, companies that have cultivated records of ethical conduct by using other, less formal alternatives. Despite the skepticism with respect to their effectiveness, there are two reasons why the use of ethics offices will most likely continue to increase: (1) According to federal sentencing guidelines effective November 1, 1991, judges are asked to look more favorably on firms that can provide evidence of a substantial investment in programs and procedures designed to facilitate ethical behavior; and (2) the demise of several of the large Wall Street investment firms has awakened companies to the fact that the unethical conduct of a few employees can have detrimental effects on the entire organization.

Financial concerns factor into the decision of whether to set up an ethics office. As stated earlier, many companies, such as Nynex, are investing in these programs in response to a public scandal or known misconduct. Others, such as Texas Instruments (TI), have seen competitors struggling with issues of ethical conduct and have implemented ethics offices to reinforce their previously written company code of ethics. According to Carl Skoogland, TI's first ethics director, "We have had a written code for over 30 years but we wanted a formal focal point for reinforcing what we felt was an already strong culture." Whatever the motivation, ethics offices appear to be an effective means of handling a variety of personnel and moral issues in the workplace.

SUMMARY

This chapter focuses on the issue of whether corporations have a "conscience." Two opposing views are presented: The first view defines the corporation as having no conscience and as having responsibility to stockholders only. A second view discusses the corporation as a stakeholder with a conscience similar to that of an individual person.

A third perspective, supported in this book, attempts to reconcile the two previous views. In this case, the corporation is seen as a social and economic stakeholder. The corporation is obliged to act in morally responsible ways toward its constituencies. Corporations must balance their moral, social, economic, and legal responsibilities with its stakeholders.

The concepts of "social contract" and "covenantal ethic" underlie the stakeholder view of the firm. These concepts argue that corporations do have social and moral obligations to their stakeholders. These concepts also strongly base the success of a corporation on its relationships with its stakeholders.

Leadership, culture, and moral responsibility are influenced by corporate strategy and structure. There are at least four levels of strategy that influence and guide corporate moral responsibility. These include enterprise, corporate, business, and functional strategies.

As a corporation implements and evaluates its strategic plans, social and moral responsibility issues must also be identified and addressed. Social audits are one method corporations have employed to monitor their performance on social responsibility issues.

Corporate structure is influenced by strategy and also affects ethical behavior. Decentralized supervision or lack of explicit policies regarding ethical conduct, leadership expectations, and overemphasis on short-term profits can lead to immoral conduct.

Two models of moral leadership are presented. The first perspective explains leadership across a continuum (manipulator, bureaucratic administrator, professional manager, and transforming leader). The second explains moral leadership in three "acts" (from issue originators, Act I; to issue legislators, Act II; to issue institutionalizers, Act III).

Corporate culture is defined, and four principles of "high-ethics" cultures in firms are characterized.

Finally, the roles of shareholders, boards of directors, and CEOs are discussed. Recommendations for enhancing the effectiveness of the governance of these groups are presented. Ethics codes, ombudsman programs, peer review programs, and ethics offices are explained as self-regulating moral vehicles in corporations.

Questions

1. Does a corporation have a "conscience"? Explain.

2. What are the problems in discussing corporations as persons? Do you agree? Why or why not?

3. Briefly explain the concept of "corporate internal decision structure." State your opinion of this concept.

4. Explain the "social contract" and "covenantal ethic" concepts. How do they relate to a stakeholder view of the corporation?

5. Identify limitations of the stakeholder perspective. How is this perspective useful?

6. In what ways does strategy influence other dimensions of an organization? Explain.

7. What are the differences between Act I, II, and III moral leadership? Identify an example of each type.

8. How is corporate culture related to ethics? Explain.

Exercises

1. Keith Davis states that "in the long run, those who do not use power in a manner in which society considers responsible will tend to lose it." Identify a real-life example of such a company and describe the situation. What is the status of the company currently?

2. Choose a corporation with which you have some experience or knowledge. What is the basic corporate strategy? How is that reflected in the corporate structure and culture? Does the firm place an emphasis on social responsibility? How?

3. Identify a moral leadership style with which you have worked. Did you work well or poorly with/under that style? Why? If you could go back and reverse roles with this individual, how would you do things differently? What type of leader would you be? Why?

4. Identify an example of a recent corporate merger, acquisition, or takeover. Do you agree or disagree with the actions taken? Why or why not? Do mergers, acquisitions, and takeovers constitute responsible or immoral business practices? Why or why not?

References and Suggested Readings

Baver, Raymond, and Dan Fenn, Jr. "What *Is* a Corporate Social Audit?" *Harvard Business Review* (January/February 1973).

Bowie, Norman, and Ronald Duska. *Business Ethics.* 2d ed. Englewood Cliffs, N.J.: Prentice-Hall, 1990.

Brooks, Leonard. "Corporate Codes of Ethics." *Journal of Business Ethics,* 8 (1989): 117–129.

Buchholz, Rogene. "Corporate Responsibility and the Good Society: From Economics to Ecology." *Business Horizons* (July/August 1991): 24.

Buchholz, Roger A. *Fundamental Concepts and Problems in Business Ethics.* Englewood Cliffs, N.J.: Prentice-Hall, 1989.

Burns, James M. *Leadership.* New York: Harper & Row, 1978.

Business Week "Where Ombudsmen Work Out," May 3, 1976, 114, 116.

Carroll, Archie B. *Business and Society: Ethics and Stakeholder Management.* 1st and 3d eds. Cincinnati: South-Western Publishing Co., 1989 and 1993.

———. "Management Ethics: A Post-Watergate View." *Business Horizons* (April 1975): 75–80.

———. "The Pyramid of Corporate Social Responsibility." *Business Horizons* 34 (July/August 1991).

Carroll, Archie B., and George Beiler. "Landmarks in the Evolution of the Social Audit." *Academy of Management Journal* (September 1975): 589–599.

Corson, John, and George Steiner. *Measuring Business's Performance: The Corporate Social Audit.* New York: Committee for Economic Development, 1974.

Cronin, Thomas. "The Concept of Acts I, II, III." Lecture at Bentley College, 1991.

Cullen, John, Bart Victor, and Carrol Stephens. "An Ethical Weather Report: Assessing the Organization's Ethical Climate." *Organizational Dynamics* 18 (Autumn 1989).

Dahl, Jonathan. "Manville Offers $2.5 Billion to Settle Claims." *The Wall Street Journal,* August 5, 1985, 3.

Davis, Keith. "Five Propositions for Social Responsibility." *Business Horizons* (June 1975): 20–23.

Deal, Terrance, and A. Kennedy. *Corporate Cultures: The Rites and Rituals of Corporate Life.* Reading, Mass.: Addison-Wesley, 1982.

DeGeorge, Richard. *Business Ethics.* 3d ed. New York: MacMillan, 1990.

Des Jardins, Joseph R., and John McCall, eds. *Contemporary Issues in Business Ethics.* 2d ed. Belmont, Calif.: Wadsworth, 1990.

Donaldson, Thomas. *The Ethics of International Business.* New York: Oxford Press, 1989.

Drucker, Peter. *Management: Tasks—Responsibilities—Practices.* New York: Harper & Row, 1978.

Estes, Ralph. *Corporate Social Accounting.* New York: John Wiley & Sons, 1976.

Evan, William, and R. Edward Freeman. "A Stakeholder Theory of the Modern Corporation: Kantian Capitalism." In *Ethical Theory and Business.* 3d ed. Edited by Tom Beauchamp and Norman Bowie. Englewood Cliffs, N.J.: Prentice-Hall, 1988.

Fahey, L. "Environmental Analysis for Strategy Formulation." In *Strategic Planning and Management Handbook,* edited by William King and D. Cleland. New York: Van Nostrand Rienhold, 1987.

Fleming, John E. "Public Issues Scanning." In *Research in Corporate Social Performance and Policy,* edited by Lee Preston. Greenwich, Conn.: JAI Press, 1978–1985.

Frankel, Mark. "Professional Codes: Why, How, and with What Impact?" *Journal of Business Ethics* 8 (1989): 109–115.

Freeman, R. Edward. *Strategic Management: A Stakeholder Approach.* Boston: Pitman, 1984.

Freeman, R. Edward, and Daniel Gilbert, Jr. *Corporate Strategy and the Search for Ethics.* Englewood Cliffs, N.J.: Prentice-Hall, 1988.

French, Peter. "The Corporation as a Moral Person." Paper delivered at the Ethics and Economics Conference, University of Delaware, November 11, 1977.

Friedman, Milton. "The Social Responsibility of Business Is to Increase Its Profits." *The New York Times Magazine,* September 13, 1970, 126.

Galbraith, John Kenneth. *American Capitalism: The Concept of Countervailing Power.* Rev. ed. Cambridge, Mass.: Riverside Press, 1956.

Geneen, Harold (with Alvin Moscow). In *Managing.* Garden City, New York: Doubleday, 1984. Excerpts are found in Hoffman and Moore (1990).

Gerth, H. H., and C. Wright Mills, trans. *From Max Weber: Essays in Sociology.* Oxford University Press, 1946.

Goodpaster, Kenneth. "The H. J. Heinz Company: The Administration of Policy," #382-055. Boston: Harvard Business School, 1981.

Goodpaster, Kenneth and John Matthews. "Can a Corporation Have a Conscience?" *Harvard Business Review* (January/February 1982).

Gordon, Judith, R. Mondy, A. Sharplin, and S. Premeaux. *Management and Organizational Behavior.* Boston: Allyn & Bacon, 1990.

Harrington, Susan. "What Corporate America Is Teaching About Ethics." *The Executive* 5, no. 1 (February 1991): 21–30.

Hitt, William. *Ethics and Leadership: Putting Theory Into Practice.* Columbus, Ohio: Battelle Press, 1990.

Hofer, Charles, and Dan Schendel. *Strategic Management: A New View of Business Policy and Planning.* Boston: Little, Brown, 1979.

Hoffman, W. Michael, and Jennifer Mills Moore, eds. *Business Ethics.* 2d ed. New York: McGraw-Hill, 1990.

Hosmer, LaRue. *The Ethics of Management.* Homewood, Ill.: Irwin, 1987.

Hyman, Michael, Robert Skipper, and Richard Tansey. "Ethical Codes are Not Enough." *Business Horizons* (March/April 1990): 15–22.

Jackall, Robert. *Moral Mazes: The World of Corporate Managers.* New York: Oxford Press, 1988.

Janis, Irving. *Groupthink: Psychological Studies of Policy Decisions and Fiascoes.* Boston: Houghton Mifflin, 1972.

Jensen, Michael. "Takeovers: Folklore and Science." *Harvard Business Review* (November/December 1984).

Keogh, James, ed. "The Business Roundtable." *Corporate Ethics: A Prime Business Asset. A Report on Policy and Practice in Company Conduct.* New York: The Business Roundtable, February 1988.

Lanza, A. J., et al. "Effects of the Inhalation of Asbestos on the Lungs of Asbestos Workers." *Public Health Reports* 4 (January 1935): 1–12.

Levitt, Theodore. "The Dangers of Social Responsibility." *Harvard Business Review* 26 (September/October 1958).

Lipin, Steven. "Citicorp Unit's Top Officials Are Dismissed." *The Wall Street Journal,* November 11, 1991, A3.

Lublin, Joann. "Firms Rethink Lucrative Severance Pacts for Top Executives as Criticism Swells." *The Wall Street Journal,* November 11, 1991, B1, B2.

Machiavelli, Niccolò. *The Prince.* New York: Macmillan, 1966.

Nader, Ralph, et al. "Who Rules the Corporation?" Quoted in Hoffman and Moore (1990, 213).

Nader, Ralph, Mark Green, and Joel Seligman. *Taming the Giant Corporation.* New York: W. W. Norton, 1976. Also excerpted in Hoffman and Moore (1990, 210–219).

Naisbitt, John. *Megatrends: Ten New Directions Transforming Our Lives.* New York: Warner Books, 1982.

Naisbitt, John, and Patricia Aburdene. *Megatrends 2000: Ten New Directions for the 1990s.* New York: Avon, 1991.

———. *Megatrends 2000: Ten New Directions for the 1990s.* New York: Morrow, 1990.

Nash, Laura. *Good Intentions Aside: A Manager's Guide to Resolving Ethical Problems.* Boston: Harvard Business School, 1990.

Pastin, Mark. "Lessons from High Profit, High-Ethics Companies: An Agenda for Managerial Action." In *The Hard Problems of Management: Gaining the*

Ethics Edge. Chapter 11, 218–228. San Francisco: Jossey-Bass, 1986. Also quoted in Hoffman and Moore (1990, 624–628).

Posner, Barry, and W. Schmidt. "Value and the American Manager: An Update." *California Management Review* (Spring 1984): 202–216.

Preston, Lee, ed. *Research in Corporate Social Performance and Policy.* Vol. 1–7. Greenwich, Conn.: JAI Press, 1978–1985.

Prokesch, Steven. "Too Much Gold in the Parachutes?" *The New York Times,* January 26, 1988, 3-1, 28f.

Reich, Robert. "Leveraged Buyouts: America Pays the Price." *The New York Times,* January 14, 1989, 25.

Rotbart, Dean. "Manville Corp. Faces Increasing Opposition to Bankruptcy Filing." *The Wall Street Journal,* January 1, 1984, 1.

Rubenstein, Larry. "More Firms Use Peer Review Panel to Resolve Employee Grievances." *The Wall Street Journal,* December 3, 1986, 29.

Shapiro, Irving. "Power and Accountability: The Changing Role of the Corporate Board of Directors." Paper presented at Carnegie-Mellon University, October 24, 1979.

Sharplin, Arthur. "Manville Lives on as Victims Continue to Die." *Business and Society Review* (Spring 1988): 25–29.

Shaw, James B., et al. "From Maternalism to Accountability: The Changing Cultures of MA BELL and Mother Russia." *The Executive* 5, no. 1 (February, 1991): 7–21.

Shaw, William, *Business Ethics.* Belmont, Cal.: Wadsworth 1991.

Sturdivant, Frederick, and Heidi Vernon-Wortzel. *Business and Society, A Managerial Approach.* 4th ed. Homewood, Ill.: Irwin, 1990.

Thompson, Arthur, Jr., and A. J. Strictland, III. *Strategy Formulation and Implementation.* Plano, Tex.: Business Publications, 1980.

Toffler, Alan. *Future Shock.* New York: Random House, 1970.

Torabzadeh, Khalil, et al. "The Effect of the Recent Insider-Trading Scandal on Stock Prices of Securities Firms." *Journal of Business Ethics* 8 (1989): 303.

Velasquez, Manuel. *Business Ethics: Concepts and Cases.* Englewood Cliffs, N. J.: Prentice-Hall, 1982.

Weiss, Joseph W. *Act I, II, II Leaders: Building A Social Responsibility Model.* Waltham, Mass.: Bentley College, 1991.

Werhane, Patricia. "The Ethics of Insider Trading." *Journal of Business Ethics* 8 (1989): 177.

5

The Corporation and External Stakeholders

Managing Moral Responsibility
in the Marketplace

The Ford Pinto entered the marketplace in September 1970. By 1976, it was Ford's most popular small car—over 2 million were sold. In 1978, in a landmark product liability case $128.5 million was awarded to a 19-year-old who, at age 13, was severely injured while riding with a friend in a Pinto. The car was hit in the rear; the gas tank erupted, killing the friend and burning most of the other boy's body. The fuel tank was located 7 inches from the car's rear bumper. Any significant impact from behind rendered the car a death trap. In June 1978, Ford recalled 1.5 million subcompacts.

(Time 1978; Weinberger and Romeo 1989)

In July 1989, Ford Motor Company reported that it recalled 518,000 subcompact cars to repair defects that caused engine fires. The 1984 Escort, the Mercury Lynx, and the EXP had defects that could cause oil to leak onto the hot engine manifolds. Ford stated it did not tally the actual number of fires reported.

(Templin 1989)

Managing legal and moral responsibility in the marketplace is a major business of corporations. At stake are sizable lawsuits from consumers, boycotts of products, loss of image, reputation, namebrand loyalty, competitiveness, and even survival. As the now classic Ford Pinto example shows, judges and juries can and do hold liable manufacturers who do not prevent and/or adequately manage dangerous products.

There are other classic cases of corporations having to manage moral and legal obligations in the marketplace (see, for example, Barett [1985]; Buchholz [1989]; Geyelin [1991]; Matthews et al. [1991]; Weinberger and Romeo [1989]), including the following cases: (1) Between 1971 and 1974, more than 5,000 product liability lawsuits were issued by women who suffered severe gynecological damage from A. H. Robins Company's Dalkon Shield, an intrauterine contraceptive device. Although the company never recalled its product, it paid over $314 million to settle 8,300 suits. It also established a $1.75 billion trust to settle ongoing claims. (2) Procter & Gamble's Rely tampon was pulled from the market in 1980 after 25 deaths were allegedly associated with toxic shock syndrome. (3) In 1982, someone inserted cyanide into Johnson & Johnson's Extra-Strength Tylenol tablets, killing seven people. The company acted swiftly to remove the product until safety procedures were ensured. (4) In 1978, the Center for Auto Safety said it had reports that Firestone's steel-belted radial TPC 500 tire was responsible for 15 deaths and 12 injuries. In October 1978, after attacking the publicity this product received, Firestone executives recalled 10 million of the 500-series tires. (5) More recently, the Dow Corning Corporation faces liability suits on its silicone-gel breast-implant products. A number of women have reported ill-nesses due to the implants. A jury already awarded $7.3 million to one woman whose implant burst, causing her illness. Over 600,000 implants have been performed over the past 30 years. The company is alleged to have rushed the product to market in 1975 without proper safety tests and to have misled plastic surgeons about the potential for silicone to leak out of the surgically implanted devices. Dow spokespersons have stated the breast implants are "safe and effective." There is an FDA moratorium on breast implants, and Dow has stopped manufacturing the product, even though it is not recalling any products as of this writing (*The Wall Street Journal* January 14, 1992, A3).

These are only a few of numerous examples of corporations that have produced questionably safe and/or poor products that have had damaging effects in the marketplace, or of firms that have had to manage sabotage or misuse of products—as with the Tylenol case.

Managing corporate responsibility in the marketplace is a negotiated process, usually involving numerous stakeholders. The media, industry and consumer groups, government agencies, community watchdog groups, scientific organizations, and PACs (political action committees) debate and negotiate the reasonableness and acceptability of controversial ads and questionable product safety in the marketplace. Even the standards that affect the public's health and uses of the environment are negotiated among a variety of stakeholders. While many unsolved disputes between corporations and stakeholders go to courts for decisions, the competing claims also are settled through negotiated logic and ethics of judges and juries.

This chapter raises the question, What ethical principles and standards are appropriate for corporations and their stakeholders who negotiate differing moral claims over controversial advertisements, unsafe products, and questionable uses of the environment? As discussed in Chapter 3, we ask, Is utilitarianism always a sufficient principle in these types of stakeholder debates and settlements? How relevant and applicable are the principles of justice, duty, and rights regarding corporations' and their stakeholders' activities in dealing with these kinds of issues and their settlement?

This chapter also provides an overview of ethical obligations and problems that corporations across industries manage in their pursuit of or flight from moral and legal responsibility to their stockholders and stakeholders. We begin by extending the discussion started in Chapter 4: the corporation's moral responsibility to the public and consumer stakeholders, in particular. What specific and realistic moral obligations do corporations have to consumers, other than to produce a reliable, salable product? Next, we present an overview of businesses' ethical responsibility in advertising. This is an important topic, since public consumption begins when a firm persuades customers to buy products or services. What is the relationship between ethics and advertising? We also discuss the topic of product safety and liability. Who is liable for unsafe products? What is the price to be paid and by whom for the use of questionable products that may be unsafe, or that may be safe but used improperly? Then, we turn to the topic of a corporation's ethical responsibility to the environment. To what extent are corporations responsible for their industrial use of the environment? To whom does the environment belong? What is the relationship between ethics and ecology? We then discuss the moral challenges that corporations face and the methods several use to manage strategic issues. We also present an overview of how corporations can understand and manage crises—which can have profound moral effects on the firm and its stakeholders. Finally, we close the chapter by discussing another powerful marketplace stakeholder of corporations: the government. In Chapter 4 we discussed methods firms use to regulate themselves; here we discuss the business/government regulatory process. How does the stakeholder approach enhance our understanding of the business/government regulatory process? Is government regulation of business activities really necessary?

5.1   CORPORATE RESPONSIBILITY TOWARD CONSUMER STAKEHOLDERS

Consumers are most important stakeholders of business. If consumers don't buy, commercial businesses cease to exist. "Consumer confidence" and spending are also important indicators of economic activity as well as business prosperity. Because this is the case, businesses should theoretically put consumer interests foremost when designing, delivering, and servicing products. Unfortunately, this often is not the case. As the examples at the beginning of this chapter illustrate, many companies continue to manufacture or distribute unreliable products, placing consumers at risk; many advertisers continue to make false and misleading claims about products; many food labels continue to have unclear and untrue statements about nutritional content. What, then, is the nature of corporate responsibility toward consumers as stakeholders?

Free Market Theory

The **free-market theory** holds that the primary aim of business is to make a profit. As far as the obligations of business toward consumers, this view assumes that there is an equal balance of power, knowledge, and sophistication of choice in the buying and selling of products and services between company and customer. If businesses deliver what customers want, customers buy. Customers have the freedom and wisdom to select what they want and reject what they do not want. Faulty or undesirable products are not supposed to sell. If businesses do not sell well, it is their own fault. The marketplace is an arena of arbitration. Consumers and corporations are protected and regulated, according to this view, by the "invisible hand."

Problems with the Free-Market Theory

Although there is some validity to this theory, there is also controversy regarding the assumptions with respect to the consumer/business relationship in particular. For example (1) most businesses are not on equal footing with consumers at large. Large firms spend sizable amounts on research aimed at analyzing, creating, and—some argue—manipulating demand of targeted buyers. Children, for example, are not aware of the effects of advertising on their buying choices. (2) There is also a question about whether many firms' advertising activities truthfully inform consumers about products: their reliability, their possible dangers, and their proper use. There is, as we discuss in the next section, a thin line between deceit and artistic exaggeration in advertising. (3) The "invisible hand" is often nonexistent regarding consumer protection against questionable advertising and poorly manufactured products released to market. One reason a stakeholder view has become a useful approach for determining moral, legal, and economic responsibility is because the issues surrounding product safety, for example, are complex and controversial. Who is right and who is wrong, who is innocent and who is liable, are problems that must be examined before informed judgments are made. The question then arises, what are realistic obligations of companies toward consumers in marketplace relationships and exchanges?

Social Contract View: Corporate Duties and Consumer Rights

In Chapter 4, we discussed the stakeholder view as based on a social contract between a corporation and its stakeholders. The social contract concept is grounded on certain obligations a firm has toward its constituencies, in this case consumers, and to society and the public at large. Some of the more obvious but substantial duties of firms include the following (from Velasquez 1988):

1. The duty to inform consumers truthfully and fully of a product and service's content, purpose, and uses;

2. The duty not to misrepresent or withhold information about a product or service that would hinder the free choice of a consumer;

3. The duty not to force or take undue advantage of a consumer through fear or stress, or by other means that constrain rational choice; and

4. The duty to take "due care" in preventing any foreseen injuries or mishaps a product (in its design and production) or its use may have on consumers.

Additional and related rights consumers have in their social contract with corporations include (1) the right to safety—to be protected from harmful commodities that injure; (2) the right to free and rational choice—to be able to select among alternative products; (3) the right to know—to have easy access to truthful information that can help decide on products to select; (4) the right to be heard—to have available a party who will acknowledge and act on reliable complaints about injustices that happened with products and business transactions; and (5) the right to be compensated—to have a means to receive compensation for harm done to a person because of faulty products or damage done in the business transaction (Buchholz 1992; Holloway and Hancock 1973).

These ethical guidelines can be used and applied to everyday individual business transactions as well as to more complicated exchanges between corporations and consumer groups. The guidelines also serve as the legal and moral foundation of corporate and consumer stakeholder relationships regarding advertising and issues surrounding product safety and liability.

5.2 CORPORATE RESPONSIBILITY IN ADVERTISING, PRODUCT SAFETY, AND LIABILITY

Advertising is big business in itself. In 1991, $126.7 billion was spent on this enterprise (*The Wall Street Journal* January 13, 1992, B1). Advertising is also a changing and innovative field. Recently, for example, **infomer-**

cials have been introduced on TV. These are program-length, soft-sell, pseudodocumentary ads that air late at night and imitate "Donahue" and "Nightline" in selling products. Sears, MCI, Volvo, GM, and a number of brand-name products are used in infomercials. The Home Shopping Network is considered an all-infomercial channel. At issue is whether consumers can distinguish infomercials from factual news documentaries. The Food and Drug Administration (FDA) has filed a dozen lawsuits since 1988 and has collected several million dollars in fines, judgments, and settlements from firms and ad agencies—including a baldness remedy company—which aired infomercials (*The Wall Street Journal* January 14, 1992, B6).

The purposes of advertising are to inform customers about products and services and to influence and persuade them to purchase them. A corporation's ethical responsibility in advertising is to inform and persuade consumer stakeholders in ways that do not lie, deceive, conceal, or withhold the truth. This does not always happen.

Paternalism or Manipulation?

Moral responsibility toward consumers in advertising can be viewed as a continuum. At one end or extreme of the spectrum is paternalism; that is, "Big Brother" (or government) regulates the free market to ban and control what consumers can or should be allowed to hear and see. Too much protection could lead to much control and enforcement over free choice. This is not desirable in a democratic market economy. At the other extreme of the continuum is corporate manipulation and control over consumers' free choice through cleverly researched ads aimed at deception. This is also undesirable, since consumer choice and knowledge are limited. Ideally, corporations should seek to inform consumers truthfully while, at the same time, using nonmanipulative persuasion techniques to sell their products.

Enforcement of advertising also can be viewed along this continuum. Outright bans on ads can result in court decisions that rule that free choice has been violated and/or that a party was or could be harmed. On the other hand, companies and industry groups can also police themselves, as has been the case in the alcohol industry with the U.S. Brewers Association issuing guidelines against beer ads that promote overindulgence. Where moral and legal disputes over specific ads actually occur on the continuum is a matter of perception and judgment. Therefore, the general debate over the pros and cons of what constitutes ethical advertising continues—whether the topic centers on claims that women are discriminated against in beer ads; or that the general public is being deceived by food labels that show half-truths about fat and cholesterol content; or that tobacco ads target unsophisticated buyers by promoting smokers who live enviable, successful life-styles; or that jeans and lingerie ads may be too sexually explicit. The following discussion summarizes the major arguments for and against advertising.

Arguments for Advertising

Arguments that justify advertising and the tactics of "puffery" and exaggeration include the following:

1. Advertising introduces and influences people to buy goods and services. Without advertising, consumers would be uninformed about products.

2. Advertising enables companies to be competitive in domestic and international markets with other firms. Firms across the globe use advertisements as competitive weapons to compete.

3. Advertising helps a nation to maintain a prosperous economy. Advertising increases consumption and spending, which in turn creates economic growth and jobs which benefits all. "A rising tide lifts all ships." The tobacco industry alone adds 350,000 jobs to the economy. It indirectly affects the employment of another 1.5 million in related industries, and it contributed $10 billion in taxes in 1988. The alcohol industry earned revenues of over $40 billion in 1988 (Steiner and Steiner 1991, 582, 591).

4. Advertising helps a nation's balance of trade and payments, especially in larger industries such as food, automobiles, alcoholic beverages, and computer technologies whose exports help the country's economy.

5. Proponents of advertising also argue that customers' lives are enriched by the images and metaphors that advertising creates. Customers pay for the illusion as well as the product that advertisements promote (Levitt 1990; cited in Hoffman and Moore 1990).

6. Those who defend the general practice of advertising claim that consumers are not ignorant. Buyers know the difference between lying, manipulation, and colorful hyperbole aimed at attracting attention. Consumers have freedom of choice. Ads do not coerce anyone to buy anything. Ads try to persuade and influence desires that are already present in the minds of people. Companies have a constitutional right to advertise in free and democratic societies.

Moreover, studies tend to show that advertising does not effectively cause people to buy products or services. In fact, the effectiveness of advertising in general is questionable (Velasquez 1988, 292–294).

Arguments Against Questionable Advertising

Critics of questionable advertising practices argue that advertising can be harmful for the following reasons: First, there is a thin line between "puffery" and deception that advertisements often cross. For example, unsophisticated buyers, especially children and youth, are targeted by companies. The American Academy of Pediatrics, a consumer-oriented group, for example, recently called for a ban on all televised food ads aimed at children. The charge is against sugary cereals, candy, and cookies. It is reported that 96% of Saturday morning food ads are for such products that lead to obesity. The Academy charged that "young children are unable to distinguish between programs and commercials and do not understand that commercials are designed to sell products" (Lipman 1991a).

Another argument against questionable advertising is that advertisements tell half-truths, conceal facts, and intentionally deceive with the goal of profit in mind, not consumer welfare. For example, the $300 to $400 billion food industry is increasingly being watched by the FDA for printing misleading labels that undermine nutritional information. Misleading labels using terms such as "cholesterol free," "lite," and "all natural" are under attack with added push from the Nutritional Education and Labeling Act of 1990. Consumers need to know quickly how much fat (a significant factor in heart disease) is in food, what are standard and understandable serving sizes, and what exact nutritional contents are in foods (Noble 1991). At stake in the short term for food companies, for example, is an outlay of between $100 million and $600 million for relabeling. In the long term, product sales could be at risk.

Critics of advertisements also argue that advertising stereotypes women—and men—and uses sex in manipulative ways to sell products. Stroh's Brewery Company recently spent millions on a TV ad for Old Milwaukee beer, featuring a "Swedish Bikini Team." The brewer was charged with sexual harassment by five female employees. Stroh's ad agency, the Hal Riney and Partners firm, was also sued by a female employee for sexual harassment. Further compounding the issue for Stroh's was the bikini team's nude appearance in the January 1991 issue of *Playboy*. It was discovered that members of the team also had a $3-a-minute call-in "900" number for sexually explicit conversations (Lipman 1991b).

Other industries also use sex to sell products. Calvin Klein's TV perfume ads (for Escape and Obsession products) feature models in sexually explicit poses. Calvin Klein's jeans ads feature fully nude models. Coors beer TV ads feature seminude adults. Davidoff's Cool Water fragrance ad features water-drenched male nudes in the sun. Jockey's underwear ads show baseball star Jim Palmer scantily clad. Sony shows seminudes advertising photo print paper. A Teledyne TV ad shows angled shots of a nude man demonstrating the Water Pik massage shower head (Elliot 1991). The debate on the increasing use of nudity in ads centers on (1) whether the United States is becoming more European in its tastes, helped along by company owners who are Europeans with more liberal attitudes, or (2) whether consumers are being exploited without their consent or approval.

Critics also argue that tobacco and alcohol advertising, in particular, continues to unjustifiably promote ads for products that are dangerous to health and the effects of which endanger others. The tobacco industry spent $6.54 billion in magazine advertising in 1991. Cigarette companies are reportedly targeting ads at lower-income women and minorities, and less at the educated. The December 1991 issue of the *Journal of the American Medical Association* reported that Old Joe Camel, the cartoon ad campaign for Camel cigarettes, lures youth to smoking. Surveys of 1,055 students ages 12 to 19 years showed that 97.7% have seen the ad, 97.5% know the product, 58% "think the ads look cool," 35% "like Joe as friend," and 33% report Camel as their favorite brand. R. J. Reynolds Company contests these reports, noting that the average Camel smoker is 35 years of age (*Business Week* December 23, 1991, 34). The FDA recently asked R. J. Reynolds Company to remove the ad voluntarily. The company refused. At stake for consumers who have a history of smoking, and for passive consumers (those indirectly affected by smokers), is the likelihood of getting lung cancer, heart disease, and other physical ailments. (Almost 400,000 people die each year from diseases related to smoking.) Also, smoking-related diseases reportedly cost the United States $52 billion annually in increased insurance premiums, health care charges, and lost productivity (*The Los Angeles Times* February 25, 1990, 591). Alcohol ads also raise problems for consumers. Critics against alcohol ads argue that targeted youth, in particular, are enticed by suggestive messages linking drinking to contemporary lifestyles, popularity and success. Consumer and public lobbying groups like Mothers Against Drunk Driving (MADD) attest to the problems that uses of alcohol cause in society.

Ethics and Advertising

The debate on these issues in advertising will continue. Given the pros and cons presented above, the controversial questions cannot be absolutely determined. These issues are matters of judgment, values, and changing standards in society. As stated earlier, the moral responsibility of firms in their advertising to consumers must be reasoned on a case-by-case basis.

Ethically, the following questions can be used to address the moral responsibility of corporations' advertising activities: (1) Is the consumer being treated as a means to an end or as an end? What and whose end? (2) Whose rights are being protected or violated intentionally and inadvertently? At what and whose costs? (3) Are consumers being justly and fairly treated? (4) Is the public welfare and good taken into consideration in the effects as well as the intention of advertisements? At the same time, companies have a right to promote their products through advertising. The ethical questions, again, concern issues of who is unfairly harmed by information in certain ads.

Advertising and Free Speech

Should certain ads be banned or restricted by courts? A distinction has been made in the Supreme Court differentiating **commercial speech** from **pure speech** in the context of the First Amendment. (See *Central Hudson Gas and Electric Corporation* v. *Public Service Commission*, 1980, and *Posadas de Puerto Rico Associates* v. *Tourism Company of Puerto Rico* [54 LW 4960]; see also Steiner and Steiner [1991, 596, 597] for a discussion of this topic.) "Commercial speech" in ads and business transactions has not been as protected in courts as "pure speech." Pure speech is more generalized to ideas, relating to political, scientific, and artistic expression in marketplace dealings. Commercial speech refers to language in ads and business dealings. The court balances both these concepts of speech against the general principle that freedom of speech will be weighed against the public's general welfare. The four-step test developed by Justice Powell and used to determine whether commercial speech in advertisement could be banned or restricted (see Steiner and Steiner 1991) is as follows:

1. Is the ad accurate and does it promote a lawful product?
2. Is the government's interest in banning or restricting the commercial speech important, nontrivial, and substantial?
3. Does the proposed restriction of commercial speech assist the government in obtaining a public policy goal?

4. Is the proposed restriction of commercial speech limited only to achieving the government's purpose?

In the following section, we explore corporations' responsibility to consumer stakeholders regarding the manufacture, distribution, and sale of products.

Product Safety and Liability

Managing product safety is one of the most important tasks of corporations. Ethical responsibilities and economic issues go hand in hand in this area. A sign in one engineering facility reads, "Get it right the first time or everyone pays!" Product quality, safety, and liability are interrelated topics that increase in importance as the technology of products advances, along with the risks for end-users and consumers.

Product quality, competitiveness and safety, and liability are also sides of the same coin, whether the industry is drugs, toys, household items, automotive products, asbestos, or silicone-gel implants. Manufacturers and businesses must be innovative to be competitive and profitable, but products must also be safe in order to protect individuals and to prevent damaging liability suits that cost companies millions of dollars and sometimes their survival. In this section we discuss the ethics of product safety and the nature of product liability.

How Safe is Safe? The Ethics of Product Safety

It is estimated that 29,000 people die and 33 million others are injured each year using consumer products such as toys, lawn mowers, appliances, power tools, and household chemicals (U.S. Consumer Product Safety Commission 1985). But how safe is safe? Few, if any, products are 100% safe. The manufacturing costs added to the sales price to bolster safety features would, in many instances, discourage price-sensitive consumers. Just as companies use utilitarian principles in developing products for markets, consumers also use this logic in shopping and purchasing. Risks are calculated by both manufacturer and consumer. There are, however, enough serious instances of questionable product quality and lack of manufacturing precautions taken (for example, the Ford Pinto and the Firestone 500 tires cases mentioned earlier) to warrant more than a simple utilitarian ethic in preventing and determining the safety of products for the consuming public. This is especially the case in commercial products, like air, sea, and space craft, over which consumers have little, if any, control.

The National Commission on Product Safety (NCPS) has noted that product risks should be reasonable (see Hoffman and Moore 1990). According to the NCPS, unreasonable risks are those that could be prevented or that consumers would pay to prevent if they had the knowledge and choice. Three steps that can be used to assess the safety of products from an ethical perspective include the following (DeGeorge 1990, 182, 183):

1. How much safety is technically attainable and how can it be specifically obtained with this product or service?

2. What is the level of acceptable risk of the public, the consumer, and the government regarding this product?

3. Does the product meet public and consumer standards? These steps, of course, will not be the same for commercial aircraft as for tennis shoes.

Regulating Product Safety

Because of the number of product-related casualties and injuries each year, and because of the growth of the consumer movement in the 1960s and 1970s, Congress passed the 1972 Consumer Product Safety Act, which created the Consumer Product Safety Commission (CPSC). This is the federal agency empowered to protect the public from unreasonable risk of injury and death related to consumer product use. The five-member commission is appointed by the president. The commission has regional offices across the country. The agency develops uniform safety standards for consumer products, assists industry in developing safety standards, researches possible product hazards, educates consumers about comparative product safety standards, and works to recall, repair, and ban dangerous products. Each year the commission targets and publishes a list of potentially hazardous products with consumer warnings.

The commission has been somewhat successful in its efforts. It sent 1,200 recalls that affected 7 million products between 1972 and 1978. Another estimate showed the commission issuing over 1,500 recalls, correcting 200 million products since its inception in 1972. The commission's effectiveness is related to the politics in Washington, D.C. Its budget went from $42.1 million with a staff of 978 in 1981 to $34.5 million with 519 people in 1989 (see Steiner and Steiner 1991). The Bush administration also scaled back regulations on business in many areas.

Consumer Affairs Departments

It should also be noted that many companies monitor their customers' satisfaction and safety concerns. Consumer Affairs Departments (CADs) are set up and coordinated in companies to ensure customer confidence and corporate responsiveness. Procter & Gamble, Digital Equipment Corporation, Federal Express, and Pepsi-Cola, to name only a few, have initiated such departments (see Steiner and Steiner 1991, 577, 578). Paying attention to customer suggestions and complaints is also good business.

Product Liability Doctrines

Who should pay for the effects of unsafe products and how much? Who determines who is liable? What are the punitive and compensatory limits of product liability? The doctrine of product liability has evolved in the court system since 1916, when the dominant principle of privity was used. Until the *MacPherson* v. *Buick Motor Company* case, consumers injured by faulty products could sue and receive damages from manufacturers if the manufacturer was judged to be negligent as a result of a product defect. Manufacturers were not held responsible if consumers purchased a hazardous product from a retailer or wholesaler (Des Jardins and McCall 1990, 255). In the MacPherson case, Buick, the defendant, was ruled liable for harm done to Mr. MacPherson. A wheel on the car had cracked. Although MacPherson had bought the car from a retailer, and although Buick had bought the wheel from a different manufacturer, Buick was charged with negligence. Even though Buick did not intend to deceive the client, the court ruled the company responsible for the finished product (the car), which—the jury claimed—should have tested its component parts (see Posch [1988, 3] and Sturdivant and Vernon-Wortzel [1991, 305]). The doctrine of negligence in the area of product liability was thus initiated.

The negligence doctrine meant that all parties, including the manufacturer, the wholesaler, the distributor, and sales professionals, could be held liable if reasonable care in producing and selling a product that injured a person was not observed.

The doctrine of strict liability is an extension of the negligence standard. Strict liability holds that the manufacturer is liable for a person's injury or death if a product goes to market that is dangerous because of a known or knowable defect. A consumer has to prove three things to win the suit: (1) an injury happened, (2) the injury resulted from a product defect, and (3) the defective product was delivered by the manufacturer being sued (Carroll 1989, 258; Des Jardins and McCall 1990, 255).

Absolute liability is a further extension of the strict liability doctrine. Absolute liability was used in 1982 in the *Beshada* v. *Johns Manville Corporation* case. Employees sued Manville for diseases related to later exposure to asbestos. The court ruled the manufacturer liable for not warning of product dangers, even though the danger was scientifically unknown at the time of the production and sale of the product (Carroll 1989, 259). Medical and chemical companies, in particular, whose products could produce harmful, but unknowable, side effects years later would be held liable under this doctrine.

Legal and Moral Limits of Product Liability

The legal and moral limits to product liability suits evolve and change historically and are, to a large degree, determined through political as well as legal stakeholder negotiations and settlements. Consumer advocates and stakeholders (for example, the Consumer Federation of America, the National Conference of State Legislators, the Conference of State Supreme Court Justices, and activist groups) argue and lobby for strong liability doctrines and laws to protect consumers against powerful firms that, these stakeholders contend, seek profits over consumer safety. On the other hand, advocates of product liability law reform (for example, advocates led by former Vice President Dan Quayle, corporate stockholders, Washington lobbyists for businesses and manufacturers, and the President's Council on Competitiveness) argue that liability laws in the United States have become too costly, excessive, routine, and arbitrary. Liability laws inhibit companies' competitiveness and willingness to innovate, they claim. Insurance companies also claim that all insurance-paying citizens are hurt by excessive liability laws that allow juries to award hundreds of millions in punitive cases; as a result, insurance rates rise.

However, a recent 2-year study of product liability cases concluded that punitive damages are rarely awarded, more rarely paid, and often reduced after the trial (*The Wall Street Journal* January 6, 1992, B1). The study, partly funded by the Roscoe Pound Foundation in Washington, D.C., is the most comprehensive effort to date to show the patterns of punitive damage awards in product liability cases over the last 25 years.

The results of the study were as follows (1) Only 355 punitive damage verdicts were given by state and federal court juries during this period. One fourth of those awards involved a single product—asbestos.

(2) In the majority of the 276 cases in which complete posttrial information was available, punitive damage awards were abandoned or reduced by the judge or the appeals court. (3) The median punitive damage returned to all product liability cases paid since 1965 was $625,000—a little above the median compensatory damage award of $500,100. Punitive damages were significantly larger than compensatory awards in only 25% of the cases. (4) The factors that led to significant awards that lawyers most frequently cited when interviewed or surveyed were "failure to reduce risk of a known danger and failure to warn consumers of those risks.

Other studies confirm these findings. A 1990 federal study of product liability suits in five states showed that plaintiffs won less than 50% of the cases; a Rand Corporation study that surveyed 26,000 households nationwide found that only 1 in 10 of an estimated 23 million people injured each year thinks about suing; and the National Center for State Courts surveyed 13 state court systems from 1984 to 1989 and found that in 1991 the increase in civil caseloads was for real property rights cases, not suits involving accidents and injuries (*The Wall Street Journal* January 6, 1992, B1).

Presently, 33 states have laws in the making to limit liability and reduce damage awards. Seven states have already limited the amount of punitive damages that can be awarded (*The Wall Street Journal* January 6, 1992, B1). The different stakeholders have drawn battle lines on the issue of limiting product liability laws. We must continue to observe how tort reform, industrial competitiveness, general economic conditions, and public opinion move to understand how product liability laws will evolve. In the next section, we discuss corporations' obligations to the environment.

5.3 CORPORATE RESPONSIBILITY TOWARD THE ENVIRONMENT

There was a time when corporations used the environment as a free and unlimited resource. That time is ending, in terms of international public awareness and increasing legislative control. The magnitude of environmental abuse, not only by industries but by human activities and nature's processes, has awakened an international awareness to protect and save the environment. At risk is the most valuable stakeholder, the earth itself. Depletion and destruction of air, water, and land are at stake in terms of natural resources. We are referring to the destruction of the rain forests in Brazil; the thinning of the ozone layer above the earth's atmosphere; climatic warming changes from carbon dioxide accumulations; the smog in Mexico City, Los Angeles, and New York City; and the pollution of the seas, lakes, rivers, and ground water supplies contaminated from toxic dumping. At the human level, environmental pollution and damage cause heart and respiratory diseases and lung and skin cancer.

Most Significant Environmental Problems

The American public and experts at the Environmental Protection Agency (EPA) differ in their identification of the nation's top four environmental problems: A national random survey of 1,413 people by the Roper Organization, Inc., found the following ranking: (1) water pollution from manufacturing plants, (2) oil spills, (3) hazardous-wastes releases, and (4) industrial air pollution. Destruction of the ozone layer was ranked fifth, and global warming was ranked fifteenth. In contrast, EPA environmental experts offered the following ranking: (1) global climate change, (2) habitat destruction, (3) species extinction, and (4) ozone-layer depletion. The EPA ranking was based on the "huge scale of the problems, their irreversible aspects and the length of time needed to solve them" (Stipp 1990). A subcommittee of EPA experts also noted the following risks to human health: air pollution, worker exposure to toxic chemicals, and drinking contaminants. These findings, based on a recent EPA report, "Reducing Risks: Setting Priorities and Strategies For Environmental Protection," are significant since EPA advisers state that the agency will begin to set priorities based not only on public concerns but also on rigorous risk assessment aimed at policies that give importance to "overall ecological destruction" as well as to lowering human health risk from specific pollutants (Stipp 1990).

The scope and seriousness of environmental abuse to which consumers and corporations, in particular, are contributing are illustrated below:

1. "The United States produces an estimated 212 million tons of hazardous waste each year—about a ton for every man, woman, and child in this nation. . . . [T]he vast bulk of this is refinery or chemical waste. . . . [O]utput of hazardous waste is estimated to be growing at the rate of about 3 percent per year. The great danger is that at some point an underground aquifer will be contaminated, which could threaten the health of thousands" (Bloom and Morton 1991, 80).

2. Over 2,500 excess cancers are linked to daily exposure to toxic air pollution. In the United States, 135 million people live in areas that are threatened by air pollution (Shabecoff 1989). Five U.S. manufacturing companies released approximately 1.3 billions of pounds of toxic chemicals into the air, water, and earth in 1988.

3. A study by the American Society of Zoologists recently announced that the Florida Keys could be destroyed at the beginning of the 21st century. Pollution from human sewage and agricultural runoff is a major cause of the harm (Keating 1991).

4. Increased amounts of carbon dioxide—from automobile exhaust—and chlorofluorocarbons (CFCs)—from coolants, aerosols, solvents, and other products—are depleting the ozone layer in the stratosphere. This is causing global warming, a condition that could lead to melting of polar glaciers, rising sea levels, and destruction of agricultural lands. Moreover, each 1% decrease in ozone is estimated to result in 4% to 6% increases in skin cancer (Shea 1989; cited in Buchholz 1992). Scientists also report that by the turn of the century, depletion of the ozone layer will cause 1.6 million additional cataracts a year and 300,000 new skin cancers worldwide. Ultraviolet radiation, also a cause of ozone layer decay, depresses the human immune system—which increases the risk of infectious diseases (*Boston Globe* November 16, 1991, 3).

5. In the United States, individuals and industries throw out 400,000 tons of solid waste—trash—each day. Landfills are overflowing; towns and communities are fighting the use of dump and incineration sites in their areas. NIMBY ("Not in My Back Yard") groups are protesting side effects of air and underground water pollution from trash dumping (Environmental Protection Agency 1988; cited in Buchholz 1992).

The list goes on. Cancer-related diseases are caused by asbestos fibers found in building insulation, automobile brakes, and scores of other products; acid rain carrying nitrogen and sulfur oxide particles in the form of water vapor is killing fish and affecting forests; a major cause of air pollution results from the burning of fossil fuels—smog has rendered Mexico City's air quality one of the worst in the world; indoor air pollution results from formaldehyde and other chemical fumes as well as from cigarette smoke; surface and ground water pollution results from runoffs that transport chemicals from agricultural sites, oil-coated roads, and construction sites. Large bodies of water have been severely damaged: the Boston Harbor, Lake Erie, the Hudson River, the Love Canal near Niagara Falls, and the Mississippi River, to name only a few. The cumulative effect of these pollutants taken together adds up to air, water, and earth damage.

Causes of Environmental Pollution

Some of the most pervasive factors which have contributed to depletion and damage of environment include:

1. A growing consumer affluence. Increased wealth—as measured by real personal per capita income—has led to increase spending, consumption, and waste.

2. Increasing materialistic cultural values. Values have evolved that emphasize consumption over conservation—a mentality that believes "bigger is better," "me first," and a throwaway ethic.

3. Increasing urbanization. Concentrations of people in cities increase pollution.

4. Population explosion. From 1900 to 1990, the global population grew from 1.2 billion to 5.5 billion. Population growth means more industrialization, product use, waste and pollution.

5. New and uncontrolled technologies. Technologies are produced by firms that prioritize profits, convenience, and consumption over environmental protection.

6. Industrial activities. The magnitude of industrial activity that, as stated earlier, has emphasized depletion of natural resources and destructive uses of the environment for economic reasons has been a significant cause of environmental decay (Steiner and Steiner 1992). It is industrial activities that abuse the environment that we are most concerned with in this book.

Enforcement of Environmental Laws

A number of governmental regulatory agencies have been created to develop and enforce policies and laws to protect the general and work-place environments. The Occupational Safety and Health Administration (OSHA), the Consumer Product Safety Commission (CPSC), the Environmental Protection Agency (EPA), and the Council on Environmental Quality (CEQ) are among the more active agencies that regulate environmental standards. The EPA, in particular, has been a lead organization vis-à-vis regulating environmental abuses by industrial firms.

In 1970, the Nixon administration concentrated EPA's mission and activities to control and decrease pollution in the following areas: toxic substances, radiation, air, water, solid waste (trash), and pesticides. The EPA has used its regulatory powers to enforce several important environmental laws:

- The Clean Air Act of 1970, 1977, and 1989. The latest revision of this law includes provisions for regulating acid rain, ozone reduction, and the capability for companies to sell or transfer their right to pollute within same state boundaries—pollution rights could be bought, sold, managed, and brokered like securities (see Sturdivant and Vernon-Wortzel 1990, 318–324).

- The Federal Water Pollution Control Act of 1972. Revised in 1977, this law controls the discharge of toxic pollutants into the water.

- The Resource Conservation and Recovery Act (RCRA). This legislation provides guidelines for the identification, control, and regulation of hazardous wastes by companies and state governments. The $1.6 billion Superfund was also created by Congress in 1980. It provides for the cleanup of chemical spills and toxic waste dumps. Chemical, petroleum, and oil firms' taxes helped keep the Superfund going, along with U.S. Treasury funds and other fees collected from pollution control. By 1989, the EPA had $8.5 billion in the program (see Sturdivant and Vernon-Wortzel 1990, 324). During 1991, the EPA's enforcement of the Superfund experienced legal setbacks because the courts were less willing to view federal environmental concerns as superseding states' statutory and constitutional language (Moses 1991).

The overall effect of enforcing and controlling environmental pollution and resource depletion is incrementally improving. An expert reports:

> Since 1975, when most of the consistent environmental measurements began, overall improvement amounts to only 15 percent. . . . In a few scattered instances, pollution levels have been significantly reduced, by 70 percent or more: lead in the air; DDT and PCBs in wildlife and people; mercury pollution in the Great Lakes; strontium 90 in the food chain; and in some local rivers, phosphate pollution. . . . Each of these pollutants has been effectively controlled not by high-tech devices, but by simply stopping its production or use. Still, the EPA continues to enforce environmental pollution laws. (Commoner 1990)

The EPA's annual enforcement scorecard for 1991 showed 125 indictments, 72 convictions, 550 months of prison sentences served by convicted defendants (a 121% increase over 1990), and $14.1 million in fines collected. Critics argue that few larger firms receive jail terms for polluting. Sixty percent of firms that were caught and convicted had sales under $1 million and fewer than 50 employees (Allen 1991). Although enforcement of corporate violations is ongoing, the effectiveness of enforcement is debatable.

The Ethics of Ecology

The role of corporations as economic institutions based primarily on a utilitarian ethic is under attack (Buchholz 1991; Sagoff 1990). Advocates of a new environmentalism argue that when the stakes approach the damage of the earth itself and human health and survival, the utilitarian ethic alone is an insufficient logic to justify continuing negligence and abuse to the earth. For example, Sagoff (1990) argues that cost–benefit analysis can measure only desires, not beliefs. Regarding environmental policy, he asks, "Why should we think economic efficiency is an important goal? Why should we take wants and preferences more seriously than beliefs and opinions? Why should we base public policy on the model of a market transaction rather than the model of a political debate?" And when it comes to setting environmental policy, Sagoff argues that "economists as a rule do not recognize one other value, namely, justice or equality, and they speak, therefore, of a 'trade-off' between efficiency and our aesthetic and moral values. What about the trade-off between efficiency and dignity, efficiency and self-respect, efficiency and the magnificence of our natural heritage, efficiency and the quality of life?" (p. 363) This line of reasoning raises such questions as "What is human life worth? What is a 'fair market' price or replacement value of Lake Erie? The Atlantic Ocean? The Brazilian rain forests? The stratosphere?"

Buchholz (1991, 19) argues for five elements of corporate social responsibility in advocating for an ecology-based organizational ethic:

1. Organizations have responsibilities that go beyond the production of goods and services at a profit.

2. These responsibilities involve helping to solve important social problems, especially those they have helped create.

3. Corporations have a broader constituency than stockholders alone.

4. Corporations have impacts that go beyond simple marketplace transactions.

5. Corporations serve a wider range of human values than can be captured by a sole focus on economic values.

While these ethical guidelines serve as an ethical basis for understanding corporate responsibility toward the environment, still utilitarian logic and cost–benefit methods will continue to play a key role in corporate decisions regarding their uses of the environment. Also, cost–benefit analysis will be used by judges, courts, and juries in trying to decide who should pay and how much in settling case-by-case environmental disputes. Costs will be estimated. For example, it has been estimated that it could cost $300 billion to clean up existing hazardous waste sites (Bloom and Morton 1991). The EPA estimates additional spending in the Clean Air Act to be between $2 billion to $8 billion a year to control acid rain, between $8 billion to $20 billion on smog control, and between $1 billion and $6 billion to control toxic air pollution (Shabecoff 1989). Some experts and industry spokespersons argue that costs for further controlling such pollutants as smog outweigh the benefits. On the other hand, an administrator of the Clean Air Working Group—the major industry lobbying organization—stated, "At stake is our hides" (Shabecoff 1989).

Rights of Future Generations and Right to a Livable Environment

The evolution of laws, regulations, and corporate practices and restrictions regarding the use and abuse of the natural environment continues. Different stakeholders will protect their turf and promote their competing interests. However, as global warming, depletion of the ozone layer, and pollution of air, land, and water continue at an accelerated pace into the 21st century, the following ethical principles will gain importance in legal and moral ecological controversies: (1) rights of future generations and (2) right to a livable environment.

The debate about the rights of future generations centers around: to what extent present generations should bear disproportionate burdens for the sake of future generations. In other words, how much of the environment can a present generation use or destroy to advance its own economic welfare? According to the ethicist John Rawls (as paraphrased by Velasquez [1988, 254]), "Justice . . . requires that we hand over to our immediate successors a world that is not in worse condition than the one we received from our ancestors."

The right to a livable environment is an issue that William Blackstone (1974) advanced (see also Velasquez [1988]). The logic is that each human being has a moral and legal right to a decent, livable environment. This "environmental right" supersedes individuals' legal property rights and is based on the belief that human life is not possible without a livable environment. Therefore, laws must enforce the protection of the environment based on human survival. It has been noted (see Velasquez [1988, 239]) that several landmark laws in the late 1960s and 1970s (Water Pollution Control Act, 1972, 1977; Clean Water Act, 1977; Air Quality Act, 1967; Clean Air Amendments, 1970, 1991) were not based on utilitarian cost–benefit analysis, but more on the logic related to Blackstone's "environmental right." While cost–benefit analysis will remain a central method in determining fault and liability in environmental court cases, principles of rights, justice, and duty as discussed above and in Chapter 3 will also serve as important criteria in determining benefits and costs, as well as for ecological legislation.

Recommendations to Managers

We conclude this section on the environment with four questions that Bloom and Morton (1991, 83) suggest as advice to managers. Although the questions are aimed at assessing corporate responsibility regarding hazardous waste, they apply to managing environmental problems as well:

1. How much is your company really worth? (This question refers to contingent liability that a firm may have to assume depending on its practices.)
2. Have you made hazardous waste risk analysis an integral part of your strategic planning process?
3. Does your information system look out for environmental problems?
4. Have you made it clear to your officers and employees that strict adherence to hazardous waste requirements is a fundamental tenet of company policy?

These are practical questions that reflect the relatedness of economic and ethical concerns.

5.4 MANAGEMENT OF STRATEGIC ISSUES AND CRISES

Managing the environment and moral responsibility in the marketplace for corporations also means managing strategic issues and crises related to advertising, product safety, as well as environmentally related problems. To act morally toward stakeholders in the marketplace, corporate executives and managers should be aware of potentially harmful issues and problems before these evolve into crises. Often at stake in strategic issue management, as well as in crises that suddenly erupt, are human lives, property, environmental damage, the firm's reputation, market-share, profits and sometimes the firm's existence—as was the case with the Manville Corporation in the asbestos lawsuits and with A. H. Robins Company in the Dalkon Shield lawsuits.

In this section, we build on the discussion from Chapter 4 by outlining how issue and crisis management are part of a firm's strategic enterprise planning process. Issue and crisis management are also related topics in the stakeholder analysis, presented in Chapter 2. Managing corporate responsibility vis à vis a firm's constituencies—especially those groups affected by critical issues and crises stemming from a firm's activities—involves issue and crisis management. Recent examples of industrial crises that threatened the environment and a wide range of stakeholders, and that involved intense media coverage, include the *Exxon Valdez* oil spill in Alaska, the Three Mile Island nuclear plant crisis in New York, the *Challenger* space shuttle disaster, the Union Carbide chemical leak in India, and the product crises discussed earlier: the discovery of cyanide in Johnson & Johnson's Tylenol, Ford Pinto's rear gas tank explosions, injuries blamed on Firestone 500 radial tires, Procter & Gamble's Rely tampon crisis, A. H. Robins' Dalkon Shield-related deaths and injuries, and Dow Corning Corporation's recent crisis in manufacturing and marketing the silicone gel used in breast implants. Because of the seriousness and scope of the stakes regarding such extraordinary events, a number of firms use management methods and techniques to manage critical issues and crises.

Strategic Issues Management

Strategic issues management attempts to (1) detect and address issues that may cause a firm and its stakeholders problems or harm and (2) contain or solve issues that could become potentially damaging crises. A number of firms (for example, Monsanto, Sears, and Arco) have issues management staff who alert top management to controversial trends that could affect operations (Carroll 1989, 486).

Managing and controlling issues involves the following steps (derived from a number of sources, including Brown [1979]; Buchholz [1982]; Carroll [1989]; and King [1987]):

1. Environmental scanning
2. Identification of issues

3. Prioritizing issues
4. Analyzing issues
5. Strategizing issue solutions
6. Responding and implementing strategies
7. Evaluating and monitoring strategies

These steps were discussed in Chapter 4 as part of a firm's corporate planning process. In the strategic issues management process, these steps are isolated and used by a firm's special issues unit's work on emerging trends as they relate to the specific industry and company.

Issues also are believed to follow a developmental, life-cycle process. There are different views (for example, see Carroll [1989]; Gottschalk [1982]; and Mahjon [1986]) on the stages and time involved in the life cycle—one source has assigned an eight-year span to an issue's life. It is instructive to understand some of the life-cycle stages suggested for purposes of tracking an issue.

Archie Carroll (1989, 489) proposed a seven-stage issue developmental process:

1. A felt need emerges (emerging events, advocate groups, books, movies).
2. Media coverage is developed (TV: "60 Minutes," "20/20"; articles, radio).
3. Interest group development and growth gains momentum.
4. Policies are adopted by leading political jurisdictions (cities, states, counties).
5. Federal government gains attention (hearings and studies).
6. Issues and policies evolve into legislation and regulation.
7. Issues and policies enter litigation.

Can you think of some contemporary issues that evolved through part or all of these stages? Did an issue change in its perceived importance or danger by society? Did the issue gain or lose public legitimacy as it evolved through the legislative stage? How did the stakes and stakeholders change as the issue evolved?

Thomas Marx (1986) offered a four-stage issue life cycle. Marx observed that issues evolved from social expectations to social control through the following steps:

1. Social expectation
2. Political issue

3. Legislation
4. Social control

Marx illustrated his framework with the auto safety belt issue. The four stages of this issue, according to Marx, were reflected in the following events: (1) Ralph Nader's book *Unsafe at Any Speed* (1964) created a social expectation. (2) The National Traffic Auto Safety Act and resulting Motor Vehicle Safety hearings in 1966 moved the expectation into the political arena. (3) In 1966, the Motor Vehicle Safety Act was passed, which was later followed by four states adopting required seat belt use in 1984. This represented the legislation stage. (4) Social control was established in 1967 when all cars were required to have seat belts. Driver fines and penalties, recall of products, and defects litigation further emphasized the control stage. Again, selecting an issue in the news and tracing its evolution through these different stages provides a window into the social, political, economic, and legislative processes of how society functions. Issues are not static or predetermined commodities. Different stakeholder groups' values and interests move or impede an issue's development. To understand how an issue develops or is killed is to understand how power works in a political system.

Issues Management and Stakeholder Analysis

After the issues are prioritized, a stakeholder analysis can be enhanced by asking the following questions (from King 1987):

- Which stakeholders are affected by the issue?
- Who has an interest in the issue?
- Who is in a position to exert influence on the issue?
- Who has expressed an opinion on the issue?
- Who ought to care about the issue?

Issues can then be ranked from highest to lowest in terms of impact on corporate-level operations and ethical obligations and responsibilities of each stakeholder. Again, Chapter 2 contains many of these considerations, which we will not repeat here. The point is, that an issues management process complements the stakeholder analysis and can be used to anticipate and resolve corporate-related issues and crises. Students of business ethics can also use these frameworks to understand and track newsbreaking incidents that present economic, legal, social, and moral problems for a company and its stakeholders.

We close this section by presenting John Naisbitt and Patricia Aburdene's (1990) list of predominant forces and issues in the "extraordinary decade" of the 1990s:

- Economic considerations transcending political ones.
- Movement is being made toward worldwide free trade.
- The importance of telecommunications is increasing.
- A relative abundance of natural resources is occurring.
- Competition is occurring for reduced taxes.
- Downsizing of economic output is happening.
- Containing inflation and interest is a trend across nations.
- An Asian consumer boom is ahead and will continue to occur.
- Advancement of democracy and free enterprise will continue.
- Obsolescence of war is occurring among major nations.
- New attention to the environment will continue.

What moral issues do these trends present to corporations and to us as individual stakeholders? Are there additional issues that this list does not identify?

Managing Crises

A crisis is a "turning point for better or worse"; a "decisive moment" or "crucial time"; or "a situation that has reached a critical phase" (Fink 1986, 15). Steven Fink (1986) states that crisis management "is the art of removing much of the risk and uncertainty to allow you to achieve more control over your destiny." Crises can, from a corporation's point of view, deteriorate if the situation escalates in intensity, comes under closer government scrutiny, interferes with normal operations, jeopardizes positive company and/or officers' image, and damages a firm's bottom line (Fink 1986, 16). We would add that a turn for the worse could also occur if any of the firm's stakeholders were seriously harmed or if the environment was damaged or destroyed.

Stages of Crises

Crises consists of four stages: (1) prodromal (precrisis); (2) acute; (3) chronic; and (4) resolution (Fink 1986, 20). Judgment and observation are required in managing these stages. Figure 5-1 illustrates these changes.

Figure 5-1 Four Crisis Management Stages

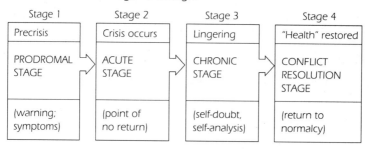

The **prodromal stage** is the warning stage. If this stage is missed, the second stage (acute crisis) can rush in, leaving damage control to follow. Clues in this stage must be carefully observed. For example, a clue could be verbal—a union leader telling upper management a strike could occur if certain contract conditions are not signed.

The second stage, **acute crisis**, is the occurrence of the actual crisis. Damage has been done at this stage. The point here is to control as much of the damage as possible. This is most times the shortest of the stages.

The third stage, **chronic crisis**, is the clean-up phase. This is a period of recovery, self-analysis, self-doubt, and healing. Congressional investigations, audits, and interviews occur during this stage. This stage can linger indefinitely, according to Fink (1986). A survey of Fortune 500 CEOs found that companies that did not have a crisis management plan stayed in this stage two and a half times longer than those that had plans.

The final stage, **crisis resolution**, is the crisis management goal. The key question here is, "What can I do to speed up this phase and resolve this crisis once and for all?" (Fink 1986, 25).

Product Crisis Management Model

Matthews, Goodpaster, and Nash (1985) also suggested five phases of corporate social responses to crises related to unsafe products. Figure 5-2 illustrates this crisis model. These phases include (1) reaction, (2) defense, (3) insight range, (4) accommodation, and (5) agency. Not all executives involved in unsafe product crises respond the same to the public, media, and other stakeholders. These phases can be used to examine and evaluate moral responsibility of corporate responses to such crises as the Firestone radial 500 tire, the Tylenol crisis, the Rely tampon, the Ford Pinto, the Dow Corning silicon-gel issue, and those presently occurring. How and to what extent executives acknowledge

Figure 5-2 Corporate Social Response Phases

Source: John Matthews, Kenneth Goodpaster, and Laura Nash. *Policies and Persons: A Casebook in Business Ethics.* 2d ed. New York: McGraw-Hill, 1991. Adapted from Archie B. Carroll, "A Three-Dimensional Conceptual Model of Corporate Performance," *Academy of Management Review* 4, no. 4 (1977): 502.

responsibility and act morally and economically responsible to their stakeholders in each response stage varies. It is interesting to observe how some executives continue to deny and avoid responsibility in crises that erupt. Knowledge of these stages would certainly be a first step toward corporate awareness.

Crisis Management Stages

The **reaction stage** occurs when a crisis has in fact occurred. Management lacks complete information and time to analyze the event thoroughly. A public reaction is required that responds to allegations about the product and the crisis. This stage is important to corporations, since the public, the media, and those stakeholders involved see for the first time who the firm selects as its spokesperson, how the firm responds, and what the message is.

The second stage, **defense**, signals that the company is overwhelmed by public attention. The firm's image is at stake. This stage usually involves the company's recoiling under media pressure. But this does not always have to be a negative or reactive situation.

The third stage, **insight range**, is the most agonizing time for the firm in the controversy. The stakes are substantial. The firm's existence may be questioned. The company must come to grips with the situation under the external circumstances. During this stage, the executives realize and confirm from evidence whether and to what extent their company is at fault in the safety issues of the product in question.

The fourth stage, **accommodation**, involves the company is acting either to remove the product from market or to refute the charges against the product's unsafe status. Addressing public pressure and anxiety is the task of this stage.

The last stage, **agency**, involves the company's attempting to understand the causes of the safety issue and developing an education program for the public.

Observe newspaper and media reports of industrially related crises. Apply this model and compare how company executives and spokespersons handle crises. Take special note of how companies respond morally to their different stakeholders. Observe whether companies give more or less attention to consumers, media, and government stakeholders. Use the frameworks in Chapter 2 to help inform your observations and judgments. Develop a time line as the crisis unfolds. Ask who the company chooses as its spokesperson. Inquire how and why the company is assuming or avoiding responsibility.

Crisis Management Recommendations

A number of suggestions that corporations can follow to respond more effectively to crises are briefly summarized here. More in-depth strategies and tactics can be found in several sources (Matthews, Goodpaster, and Nash 1985; Mitroff, Shrivastava, and Udwedia 1987).

- Face the problem; don't avoid or minimize it; tell the truth.
- "No comment" answers imply guilt; take your "lumps" in one big news story rather than in bits and pieces.
- Recognize that in the age of instant news, there's no such thing as a secret or private crisis.
- Stage "war games" to observe how your crisis plan holds up under pressure; train executives to practice press conferences; train teams to respond to crises that may affect other functional areas or divisions.
- Use the firm's philosophy, motto, or creed to respond to a crisis: For example, "We believe in our customer. Service is our business."
- Use the firm's closeness to customers and end-users for early feedback on the crisis to evaluate your effectiveness in responding and addressing the events.

Finally, issues management cannot be effective in corporations without implementing the following factors: Top management must be supportive and must participate; cross-departmental involvement is needed; the issues management unit must fit with the firm's culture; and output instead of process must be the focus (Wartick and Rude 1986).

In the last section of this chapter, we briefly discuss the relationship between business and government. The following issue remains to be addressed: Can corporations govern their own activities toward consumers and the public? To what extent, if any, is government control over corporate activities necessary? Chapter 4 dealt with characteristics and mechanisms of corporate self-regulation; here we explore the extent to which corporate self-regulation is inadequate.

5.5 THE GOVERNMENT AS CORPORATE REGULATOR AND STAKEHOLDER

Government regulation is an integral part of the economic affairs of business in America. The U.S. Constitution (Article 1, Section 8) and system of national governance define the roles of federal government as lawmaker, regulator, and enforcer over interstate and foreign commerce, taxes, duties, imports, tariffs, excises, the military, foreign affairs, bankruptcy, copyrights, and patents. Still, the nature of the changing business–government relationship in the United States is dynamic. As we discuss below, the dynamic character of this relationship is based on (1) clashing values systems between government and business, (2) an adversarial relationship between the two enterprises, and (3) the politics of the regulation process.

The nature of the government–business relationship is adversarial; that is, business and government professionals often have contrary missions, goals, and roles. Business officials see their roles as "probers, inspectors, taxers, regulators, and punishers of business transgressions" (Jacoby 1975). Business professionals, on the other hand, tend to see their roles as entrepreneurs, investors, and risktakers who do not need or desire unnecessary bureaucratic controls.

The adversarial nature of this relationship is based on an underlying set of clashing values. Government goals and operations are grounded in collectivistic values aimed at serving the public interest and good. Business goals and practices are based on individualistic values that serve private, economic self-interests (Jacoby 1975). Governmental values emphasize group self-interests; business values enhance economic return on investment for individual stockholders and stakeholders. This adversarial relationship accounts for much of the ongoing conflict of interests among businesses, government, and the public.

The business–government relationship in the United States is also political in nature. At the national level, Democratic and Republican presidents, congresses, and judicial officials and judges with different political ideologies determine and influence to a large degree the direction, nature, and extent of legislation; regulatory rules and enforcement;

and expenditures that empower regulation. President Lyndon Johnson, for example, created the concept of the "Great Society" in the 1960s and passed more social legislation than any other president. President Ronald Reagan campaigned for less government control and regulation in the 1980s and succeeded in building on President Ford's and President Carter's deregulation of railroads, airlines, trucking, financial firms, natural gas companies, and other industries.

The making, enforcement, and dispute settlement of laws and regulations also reflect the political process of coalition building, which helps shape and determine regulatory outcomes. Senators and congresspersons are generally influenced by paid lobbyists and political action committees (PACs) that promote special interests and legislation to support or inhibit the passage of specific laws, interests, and regulations regarding labor, unions, realtors, educators, home builders, medical doctors, and other professional and private groups.

The Ethics of Politics and Regulation

Two major criticisms regarding the politics of the regulatory process as it has evolved are, "Who represents the interests of the public?" and "Who regulates whom?" A retort to the first question has been, "Which public? Whose particular interests?" Without a paid lobbyist or participation in a PAC, critics of the regulatory "game" argue that it difficult, if not impossible, to implement legislation and regulations regarding particular interests. The ethical problem raised in the politics of paid lobbyists and PACs is whether and to what extent the public's exercise of its freedoms embodied in the First Amendment is being violated and even bought out. Who regulates whom seems to depend on the "golden rule": "Who has the gold, rules" (Sabato 1984). In the U.S. pluralistic, economic capitalist system, the ideal is a balance between a free, open political process and a "marketplace of political ideas" (Steiner and Steiner 1991). From an ethical perspective, we also ask to what extent is it the government's responsibility to promote and protect the rights of individual citizens? To what extent should the government ensure the just distribution of resources in the society? What is the duty of the government to ensure the public's freedom of choice in the marketplace?

Roles of Government in Regulating and Influencing Business

Government plays several regulatory and nonregulatory, even contradictory, roles with business in America. Government is a major purchaser of business goods and services (such as military hardware) as well as a regulator and controller of business activities. Government competes with businesses (such as in postal services) and at the same time finances and subsidizes businesses (for example, agriculture). Government breaks up business monopolies (for example, AT&T) and bails them out (for example, the 1979 $1.2 billion loan to Chrysler, and the ongoing Savings and Loan multimillion-dollar bailout). Depending on the climate of national and global economics, industrial competitiveness, and geopolitics, the roles of government with business change. During the Reagan years, less government was seen as better. Deregulation was emphasized, as was a "hands-off" approach. In the 1990s, with the rise of Japanese superior industrial and economic competitiveness, the automotive, computer, and auto parts industries, in particular, are calling for more government protection and intervention.

In general, the national government functions to influence business in the following ways: by (1) defining the rules of the competitive game (for example, labor–management relations, advertising, safety regulations, antitrust laws); (2) promoting and subsidizing business (for example, loan guarantees, tariff protections, tax incentives, purchase of business goods and services—$1.1 trillion by federal, state, and local governments); (3) using business as an instrument of government aims (enforcing companies to pay minimum wages, use minority hiring policies, subcontract to minority businesses); (4) setting national economic goals; (5) protecting society's social, physical, and workplace interests (such as environmental laws, safety laws, consumer laws); (6) redistributing resources to meet moral and social goals (for example, transfer payments, research and development expenditures, tax incentives); (7) promoting and conserving quality-of-life needs (for example, environmental laws); (8) setting standards to promote public interests and resolving potential business conflicts (for example, businesses sometimes seek regulation that is good for the environment but that cannot be implemented unless all competitors comply; otherwise, some businesses would profit at others' expense); and (9) controlling unfair business practices (such as monopolies) (see Steiner and Steiner 1991, 285–290). Most of these functions cannot be accomplished by individual businesses.

Types of Government Regulation in Business

Government regulation regarding business activities involves designated agencies, boards, and commissions created, empowered, and funded by Congress to set and enforce standards for particular industries and, as is the case more recently, for particular business functions and their policies across industries (that is, marketing, manufacturing, purchasing, international operations, legal, personnel, planning, finance, and so on). (See Weidenbaum [1989] for a more complete listing of Federal regulatory agencies and business functional areas.) For example, the Federal Trade Commission, the Food and Drug Administration, the Consumer Products Safety Commission, the USDA, the Department of Health, Education, and Welfare (HEW), and others work to regulate and monitor marketing and advertising activities. The Energy Department, the Treasury Department, the Drug Enforcement Administration, the Nuclear Regulatory Agency, the Environmental Protection Agency, and the Occupational Safety and Health Administration monitor manufacturing standards and activities. The Equal Employment Opportunity Commission, the National Labor Relations Board and others set guidelines and enforce personnel standards and laws. In finance, the Internal Revenue Service, the Securities and Exchange Commission (SEC), and the Federal Reserve, among others, regulate laws and guidelines. The Federal Trade Commission and the SEC regulate legal functions in companies. International operations of firms are regulated by the International Trade Commission, the Commerce Department, and the Treasury Department, to name some of the more prominent agencies.

Costs and Benefits of Government Regulation

Is government regulation worth the costs to consumer stakeholders? To business stakeholders? To society? To future generations? What are the benefits of government regulation? Who benefits; who loses? What would American society be like without government regulation? Who would suffer most? Although there are no simple answers to these questions, they do raise issues that underlie the problems associated with determining costs and benefits of regulation. Although there may be no consensus on the value or price of human health and life, air, water, and earth, the costs and benefits of regulating the environment, safety, equality, and free-market competitiveness will be estimated and debated by those who must pay the costs and by those who must bear the consequences of nonregulation.

An Arthur Andersen (1979) study showed that the incremental costs of 48 firms (that is, costs the firms would not have spent without regulations) in meeting six federal agency program standards was $2.6 billion (see also Steiner and Steiner 1991). Realistically, it is impossible to estimate all the costs to firms that conform to government regulations. Some of the more pronounced types of costs of compliance entail (1) hiring and maintaining professionals and lawyers to meet human resource standards such as affirmative action and to settle legal disputes; (2) submitting paperwork required to meet compliance standards (approximately $25 billion to $32 billion each year) (U.S. Commission on Federal Paperwork 1977); and (3) purchasing equipment and maintaining manufacturing costs for implementing safety standards. There are also indirect costs of regulation, such as losses in productivity from having to comply with confusing, contradictory, and time-consuming standards; losses in facility constructions that are not built because of noncompliance problems or plant closings that do not meet standards; losses in hiring and employment because of minimum wage restrictions (Buchholz 1989); and losses in innovation from pretesting requirements and over-compliance measures (Buchholz 1989; Schnee 1979).

The benefits of government regulation are as difficult to estimate as the costs. One such study estimated air pollution control benefits at $5 billion to $58 billion annually; water pollution cleanup at $9 billion; and avoidance of workday accidents and fatalities during a 2-year span at a $15 billion reduction. (Carroll 1989, 181; *Congressional Quarterly's Federal Regulatory Directory* 1985–1986).

These costs must be weighed against the many intangible and often inestimable benefits that government regulation serves. What would our society be like without any government regulations? Would the environment benefit without the Clean Air Act or the Federal Water Pollution Control Act? Would consumers be as protected without product liability and safety regulatory legislation? Would minorities have equal opportunities in the marketplace without civil rights legislation? Would consumers be better off without antimonopoly legislation? Without government regulation, social aims and direction would not be set for our society. The issue of costs and benefits should, perhaps, center more on the specific methods, volume, and costs of regulation than on whether regulation is needed to set social goals and monitor industries' moral and economic obligations toward stakeholders and the public (see Steiner and Steiner 1991).

Again, it is difficult to evaluate the benefits of the Clean Air Act, the Toxic Substances Control Act, the Clean Water Act, and OSHA and EPA regulatory standards for the workplace and the environment. A key issue concerning the controversial topic of costs versus benefits of environmental protection continues: "What would be the effects on the environment, on the workplace, and on employee safety and equality without laws and regulations addressing and enforcing such issues?" Cost–benefit analysis and principles of justice, duty, rights, and obligations will continue to be weighed and considered in decisions and disputes by managers, judges, and juries regarding administrative, judicial, legal, and business stakeholder concerns.

Although corporate self-regulation is certainly necessary, we argue that it is not sufficient in a complex society in which public health and safety and the environment must be protected against the uses of changing technologies and industrial activities aimed primarily at profit making.

SUMMARY

Businesses have a legal and moral obligation to provide their consumers with safe products, without the use of false advertising and without doing harm to the environment. The complexities and controversies with respect to this obligation stem from attempts to define "safety," "truth in advertising," and levels of "harm" caused to the environment.

Corporations need to balance their social responsibilities toward the consuming public with the return on investment demands of their stockholders. Increasing concern over the destruction of the ozone layer, destruction of the rain forests, and other environmental issues has presented firms with another area in which economic and social responsibilities must be balanced.

The very survival of many corporations can depend on how quickly and responsively it deals with a crisis of public confidence brought on by sabotage or faulty products. Crisis and issues management models complement the stakeholder approach by adding a dynamic dimension of tracing and evaluating changing issues in the environment.

Crisis management is a process of minimizing the risk and uncertainty and restoring as much control as possible to the corporation's future management. The four stages of a crisis are the prodromal, acute, chronic, and resolution stages, each of which requires accurate observation and informed judgment.

Issues management deals with anticipating and addressing issues that may harm the firm or its stakeholders. Issues develop through a "life cycle." Two issues development models are presented. The issues management process also adds to the stakeholder analysis not only by identifying issues but also by prioritizing them and by detecting and resolving potential or existing business-related crises.

The government also has a stake in helping to manage the social obligations of business to its stakeholders. The relationship of business and government tends to be adversarial because of business's pursuit of individualistic values that conflict with the collectivist public value goals of government. However, because of the difficulty in measuring the specific cost or value associated with human health, quality of life, and environmental damage, some government regulation is necessary in order to assist in balancing corporate goals of profit maximization with its social and moral obligations. Arguments for and critical of government regulation of business are discussed.

Questions

1. What is the "free-market theory" of corporate responsibility toward consumers, and what are some of the problems associated with this view? Compare this view with the "social contract" and stakeholder perspective of social corporate responsibility.

2. Identify arguments for and against questionable ethical advertising. Which do you *not* agree with? Explain.

3. Describe an advertisement on TV or in the press that you believe is unethical. Explain your argument.

4. What is the four-step process developed by Justice Powell to determine whether commercial speech in advertising can be restricted or banned?

5. What constitutes "unreasonable risk" concerning the safety of a product? Identify considerations that define the safety of a product from an ethical perspective.

6. Explain the differences between the doctrines of negligence, strict liability, and absolute liability. What do you believe should be the "limits" to product liability doctrine? Explain.

7. Identify moral arguments for corporate responsibility toward the environment. Do you believe trees, lakes, oceans, and animals should have rights? Explain.

8. What are the stages involved in product crisis management? Briefly explain each one. Identify a product crisis recently or in the past. Explain and evaluate how the company handled the crisis.

9. What are some of the ways in which the federal government acts to influence business behavior? Do you agree or disagree that the government should regulate businesses?

10. What are some areas of business in which federal or state governments should not be involved of intervene? Explain.

Exercises

1. Identify a recent example of a corporation accused of false or deceitful advertising. How did the company justify the claims made in its ad? Do you agree or disagree with the company's claims? Explain.

2. In a few paragraphs, explain your opinion regarding whether advertising is a valid or legitimate industry.

3. Can you think of an instance when you or someone you know was affected by corporate negligence in product safety standards? If so, did you communicate the problem to the company? Did the company respond to the complaint? Characterize the company's response. How could/should the company have responded differently?

4. Find an article discussing environmental damage caused by corporate activities. Recommend methods the firm in the article should employ to reduce harmful effects on the environment.

5. Give a recent example of a corporation that had to manage a crisis in public confidence. Did the company representative respond effectively or ineffectively to its stakeholders regarding the crisis? What should the company have done differently in its handling of the crisis?

6. Using a framework from the chapter, identify a controversial societal issue and explain how the issue evolved and changed. Predict how the issue *will evolve*. Defend and substantiate your prediction.

References and Suggested Readings

Alexander, George. *Honesty and Competition.* Syracuse, N.Y.: Syracuse University Press, 1967.

Allen, Frank, "Few Big Firms Get Jail Time for Polluting." *The Wall Street Journal,* December 9, 1991, B1.

Arthur Andersen and Co. *Cost of Government Regulation Study for the Business Roundtable.* New York: Arthur Andersen, 1979.

Barett, William. "Dalkon Shield Maker Concedes Possible User Injuries." *Dallas Times Herald,* April 3, 1985, A8. Cited in Rogene Buchholz. *Fundamental Concepts and Problems in Business Ethics.* Englewood Cliffs, N.J.: Prentice-Hall, 1989, p. 202.

Beauchamp, Tom, and Norman Bowie. *Ethical Theory and Business.* 3d ed. Englewood Cliffs, N.J.: Prentice-Hall 1988.

Blackstone, William. "Ethics and Ecology." In *Philosophy and Environmental Crisis,* edited by W. Blackstone. Athens, Ga.: University of Georgia Press, 1974.

Bloom, Gordon F., and Michael Morton. "Hazardous Waste Is Every Manager's Problem." *Sloan Management Review* (Summer 1991): 80.

The Boston Globe. November 16, 1991, 3, "Ozone Depletion Is Said to Harm Immune System."

Brown, James. *This Business of Issues: Coping with the Company's Environment.* New York: Conference Board, 1979.

Buchholz, Rogene. "Education for Public Issues Management: Key Insights from a Survey of Top Practitioners." *Public Affairs Review* 3 (1982): 65–76.

————. *Fundamental Concepts and Problems in Business Ethics*. Englewood Cliffs, N.J.: Prentice-Hall, 1989.

————. "Corporate Responsibility and the Good Society: From Economics to Ecology." *Business Horizons* (July-August, 1991): 19–31.

————. *Business Environment and Public Policy: Implications for Management and Strategy*. 4th ed. Englewood Cliffs, N.J.: Prentice-Hall, 1992.

Business Week. December 23, 1991, 34.

Carroll, Archie B. *Business and Society: Ethics and Stakeholder Management,* 1st and 3d eds. Cincinnati: South-Western Publishing Co., 1989 and 1993.

Commoner, Barry. "Failure of the Environmental Effort." In *Contemporary Issues in Business Ethics,* edited by Joseph Des Jardins and John McCall. Belmont, Calif.: Wadsworth, 1990.

Congressional Quarterly's Federal Regulatory Directory. 1985–1986, 30. Also cited in Carroll (1989, 181).

DeGeorge, Richard. *Business Ethics* 3d ed. New York: Macmillan, 1990.

Des Jardins, Joseph, and John McCall, eds. *Contemporary Issues in Business Ethics.* Belmont, Calif.: Wadsworth, 1990.

Elliott, Stuart. "Has Madison Avenue Gone Too Far?" *The New York Times,* December 15, 1991, Business section, 1, 6.

Environmental Protection Agency. *Environmental Progress and Challenges: Update.* Washington, D.C.: Government Printing Office, 1988, 87. Also cited in Buchholz (1992, 441).

Fink, Steven. *Crisis Management.* New York: AMACOM, 1986.

Galbraith, John Kenneth. *The Affluent Society.* Boston: Houghton Mifflin, 1958.

————. *The New Industrial State.* New York: New American Library, 1967.

Geyelin, Milo. "Dalkon Shield Trust Lawyers Draw Fire." *The Wall Street Journal,* November 12, 1991, B5.

Gottschalk, Earl, Jr. "Firms Hiring New Type of Manager to Study Issues, Emerging Troubles." *The Wall Street Journal,* June 10, 1982, 33, 36.

Gray, Irwin. *Product Liability: A Management Response.* New York: AMACOM, 1975.

Hoffman, Michael, and Jennifer Moore. *Business Ethics: Readings and Cases in Corporate Morality.* 2d ed. New York: McGraw-Hill, 1990.

Holloway, Robert, and Robert Hancock. *Marketing in a Changing Environment.* 2d ed. New York: John Wiley and Sons, 1973.

Iannone, A. Pablo, ed. *Contemporary Moral Controversies in Business.* New York: Oxford University Press, 1989.

Jacoby, Neil, ed. *The Business Government Relationship: A Reassessment.* Pacific Palisades, Calif.: Goodyear, 1975.

Keating, Dan. "Florida Keys May Be Dying by the Year 2000, Study Finds." *The Boston Sunday Globe,* December 29, 1991, 9.

King, William. "Strategic Issue Management." In *Strategic Planning and Management Handbook,* edited by W. King and D. Cleland. New York: Van Nostrand Reinhold, 1987, 256.

Levitt, Theodore. "The Morality (?) of Advertising." *Harvard Business Review* (July/August 1970), as cited in Hoffman and Moore (1990, 422).

Lipman, Joanne. "Pediatric Academy Prescribes Ban On Food Ads Aimed at Children." *The Wall Street Journal,* July 24, 1991a, B8.

———. "Stroh's Ad Campaign Spins Out of Control." *The Wall Street Journal,* December 12, 1991b, B6.

The Los Angeles Times. "Smoking: All Clear (Cough, Cough)." February 25, 1990. Also cited in Steiner and Steiner (1991, 591).

Mahjon, John. "Issues Management: The Issue of Definition." *Strategic Planning Management* (November, 1986): 81–85.

Marx, Thomas. "Integrating Public Affairs and Strategic Planning." *California Management Review* (Fall 1986): 145.

Matthews, John B., Kenneth Goodpaster, and Laura Nash. *Policies and Persons: A Casebook in Business Ethics.* New York: McGraw-Hill, 1985.

———. *Policies And Persons: A Casebook in Business Ethics.* 2d ed. New York: McGraw-Hill, 1991.

Mitroff, Ian, Paul Shrivastava, and Firdaus Udwadia. "Effective Crisis Management." *Academy of Management Executive* 1, no. 7 (November 1987), 283–292.

Moses, Jonathan. "Court Sets Back EPA on Enforcement for Superfund." *The Wall Street Journal,* November 6, 1991, B5.

Naisbitt, John, and Patricia Aburdene. *Megatrends 2000: Ten New Directions for the 1990s.* New York: William Morrow and Company, 1990.

Noble, Barbara P. "After Years of Deregulation, a New Push to Inform the Public," *The New York Times,* October 27, 1991, F5.

Posch, Robert. *The Complete Guide to Marketing and the Law.* Englewood Cliffs, N.J.: Prentice-Hall, 1988.

Sabato, Larry. "PAC-Man Goes to Washington." *Across the Board* (October 1984): 16.

Sagoff, Mark. "Economic Theory and Environmental Law." In *Contemporary Issues in Business Ethics,* edited by Joseph Des Jardins and John McCall, 360–364. Belmont, Calif.: Wadsworth, 1990.

Schnee, Jerome. "Regulation and Innovation: U.S. Pharmaceutical Industry." *California Management Review* 22, no. 1 (Fall 1979): 23–32. Also cited in Buchholz (1989, 129).

Shabecoff, Phil. "In Search of a Better Law to Clear the Air." *The New York Times,* May 14, 1989, sec. 4, p. 1.

Shea, Cynthia P. "Protecting the Ozone Layer." In *State of the World 1989,* 82. New York: Norton, 1989. Cited in Buchholz (1992, 581).

Steiner, George, and John Steiner. *Business, Government, and Society: A Managerial Perspective, Text and Cases.* 6th ed. New York: McGraw-Hill, 1991.

Stern, Louis. "Consumer Protection via Increased Information." *Journal of Marketing.* 31, no. 2 (April 1967): 48–52.

Stipp, David. "EPA, Public Differ Over Major Risks." *The Wall Street Journal,* October 1, 1990, B1, Col. 6

Sturdivant, Frederick, and Heidi Vernon-Wortzel. *Business and Society: A Managerial Approach.* 4th ed. Homewood, Ill.: Irwin, 1991.

Templin, Neal. "Ford Is Recalling 581,000 Cars Tied to Engine Fires." *The Wall Street Journal,* July 18, 1989, C25.

Time. "Ford's $128.5 Million Headache," February 10, 1978, 65.

U.S. Commission on Federal Paperwork. *Final Report Summary.* Washington, D.C., 1977.

U.S. Constitution. Article 1, Section 8.

U.S. Consumer Product Safety Commission, Washington, D.C.: September 1985, p. 1.

Velasquez, Manuel. *Business Ethics Concepts and Cases.* 2d and 3d eds. Englewood Cliffs, N.J.: Prentice-Hall, 1988 and 1992.

The Wall Street Journal. January 6, 1992, B1.

————. January 13, 1992, B1.

————. January 14, 1992, A3.

————. January 14, 1992, B6.

Wartick, Steven, and Robert Rude. "Issues Management: Fad or Function?" *California Management Review* (Fall 1986): 134–140.

Weidenbaum, Murray. *The Future of Business Regulation.* New York: AMACOM, 1979.

————. *Business, Government, and the Public.* 2d ed. Englewood Cliffs, N.J.: Prentice-Hall, 1981.

Weinberger, Marc, and Jean Romeo. "The Impact of Negative Product News." *Business Horizons* (January/February 1989): 44–50.

6

Employee Stakeholders and the Corporation

> When Richard Rathemacer, a systems engineering manager, left IBM in
> August 1987, he wasn't really fired, the company says. And the 30-year
> veteran agrees. Instead, he says IBM threatened him with an "unsatisfac-
> tory" job rating and then "suggested" he sign up for a 1986 early retirement
> plan. He initially signed up under duress but then wavered. IBM, meantime,
> stripped him of his title and duties and reassigned him to an abandoned
> office, with no supplies, no switchboard, and no secretary. Weeks later,
> Rathemacer, then 55, arrived at work to find that his office had been cleared
> out the night before.   *(Galen 1991, 33)*

The employee in this case sued IBM for lost pay of $75,000 a year, along
with punitive and other damages. Rathemacer had been an excellent per-
former at IBM for most of his tenure. He won numerous sales and
achievement awards. IBM denies Rathemacer was mistreated and claims
he left "voluntarily" with a "very generous severance and retirement
package" (Galen 1991). Further, IBM denies this is a case of age discrimination and claims Rathemacer had serious performance problems.
Rathemacer counters that IBM used negative job appraisals to force early
retirement. Moreover, Charles Quinn, a new manager in 1985, denied
Rathemacer a promotion, opting instead—according to Rathemacer—for
"new young blood in that job." Court records in 1986 state that Quinn
reorganized the unit and put Rathemacer in charge of mainframe com-
puters. All Rathemacer's experience had been in small systems. His performance was subsequently downgraded. Rathemacer stated that he
protested to superiors about age discrimination and that he formally
filed an open-door complaint with the office of IBM's CEO (Akers) in
March 1987. In June, Rathemacer sought a rehearing. IBM claims
Rathemacer's performance showed "persistent negativism, insensitivity,
rudeness, verbal abuse, and poor interpersonal relations with his coworkers" (Galen 1991).

IBM has a lot at stake in this particular case. First, this case challenges the firm's capability to downsize using early retirement incentives
as a strategy during a severe industry downturn—accompanied by
increasing international competition. IBM, at the time of this incident,
announced plans to cut 17,000 more workers, mainly through retirement
incentives. IBM also faces the charge that it used early-retirement plans
to cover age discrimination. This charge questions the firm's image and
integrity with its work force, particularly its aging work force. IBM could
also be forced to change its performance standards as well as its practices and the principles that underlie these standards.

The question of age discrimination is only one of the personnel and moral problems facing corporations in America in this and the coming decade. Work force problems discussed in this chapter involve one of the corporation's most important stakeholders—its employees. We begin by addressing significant changing characteristics of the work force in the United States. What is different about the work force, and how does this affect the corporation's ethical responsibilities? We then discuss the following questions: "What binds employees to their companies? What is the nature of the employer/employee social contract? How has this contract changed historically?" Then, rights and obligations of employer and employee are briefly presented to offer a perspective on what employers and employees expect from each other. Problems of discrimination in the workplace and affirmative action legislation are presented next. We address the question, "What is illegal and immoral regarding workplace discrimination?" Then we define sexual harassment and the law and offer recommendations for organizations and individuals for preventing and dealing with this problem. Finally, we look at issues surrounding whistle-blowing versus loyalty to the firm. What are the boundaries of employee loyalty? When do employees have the right or obligation to "blow the whistle" on the company?

6.1 EMPLOYEE STAKEHOLDERS: WORK FORCE 2000

The work force and the workplace in America are significantly changing in ways that are affecting management practices and moral issues. David Jamieson and Julie O'Mara (1991), in their book, *Managing Workforce 2000: Gaining the Diversity Advantage,* described the following major trends that are affecting the workplace: The work force is aging; women entrants are increasing in number; cultures are mixing, as are values; the education gap is increasing; and the number of workers with disabilities is expanding. These trends are based on statistical projections as well as ongoing occurrences. We will discuss the ethical implications for the corporation of these changes after we summarize the major trends.

The Aging Work Force

The work force is aging. By the year 2000, half of the work force—the Baby Boomers (those born between 1946 and 1964)—will be middle-aged. At the same time, those aged 16 to 24—the Baby Busters (those born after the Boomers)—will make up 16% of the work force and will continue to decline. The seniors—those over age 55—will represent about 13% of the work force (Jamieson and O'Mara 1991, 16).

Women in the Work Force

By the year 2000, women will represent 50% of the work force. Six out of seven working-age women will be in the work force. Two thirds of the new entrants between 1985 and 2000 will be female. Three fourths of all working women will be in their childbearing years; women with children under 6 years old represent the most rapidly increasing segment of the work force. Female managers, administrators, and executives are also increasing—up 35% in 1987. Moreover, dual-career families will also increase by 75% (Jamieson and O'Mara 1991, 18).

The Increasing Cultural Mix

By the year 2080, over 27% of Americans will be nonwhite; nonwhites will consist of 15% of the U.S. work force. Between the years 1985 and 2000, American-born people of color and immigrants are projected to make up 43% of newcomers to the workplace. The large increase of immigrants and people of color to the work force will consist of Hispanics, Asians, Latin Americans, and blacks. Presently, California is projected to have a minority work force exceeding 50% by the year 2005 (Jamieson and O'Mara 1991, 21).

The Growing Education Gap

There is a growing dichotomy in education levels of those in and those entering the work force. While the United States has the most educated work force in its history, the number of less-educated entrants is also increasing. For example, in the mid-1980s, 86% of 25- to 29-year-olds graduated from high school; but in 1988, there were 20 million functionally illiterate people in the United States. Of the 18- to 21-year-old population, 13.6% did not complete high school. A *Business Week* (September 19, 1988) article reported that "most 17-year-olds in school cannot summarize a newspaper article, write a good letter requesting a job, solve real-life math problems, or follow a bus schedule" (see also Jamieson and O'Mara 1991, 24).

Mainstreaming Disabled Workers

Hiring and mainstreaming qualified disabled workers is increasing in importance because of the combined effects of the shrinking and aging work force. A survey by the International Center for the Disabled found that two thirds of the working-age disabled are not in the work force, while a "large majority" say they prefer to work (Jamieson and O'Mara 1991, 25). Disabilities affect a large number of the work force. Disabilities are categorized as permanent (for example, physical disabilities), temporary (for example, resulting from injury or stress), and progressive (for example, AIDS, alcohol and drug addiction, cancer) (Jamieson and O'Mara 1991, 26). According to these definitions, disabled workers can and will number into the millions. One alarming statistic, for example, is that 10,000 to 15,000 heterosexuals are getting AIDS every year (Bunzel 1991, A20).

Ethical Implications and the Changing Work Force*

The aging work force will necessitate changes in managing employees' motivations, rewards, and career opportunities. Moral and legal conflict will likely increase in workplace situations with regard to:

1. *Age discrimination* (as illustrated in the opening case): "When are experienced workers not able to work? According to whose and what standards? Should companies, like IBM in the opening case, treat aging employees differently during economic downturns or when technologies require new or different skills?"

2. *Clashes of values and expectations between managers and employees:* "Will the experience of aging workers be devalued? How well will aging, experienced workers and younger, better educated workers integrate with different compensation and reward systems?"

3. *Health care cost increases:* "How will companies deal with increasing health care costs of aging employees, especially during economic recessions and in industries that are losing international competitiveness?"

Increasing numbers of women in the work force are already signaling changes in the tensions and moral problems in what has been a

---

*This discussion is based on Jamieson and O'Mara (1991, 17–27).

white, male-dominated work force. These tensions translate into the following moral and management problems:

1. *Sexual harassment and discrimination in the workplace.* More women are speaking out under the protection of Title VII of the amended Civil Rights Act, which we discuss in section 6.5 of this chapter.

2. *Miscommunication differences and conflict between genders in the workplace, especially between male bosses and female subordinates.* A recent book, *You Just Don't Understand* by Deborah Tannen (1990) illustrates the different communication styles of men and women. Some consulting companies (such as Arthur Andersen and Harbridge House) are also offering "gender training" to ease the tensions and miscommunications between men and women in the workplace.

3. *Policy demands that strain corporate relationships and finances and cause conflict between management and workers.* Requests for child-birth and childcare leave programs will increase. Requests for flex-time, part-time, and work-at-home jobs will also increase. Less willingness to relocate will strain corporate decisions.

The incoming mix of cross-cultural backgrounds is introducing different values, norms, ways of communicating, motivations, expectations, work styles, and work ethics into the workplace. What is right and wrong for members of one cultural group may be different or unacceptable to others. Again, the potential for conflict will be enhanced.

The growing educational gap will increase workplace problems. Highly educated workers demand more involvement and autonomy, less control, more information, more career opportunities, and rewards commensurate with performance. The less educated often require more training, more educational opportunities, more supervision, and structured opportunities to increase mobility. The mix of the two educational levels will strain work, personal, moral, and managerial/employee relationships.

Finally, mainstreaming workers with disabilities challenges corporations to accommodate legislation and to collaborate with other social, medical, and educational institutions in society, which are also becoming stakeholders of the corporation. A range of moral issues in this area is already confronting management, such as (1) discrimination issues over drug and AIDS testing and violation of privacy rights and (2) health care and other organizational costs from workers suffering from addictions and such diseases as AIDS. While many of these problems present management with costly economic and moral dilemmas, the fact is that society and the work force is changing. Corporations must change with the people it manages in order to succeed.

Changing Work Force Values

From surveying 350 managers and human service professionals, Jamieson and O'Mara (1991, 28–29) identified the following work-related values that are now considered most important and that would continue to be valued in the near future:

- Recognition for competence and accomplishment
- Respect and dignity
- Personal choice and freedom
- Involvement at work
- Pride in work
- Quality of life-style
- Financial security
- Self-development
- Health and wellness

As work force demographics and values change, a central question regarding ethics in the workplace is, "What are the social doctrines that have and presently define the legal and moral basis of the employer/ employee relationship?" This is an important subject, since the social contract between employer and employee serves as the rationale that influences management decisions and conflict resolution. We discuss the changing employer/employee social contract in the following section.

6.2 THE SOCIAL CONTRACT BETWEEN CORPORATION AND EMPLOYEE

The social contract that has historically defined the employee/employer relationship is known as the **employment-at-will (EAW) doctrine.** This implied legal agreement has been in effect since 1884, when the *Payne* v. *Western A.R.R. Co.* judgment ruled that "all may dismiss their employees at will, be they many or few, for good cause, for no cause, or even for cause morally wrong without being thereby guilty of legal wrong" (cited in Steiner and Steiner 1991, 625).

Essentially, the EAW doctrine can be defined as "the right of an employer to fire an employee without giving a reason and the right of an employee to quit when he or she chooses" (Fulmer and Casey 1990, 102). If employees are unprotected by unions or other written contracts, they can be fired, according to this doctrine.

The EAW doctrine evolved as part of the laissez-faire philosophy of the Industrial Revolution. Between the 1930s and 1960s, however, exceptions to the doctrine have appeared. Federal legislation has, since the 1960s, been enacted to protect employees against racial discrimination and to provide rights to a minimum wage, equal hiring and employment opportunity, and the right to participate in labor unions.

Moreover, since the 1970s, state court decisions have also limited the EAW doctrine. Specifically, state courts have upheld employees' rights to use legal action against their employers if an employee termination violated "public policy" principles: for example, if employees were pressured to commit perjury or fix prices; if employees were not permitted to perform jury duty or file for workman's compensation; if employees were terminated because they refused to support a merger; or if employees reported alleged employer violations of statutory policy (whistle-blowing).

An important 1981 California Appeals Court decision, *Pugh* v. *See's Candies, Inc.*, ruled that in a noncontractual employment arrangement, an implied promise from the employer existed. The employer could not act arbitrarily with its employees regarding termination decisions, when considering the following factors: (1) duration of employment, (2) recommendation and promotion received, (3) lack of direct criticism of work, (4) assurances given, and (5) the employer's acknowledged policies (Fulmer and Casey 1990, 103, 104).

Although the EAW doctrine has undergone change, it is not dead. There still are large numbers of people who are fired at will. For example, upper-level and mid-level white-collar management positions are vulnerable during economic recessions and with increasing global competitiveness; nonunionized beginners are threatened; workers without union contracts and temporary workers can be terminated at will; and sports coaches and professional athletics are frequently fired (DeGeorge 1990, 334).

Presently, the courts have demonstrated that when employers make a promise of job security, whether it is implied verbally or in writing (as in a personnel handbook, contract, or other document), employers are bound by that promise. The courts have also not ruled that employers must state how employees will be terminated and under what conditions they may be fired. Employers can eliminate references to or promises of job security in their documents. Some employers, such as Sears, have asked employees to sign disclaimers when hired, stating that there is no binding contract between employer and employee. Sears has won employee termination judgments based on their disclaimer statements (Fulmer and Casey 1990, 105). There is no hard and fast rule employers can use to protect against employee terminations. Courts to date have generally ruled to reverse decisions based on EAW principles (Beauchamp and Bowie 1988, 259).

In the next section, we present specific employee rights and employer obligations and offer recommendations that managers can use in avoiding arbitrary and immoral termination decisions.

6.3 RIGHTS AND OBLIGATIONS BETWEEN EMPLOYEE AND CORPORATION

The relationship between employer and employee in the United States has evolved from the employment-at-will doctrine, described above, to expanded federal and state legislation, aimed at protecting workers and promoting minority employees' rights and opportunities. The transition has evolved from a feudal, European governance context to a contemporary American, pluralistic setting. Employee rights in the workplace are still evolving. Changing social, political, legal, technological, scientific, and competitive forces present new issues, opportunities, and controversies between employee rights and corporate duties.

Moreover, in a market economy, employer/employee rights and obligations are based on contrasting, sometimes conflicting assumptions and values. Employers control private property and proprietary rights over their intellectual property. Employees claim their constitutional rights to individual freedom, liberty, and control over their private lives. Employers look to maximize productivity and profits, sustain financial growth and stability, minimize costs, improve quality, increase market-share, and stabilize wages. Employees seek to increase their wages and benefits, improve working conditions, enhance mobility, and ensure job security. These differences can collide in policy decisions, especially during economic downturns and increased competition. Although there is no perfect boundary to the intersection of employer/employee rights in a capitalist market economy, there are moral principles that can guide and help resolve some of the differences among employer/employee stakeholder interests and conflicts.

Before discussing specific rights and obligations between employer and employee, we begin by presenting three organizing concepts that underlie employee rights. These include the concepts of: (1) balance, (2) governmental rights, and (3) moral entitlement. The concept of balance is based on utilitarian ethical reasoning; the concept of governmental rights is based on reasoning related to inalienable individual rights; the concept of moral entitlement is based on Kantian, nonconsequentialist reasoning. Although these concepts are not mutually exclusive, it is helpful to understand their distinctive logic in order to argue their merits and shortcomings as they apply to specific workplace controversies.

The Social Contract Between Employer and Employee

As common law and custom have evolved from the EAW doctrine to implied employee rights, employers must now consider more than stockholder and financial interests in dealing with employee stakeholders. Since the development of the EAW doctrine, the social contract that has evolved between employer/employee is based on a more symmetrical contractual relationship, justified by a principle of balance and mutual fairness: the employer's interest in operating the business as she or he so determines, as balanced against the welfare and interest of the employee (Steiner and Steiner 1991, 624). Employers generally have more power than employees in the contractual relationship. Nevertheless, employees have implied as well as explicit rights in the relationship, as discussed above. According to the logic of this view, employees can negotiate and dispute employers' arbitrary uses of their power over employees.

The concept of balance has been expanded beyond the historically narrow limits in the EAW doctrine. With reference to termination decisions, courts weigh employer rights against the interests of the "economic system" and "public good" (*Monge v. Beebe Rubber Co.*, 1974). The concept of balance, then, can exceed employer/employee interests and stakes in adversial termination questions.

Rights in Government Legislation

Employee rights are also based on principles determined by law, as we will discuss in the next section. Certain employee rights are not negotiable in written or implied contracts: for example, the minimum wage; sexual harassment; discrimination based on race, creed, age, national origin, sex, or disability; and the right to assemble. While employee rights based on certain legislation are not normally negotiated according to employer/employee self-interests, these rights can be disputed, depending on circumstances. Reverse discrimination, as we will discuss later, is one such example.

Rights of Moral Entitlement

Joseph Des Jardins and John McCall (1985) argue that employees also have "rights possessed independently of any contractual agreement or legislation." Due process is one such principle based on **moral entitlement**. Moral entitlements differ from rights established in either contracts or legislation, since the latter can be negotiated among business and employee interests. Rights based on moral entitlement are nonnegotiable. Rights based on this principle represent "a general and presumptive moral entitlement of any employee to receive certain goods to be protected from certain harms in the workplace." Moral entitlements and rights such as due process are also different from rights based on contracts or legislation because "the basic moral rights of human persons can place constraints on the treatment those persons receive when operating within their institutional or social roles."

Des Jardins and McCall (1985) also argue that employee rights based on moral entitlements "function to prevent employees from being placed in the fundamentally coercive position of having to choose between their job and other basic human goods or treatments" (p. 369). Again, these rights are not open to normal negotiating processes (such as increasing profit margins or wage levels), although there may be instances when such rights can be overruled (for example, economic conditions requiring justifiable downsizing).

Obligations Between Employer and Employee

Employers and employees have rights, obligations, and duties to each other. In this section, we discuss these mutual obligations that stem from each party's rights.

Employer Obligations to Employees

Employers are obliged to pay employees fair wages, to provide safe working conditions, and to provide meaningful work.

Obligation to Pay Fair Wages Fair wages are determined by such factors as what the public and society support and expect, conditions of the labor market, competitive industry wages in the specific location, profitability of the company, the nature of the job and work, laws governing minimum wages, comparable salaries, and the fairness of the salary or wage negotiations (Velasquez 1988, 364, 365). As we will discuss in section 6.4, fair wages for comparable jobs held by men and women are not always paid.

Obligation to Provide Safe Working Environments Employers are also obliged to provide workers with a safe working environment and working conditions. OSHA and federal laws and regulations provide safety standards and enforce employers to institute their own safety standards. The problems for employers providing—and for employees accepting—safe working environments and conditions stem from (1) lack of knowledge and/or available, reliable information about levels of health risks; (2) lack of appropriate compensation proportional to level of occupational risk; and (3) employees accepting known risks in the absence of comparable options or mobility (Velasquez 1988, 367). When the option is employment versus no employment, workers—especially in low-income, noncompetitive employment regions—often choose jobs with hazardous risks to their health or life.

Employers are, then, obliged to pay competitive wages commensurate with the occupational risks associated with a profession, job, or work setting. For example, race car drivers would not be expected to receive the same pay as college professors. Employers are also obliged to provide full information of risks and health hazards related to work, products, and working environments to all employees exposed to those risks. Employers should also offer health insurance programs and benefits to employees exposed to workplace hazards (Velasquez 1988, 368). We know that in actuality not all employers meet these obligations.

Obligation to Provide Meaningful Work Employers are obliged to offer employees working conditions that provide meaningful work and job satisfaction. This argument is based on the view that employees as human beings work most productively when they can participate and control their tasks, when they are given responsibility and autonomy over their assignments, and when they are treated with respect. While there is some debate on this topic, studies generally support the connection between worker productivity and **quality-of-work-life** programs that provide employees with more autonomy, participation, satisfaction, and control over work tasks (Bjork 1975; Simmons and Mares 1983). Many companies are presently organizing self-designing work teams and quality circles in order to use employee creativity and ability. Workers and management both gain from such programs and new organizational forms.

Employee Obligations to Employers

Employees are obliged to fulfill their contracted responsibilities to the corporation; to follow the goals, procedural rules, and work plans of the organization; to offer competence commensurate with the work and job they are assigned; and to perform productively according to the required tasks. Other obligations include being on time and avoiding absenteeism; acting legally and morally in the workplace and while on work assignments; and respecting the intellectual and private property rights of the employer.

Conflicts of Interest

The problem regarding employee obligations to employers becomes complicated when conflicts of interest appear, that is, when an employee's private interests compete or are not aligned with the interests of the company. More obvious conflicts of interest arise in a number of situations, such as taking or offering commercial and/or personal bribes, kickbacks, gifts, and insider information for personal gain.

It is the so-called "gray areas" that are more problematic in determining whose interests are violated at the expense of the other's: for example, when an employee quits a firm, joins a competitor, and is accused by the former company of stealing proprietary property (that is, passing on intellectual property, sharing trade secrets, and offering competitive advantage by divulging confidential information). Whose interests are violated? Beauchamp and Bowie (1988) note that some courts have used a "balancing model" based on utilitarian logic in resolving trade secret protection cases; that is, an employee's interest in mobility and opportunity is weighed against the employer's rights in deciding the extent of protection given to confidential information. For example, the following three criteria (from Beauchamp and Bowie 1988, 264) have been used to decide whether trade secrets have been divulged by employees:

1. True trade secrecy and established ownership must be shown.
2. A trade secret must have been disclosed by an employee, thus breaching a duty of confidentiality.

3. The employer's interest in keeping the secret must outweigh the employee's interest in using the secret to earn a living and the public's interest in having the secret transmitted.

There are other considerations courts use in these types of rulings (for example, contract obligations, promises made, truthfulness, confidentiality, and loyalty). The point we make here is that as technology and expertise become more sophisticated and as employee mobility—as well as downsizing—increases, workplace and courtroom criteria regarding the proof of conflict of interest also grow more complicated. While a utilitarian model is used to help determine conflict of interest court cases, such as trade secrecy, ethical principles such as rights, duty, and justice also remain essential considerations in determining right and wrong; violation of loyalty, confidentiality, or truthfulness; and harm done to either employers or employees.

Employee Rights in the Workplace

Labor, along with money and materials, is considered part of capital in a free market system. However, labor is not the same as materials and money; labor also means human beings who have general, constitutional rights that should not be relinquished between 8 A.M. and 5:30 P.M. (DeGeorge 1990; Ewing 1977). However, clashes of interests and stakes between employee rights and management demands frequently occur. The boundary between an employer's private property and an employee's individual rights is often blurred in everyday experience. Employee rights are more often than not violated; this is especially the case with nonunion workers. Still, understanding employee rights is an important part of business ethics education. Implementing and protecting those rights is another matter. When employees and employers cannot agree on whose rights are seriously violated, third-party negotiation, arbitration, and even settlement may be required. In this section, we present major types of employee rights in the workplace: the right to a job and the right not to be terminated without just cause; the right to due process; the right to privacy; the right to know and workplace safety; the right to organize; and rights regarding plant closings. These rights become even more important in a society that rapidly transforms technological and scientific inventions into the human and social nature of the workplace.

The employee as stakeholder has constitutional rights as a citizen in society, and these translate into workplace rights. While many employee rights must be balanced against those of the employer, it is also true that certain employee rights are nonnegotiable moral entitlements. We begin this discussion by presenting the moral reasoning for an employee's right to a job and the right not to be arbitrarily fired.

Right to a Job and the Right Not to be Terminated Without Just Cause
Employees probably have more of a right not to be arbitrarily terminated or without just cause than they do to a job in a free-market economy. The right or moral entitlement to have a job is still a debated issue. This right is based on the argument that holding a job means having social status and self-esteem. Without work, one has no self-respect in society (Beauchamp and Bowie 1988, 260, 261).

It has also been argued that workers should have three rights regarding work to maintain self-respect: the right to employment, the right to equal opportunity, and right to participate in job-related decisions (Meyers 1988). We have already discussed an employee's right not to be terminated arbitrarily. The right to equal opportunity has been legislated for minorities, as we will discuss later in this chapter. The right to participate in job-related decisions has strong backing from those who argue that productivity, job satisfaction, and motivation are related to participation.

Right to Due Process Due process is one of the most important underlying rights employees have in the workplace, since it affects most other rights of employees. **Due process** refers to the right of employees to have an impartial and fair hearing regarding employers' decisions, procedures, and rules that affect employees. Due process, as applied in the workplace, essentially refers to grievance procedures.

At a more general level, due process rights protect employees from arbitrary and illegitimate uses of power. This right is based on the Fifth and Fourteenth Constitutional amendments, which state that no person shall be deprived of "life, liberty, or property, without the due process of law" (Des Jardins and McCall 1990, 131).

Werhane (1985) states that due process should include the following procedural mechanisms to ensure employees' right to due process:

- Have the right to a public hearing
- Be able to have peer evaluations
- Be able to obtain external arbitration
- Have an open, mutually agreed on grievance procedure

The right to due process applies to other employee rights such as privacy, safety and health, working environment conditions, right to assemble, hiring, firing, and other human resource decisions.

Right to Privacy Employees' right to privacy remains one of the most debated and controversial rights. This right raises the questions, "Where does the employer's control over employee behavior, space, time, and property begin and end? What freedoms and liberties do employees have with employer property rights? What rights do employers have to protect their private property, earnings, and costs from employees?"

Privacy Defined The U.S. Constitution does not actually refer to a person's right to "privacy." The working definition of employees' right to privacy has come to mean to be "left alone." Privacy in the workplace can also refer to one's right to autonomy and the right of employees to determine "when, how, and to what extent information about them is communicated to others" (Werhane 1985, 118).

The extent of an employee's privacy in the workplace remains an unsettled area of controversy. The definition of what constitutes an employee's privacy is still somewhat problematic. There is the notion of psychological privacy (involving one's inner life) and the notion of physical privacy (involving one's space and time) (Velasquez 1988, 376). In the 1965 *Griswold* v. *Connecticut* case, the Supreme Court ruled that the Constitution guaranteed individuals a "zone of privacy" around them that the government could not intrude on. Proponents of this definition argue that this zone includes personnel records and files, and protection against polygraph and psychological testing and surveillance in the workplace. It also is intended to protect employees in their after-work activities; their peace and quiet in the workplace; their dress, manners, and grooming; and their personal property in the workplace. Identifying this "zone of privacy" has proved complicated, especially in the technological world of changing inventions and applications in the workplace.

Polygraph and Psychological Testing Employers are particularly concerned about employee privacy rights, since these protect against polygraph and psychological testing and other techniques that many managers would like to use to prevent and detect crime in the workplace. Workplace theft is estimated to cost between $30 billion and $40 billion a year in the United States (Carroll, 1989). Issues surrounding the use of polygraphs and psychological testing include the following: (1) These tests are not reliable or valid; they are only indicators; (2) the tests can, to some extent, be manipulated and influenced by the operators; (3) the tests may include irrelevant questions (pertaining to one's sex life, religion, after-work life and activities) that invade a person's private life; and (4) employees do not have control over the test results or how the information will be used.

Workplace Surveillance Surveillance of employees at work (that is, employers using technology to spy on and invade workers' personal privacy) is also a subject of concern. Software programs are used to monitor an estimated 4 million workers who use computer terminals (Carroll 1989, 371, 372). Employers can detect the speed of employees' work, number and length of phone calls made and received, breaks taken, when machines are in use, and so on. Although some form of work-related monitoring is certainly legal and even necessary, the ethical issues raised by the American Civil Liberties Union are the possible invasion of employee privacy and fair treatment. What type of information does an employer have a right to and what effects do stress and anxiety from monitoring have on employee welfare? The Electronic Communications Privacy Act, signed during the Reagan administration, renders electronic eavesdropping, computer-to-computer transmissions, private video conferences, and cellular car phones illegal (Carroll 1989; Sitomer 1986).

Drug Testing Privacy issues also affect drug testing. Advocates for employee drug testing argue that employers' health costs and costs associated with sick and lost days are affected when employees contract serious diseases, like AIDS, as well as types of drug addiction and alcohol use. Also, in industries (such as the airline industry or nuclear plant operations) in which drug abuse can cost lives of innocent people, it is in the public's good to screen drug abusers. Those who oppose forced employee drug testing argue that the practice violates employees' rights to due process and privacy. Questions remain about the reliability of drug tests.

Guidelines that can be used in drug-testing programs include the following: (1) Tests should administered only in jobs that have a clear and present potential to cause harm to others; (2) procedural testing limitations should include prior notice to those being tested; (3) employees tested should also be notified of the results; (4) employees tested should be informed that they are entitled to appeal the results; (5) the employer should demonstrate how the information will be kept confidential (or destroyed) (Des Jardins and McCall 1990, 204–206).

Privacy and Computer-Stored Data Systems The growth and use of sophisticated computerized personal data systems has also threatened the individual privacy of employees and citizens. At stake for employees and citizens whose personal information is stored in computer data systems is access without consent to confidential information from any number of commercial sources.

At stake for executives of practically every business that relies on client credit and mailing information is the cost of the impact of regulations that govern these systems. Goldstein and Nolan (1975) noted that computer privacy regulation will affect virtually every organization that collects and uses personal information about its own employees. Several states and foreign governments have already enacted privacy laws.

Four steps that managers can use to develop corporate policy guidelines to prepare for privacy regulation include the following (from Goldstein and Nolan 1975):

1. *Prepare a "privacy impact statement":* This statement analyzes the potential privacy implications that should be taken as part of all proposals for new and expanded systems.

2. *Construct a comprehensive privacy plan:* The privacy impact statement provides the input for planning; the plan specifies all that has to be achieved.

3. *Train employees who handle personal information:* Make employees aware of protecting privacy and of the particular policies and procedures that should be followed to do so.

4. *Make privacy part of social responsibility programs:* Keep organizational members informed about organizational plans regarding privacy issues, with or without regulatory pressures.

The Right-to-Know Issue and Workplace Health and Safety Every employee is entitled to a safe, healthy workplace environment. Because 1 of 10 workers in private industry suffers from an industrial accident or disease while working, information about unsafe, hazardous workplace conditions and some form of protection from these hazards are needed (Des Jardins and McCall 1990, 213). Employees have a right to know the nature and extent of hazardous risks to which they are exposed as well as information, training, and protection from those risks. Right-to-know laws have been passed in 20 states since the mid-1980s.

The Occupational Safety and Health Administration (OSHA) is the federal agency responsible for researching, identifying, and determining workplace health hazards; setting safety and health standards; and enforcing the standards. This remains a major task. Critics of OSHA claim it is too overwhelming a task for one agency to monitor and execute effectively. As we discussed in Chapter 5, the mission and budgets of government regulatory agencies—including OSHA—are also a function of the administration's and congressional politics. For example, President Reagan's administration emphasized business and free-enterprise activities over regulation in the 1980s. Consequently, OSHA's clout and effectiveness in the area of workplace health and safety decreased. While workplace safety and health issues and standards cover an extensive range of industries and potential illnesses, in this section we will discuss two of the more notable contemporary health problems in the workplace: AIDS and smoking in the workplace.

AIDS The number of persons affected with acquired immunodeficiency syndrome (AIDS) in the United States is growing at an alarming rate. The U.S. Centers for Disease Control reported in January 1992 that the number of reported AIDS cases stood at 206,392, and 133,232 persons have died from the illness. The same source reported that of the 206,392 cases, the first 100,000 cases differed from the latest 100,000 in that (1) 7% of the newest 100,000 AIDS cases were traced to heterosexual transmission, up 44% compared with the first 100,000 cases; (2) 12% of the second 100,000 cases occurred in women, compared with 9% of the first 100,000; and (3) 31% of the second 100,000 cases occurred in blacks, compared with 27% earlier (*Boston Globe* January 17, 1992, 10).

For the workplace, AIDS spells trouble for both employee and employer. Beyond the human and emotional toil, there is also the fear and uncertainty of how the disease is transmitted, who is at risk, the privacy and due process issues of testing, and the liability of who should pay what for the costs incurred for those who transmit as well as receive the disease. Health care workers in clinics run a greater risk of being infected by patients with the human immunodeficiency virus (HIV) than do any other occupational or public group, including patients and doctors. Each year 12,000 health care workers are infected with hepatitis B virus, and others contract hepatitis C, which, like the AIDS virus, is transmitted by contact with blood. Each year 250 health care workers die of these viruses, which they receive from patient contact—usually from accidental needle sticks (Curfman 1991; Leary 1991). Statistics also show that doctors are a low-risk group for contracting HIV. Forty-seven doctors have been reported to have contracted the disease as of December 1991. Patients are at minimal risk of contracting AIDS from doctors. Federal authorities estimate that "an infected physician would have to perform 41,667 to 416,667 invasive procedures to infect one patient" (Leary 1991). The only known case of a health worker's transmitting AIDS to a patient involved a Florida dentist who died of the disease. Five of his patients, including Kimberly Bergalis (who died of AIDS

December 8, 1991) were infected with HIV, but it is not conclusively known if they were infected by the dentist.

Presently, AIDS testing of private-sector employees is not a common practice. Limited screening procedures for jobs and industries that place professionals and workers at risk with the public are under review. Although the American Medical Association does not currently approve of an AIDS risk list of procedures that doctors and health workers should perform if they are infected by AIDS, new protective gloves, surgery face masks, and other products are in place in many hospitals to protect against HIV transmission.

Employees who have been infected by HIV are protected in their employment if they are performing work responsibilities satisfactorily (Carroll 1989, 380). Employers need to provide and sponsor more proactive education and training in the workplace to dispel misconceptions that AIDS is transmitted by casual means and to relieve stress about the disease itself. In the meantime, employees have a right to their privacy and to due process regarding AIDS testing and other related issues.

Smoking in the Workplace: Whose Right? Should smoking be completely banned in all workplaces in the United States? Because it has been proved that smoking causes cancer, should nonsmokers have a right to their health and life? Whether and to what extent smoking should be restricted and banned in the workplace remains a controversial topic among major stakeholders. Among those stakeholders who argue and lobby against smoking in the workplace are the EPA, OSHA, and ASH (Action on Smoking and Health—the powerful, national antismoking group). Prosmoking advocates include the tobacco industry and its lobbying group, the Tobacco Institute, and the Bakery, Confectionery and Tobacco Workers union. OSHA has not been able to date to place an absolute ban on smoking in all workplaces. The issue reflects habits and attitudes in society as well as politics and economics in the industry.

Consider these facts. It is estimated that 28% of Americans age 18 and over are smokers. Approximately 400 city and county ordinances restrict smoking at work; only 10 ban it. Thirty-seven states adopted laws restricting smoking at work. Almost 75% of 1,794 facility managers in a survey claim they ban or segregate smoking in their workplaces (Karr and Guthfield 1992). One of OSHA's recent strategies has been to link smoking in the workplace to indoor air-quality problems and pollution and to legislate against it. The Clean Air Act is one such move to further restrict indoor smoking in public facilities. The issue remains controversial among stakeholders who argue and lobby for and against smoking in the workplace.

Right to Organize and Strike Workers have a right to organize, just as owners and managers do. Individuals, as workers and citizens, have the right of free association to seek common ends. This also means that employees have a right to form unions. Although unions have a right to exist, they have no special rights beyond those as due organizations with legal status (DeGeorge 1990, 322–324).

Unions emerged as a counterveiling force against corporations that exerted undue pressure on employees to accept immoral working conditions and practices. Unions also provided a means for employees to strike against management. Strikes are a form of pressure and protest against an action(s) of management with which organized workers disagree. Strikes usually are a last-resort effort after negotiations have failed. Unions have the right to call strikes, since each employee has the right to quit the job, with the conditions that (1) no prior negotiated agreements not to strike are broken and (2) no legitimate moral, safety, or security rights of others are violated (Velasquez 1988, 389–390).

Plant Closing and Employee Rights Companies have the right to relocate and transfer operations from and to any place they choose. If firms can find cheaper labor, raw materials, and transportation costs, lower taxes, no unions, and other business advantages for making a profit, they often will close plants and move. Companies also close plants because of loss of competitiveness, financial losses, and other legitimate economic reasons. The ethical questions that are posed to corporate managers regarding plant closings are, What rights do the individual employees have who are affected by the closing? What responsibilities does the company have toward the affected communities, and even toward the national economy?

As of August 1988, companies with over 100 employees must by law give 60 days' notice to workers before closing. Employees also have the following moral rights when companies decide to relocate or close: to be treated fairly, equally, and with justice. That is, employees have the right to be compensated for the costs of retraining, transferring, and relocating; they have the right to severance pay, outplacement and support programs that assist them in finding alternative employment; and they have the right to have their pension, health, and retirement plans honored (Velasquez 1988, 388).

Employees should also be given the right to find a new owner and/or to explore the possibility of employee ownership of the existing plant before it is closed (Carroll 1989, 330). These rights extend beyond individual workers and include the welfare of the communities in which the plant operated. Plant closings affect jobs, careers, families, and the local tax base, and can even negatively affect the regional and national economies when sizable operations are shut down or moved abroad.

Whatever the motivation for corporations' closing or transferring facilities out of local geographies, the rights of employees and local community groups stand, even though these rights are often negotiated against the utilitarian interests of the corporation in the specific economic context.

6.4 DISCRIMINATION, EQUAL EMPLOYMENT OPPORTUNITY, AND AFFIRMATIVE ACTION

It is difficult to imagine that throughout most of the 19th century, women in America could not vote, serve on juries, issue lawsuits in their own name, or initiate legal contracts if they lost their property to their husbands. In an 1873 Supreme Court decision, *Bradwell* v. *Illinois,* a woman had "no legal existence, separate from her husband, who was regarded as her head and representative in the social state" (see Kanowitz 1969, 36; also quoted in Velasquez 1988, 324).

It is also difficult to imagine the legal status of blacks in the United States in 1857. In the Dred Scott case, one of the opinions of the Supreme Court considered blacks as "beings of an inferior order . . . and so far inferior that they had no rights that the white man was bound to respect" (Fehrenbacher 1978). It is against this background that the doctrines, laws, and policies of discrimination, affirmative action, and equal opportunity must be considered.

Discrimination

Discriminatory practices in employer/employee potential or actual relationships include unequal or disparate treatment of individuals and groups (Des Jardins and McCall 1990, 377–382). Unequal or preferential treatment is based on irrelevant criteria such as sex, race, color, religion, national origin, and/or disability. Systematic and systemic discrimination is based on historical and institutionally ingrained unequal and disparate treatment against minorities, the disadvantaged, and women.

Examples of contemporary and systemic discrimination in employer/employee relationships are found in such practices as recruitment, screening, promotion, termination, and conditions of employment (Velasquez 1988, 328–329). Recruiting procedures that are biased toward certain groups and that do not openly advertise to minority groups are discriminatory. Screening practices that exclude certain groups and that use biased tests or qualifications are discriminatory. Promotion procedures that have "glass ceilings" (that is, invisible discriminatory barriers to advancement) for women and minority groups are discriminatory. Seniority tracks that favor white males or other groups over minorities or women are discriminatory. Terminating employees on the basis of sex, age, race, or national origin is discriminatory. The opening case to this chapter questions whether IBM terminated Richard Rathemacer because of his age. Paying people lower salaries, wages, and bonuses who do the same work as those compensated at a higher rate is discriminatory.

Equal Employment Opportunity and the Civil Rights Act

Title VII of the Civil Rights Act of 1964 makes discrimination in employment on the basis of sex, race, color, religion, or national origin, in any term, condition, or privilege of employment illegal. The law prohibits discrimination across the practices discussed above: hiring, classifying, referring, assigning, promoting, training, retraining, conducting apprenticeships, firing, and dispensing wages and fringe benefits. The Civil Rights Act also created the Equal Employment Opportunity Commission (EEOC) as the administrative implementation agency to investigate complaints submitted by individuals. The EEOC negotiates and works with the Justice Department regarding complaints; however, the EEOC cannot enforce the law.

The Civil Rights Act of 1991 extends for the first time punitive damages to victims of employment discrimination. This law states that job bias based on sex, harassment, disability, religion, or national origin will be punished as severely as job discrimination based on race. It also makes it easier for job bias plaintiffs to win lawsuits. This legislation shifts the legal burden to the employer, who must defend any unintentional employment bias, especially if the practice in question has a "disparate impact" on minorities or women. Under this law, the employer must demonstrate that the alleged discriminatory act is "job-related for the position in question and consistent with business necessity" (Noah and Karr 1991, 31). "Job-related" and "business necessity" are undefined and will be determined by the courts. Under this law, employers with more than 500 employees could be liable for up to $300,000 in compensatory and punitive damages. Smaller companies will be liable for less, depending on the number of workers.

The Equal Employment Opportunity Act of 1972 amended the 1964 act to empower the EEOC to enforce the law by filing grievances from individuals, job applicants, and employees in the courts. Under the revised act, all private employers with 15 or more persons were under jurisdiction of the law, with the exception of bona fide, tax-exempt, private clubs. All private and public educational institutions are covered by the law, as are all public and private employment agencies. Labor unions (local, national, and international) with 15 or more members are included in the law. Joint labor–management committees that administer apprenticeship, training, and retraining programs are also under this law's jurisdiction.

Age and Discrimination in the Workplace

The Age Discrimination in Employment Act of 1967, revised in 1978, prohibits employers from discriminating against individuals based on their age (between 40 and 70) in hiring, promotion, terminations, and other employment practices.

Comparable Worth and Equal Pay

The Equal Pay Act of 1963, amended in 1972, prohibits discriminatory payment of wages and overtime pay based on sex. The law is based, in large part, on the doctrine of "comparable worth." This doctrine and the Equal Pay Act hold that women should be paid comparable wages as men who hold jobs that require equal skill, effort, and responsibility, and that have the same working conditions. Women generally are paid 60 cents to the dollar that men earn in the marketplace. This law addresses this inequity and applies to executive, professional, sales, and administrative positions (Buchholz 1991, 318).

AIDS and Discrimination

AIDS victims are increasingly being discriminated against in the United States. In 1983 the number of reported complaints based on reports of discrimination and referrals received by legal services and HIV/AIDS organizations was zero. By 1988, that number of over 2,500. Under the Americans with Disabilities Act of 1992, it is illegal for most companies to fire or reassign an employee only on the basis that the person is HIV-positive. While many states have had such laws, this act makes employment discrimination illegal at any company with at least 25 employees (Lambert 1991). By 1996, the law will apply to companies with at least 15 employees.

This law will also make it easier for employees with HIV to sue for punitive damages from discriminatory practices. The law extends coverage to address discriminatory practices against HIV-positive people in housing, health care, and insurance areas.

This law is only the beginning of what will become more refined and detailed legislation in this area. Presently, the law does not apply if an HIV-positive employee's illness presents a threat to others and if the worker cannot find a reasonable way to eliminate that risk.

The laws discussed above certainly are not inclusive of all the equal opportunity legislation or federal policy directives passed and amended in the 1960s and 1970s, but these represent some of the more basic, prominent ones.

Laws alone cannot guarantee or equalize employment opportunity, fairness, and justice to members of groups that have been discriminated against historically and presently. Stereotypes and biases can be manipulated in subtle, legal ways through the ways job descriptions and evaluations are written and carried out, by the types of qualifications included in job descriptions, through the means of advertising for jobs, and through the creation of special, exclusionary conditions and practices of employing and terminating people. Still, equal opportunity laws and their enforcement are important—even if many do not go far enough in implementation—in a free-market system governed by law. Laws set social goals and send a message to all involved in employment that minority and disadvantaged groups have equal protection under the law.

Affirmative Action

Affirmative action programs are a proactive attempt to recruit applicants from minority groups in order to create opportunities for those who, otherwise, because of past and present discriminatory employment practices, would be excluded from the job market. Affirmative action programs attempt to make employment practices blind to color, sex, national origin, disability, and age. While the doctrine of equal opportunity states that everyone should have an equal chance at obtaining a job and promotion, affirmative action goes further. "Affirmative action implies a set of specific result-oriented procedures designed to achieve equal employment opportunity at a pace beyond that which would occur normally" (Buchholz 1990, 325). As such, affirmative action programs set goals, quotas, targets, and time frames for companies to hire and promote women and minorities in proportion to their groups in the labor force and in same or similar occupational categories within the company (Buchholz 1990).

Courts have come to regard affirmative action approaches as an integral part of the Civil Rights Act, summarized above. Federal contractors, for example, are required to analyze their labor force and to file affirmative action plans with goals and time frames to demonstrate how minority hiring will be carried out and reflected in company statistical profiles. When company labor force statistics by job classification show that minority hiring, recruitment, and promotion do not meet affirmative action goals and quotas set by the company, or when such statistics show minority "underutilization," discrimination may exist.

DeGeorge (1990) presents four arguments that explain and summarize affirmative action as it applies to hiring, promotions, and terminations. He states that:

1. Affirmative action does not justify hiring unqualified minority group members over qualified white males. All individuals must be qualified for the position in question.

2. Qualified women and minority members can, morally, be given preference on the basis of sex or race, over equally qualified male whites, in order to achieve affirmative action goals.

3. Women and minority members who are qualified can morally be given preference over better-qualified white males, also to achieve affirmative action goals.

4. Companies must make adequate progress toward achieving affirmative action goals even though preferential hiring is not mandatory.

Affirmative Action and Compensatory Justice

Affirmative action as a doctrine, and the programs and laws derived from the doctrine, are defended on the principle of compensatory justice. The argument is that because white males have historically dominated and continue to dominate the highest paying, most prestigious employment positions in society, members of those groups who have been excluded from comparable employment opportunities because of past and present discriminatory practices deserve to be compensated through affirmative action programs embodied in equal opportunity laws.

Reverse Discrimination: Arguments Against Affirmative Action

Arguments against affirmative action are directed toward the doctrine itself and against its implementation of quotas. The doctrine has been criticized on the grounds that nondiscrimination requires discrimination (that is, reverse discrimination). Reverse discrimination is alleged to occur when an equally qualified woman or member of a minority group is given preference over a white male for a job, or when less qualified minorities are given hiring preference over white males through a quota system (Buchholz 1990, 325). Affirmative action, opponents argue, discriminates against sex and race: white males. Some even say that affirmative action discriminates against age: white, middle-aged males.

Another major argument against affirmative action holds that individuals are responsible for injustices for which they were and are not responsible. Why should all contemporary and future white males as a group have to compensate for discriminatory practices others in this demographic category committed in another historical time?

Although there is some validity to these claims, proponents of affirmative action argue that historical injustices through discrimination have been institutionalized against minority groups. It happens that white males continue to benefit from the competitive disadvantages that past and present discriminatory practices have created. To compensate and correct for these systemic disadvantages based on color, sex, and other irrelevant nonemployment-related characteristics, social affirmative action goals and programs for the society must be implemented. Still, the law is not a perfect means to correct past or present injustices. Victims of all colors will continue to be hurt by discrimination and reverse discrimination practices. In the meantime, the court system will also continue to use civil rights laws, affirmative action guidelines, and moral reasoning to decide on a case-by-case basis the justice and fairness of employment-related practices. The following discussion is a summary of three notable Supreme Court cases that illustrate how affirmative action and discrimination issues have been addressed.

Supreme Court Rulings and Reverse Discrimination

The Bakke Case Allan Bakke, a white male, sued the Regents of the University of California at Davis because he was denied admission to the medical school in 1973. He sued on the basis of reverse discrimination. Bakke charged that the university gave preferential treatment to less qualified minorities. Of 100 places in the entering class of 1973, 84 were open for competitive admission; 16 places were given preference for minority candidates. In 1978, the Supreme Court ruled on a 5–4 vote in favor of Bakke. The decision argued against strict quotas but upheld the criterion of race as a consideration in admissions policies. The ruling sent the message that quotas that were based on race in instances where no previous discrimination had been proved were illegal. On the other hand, quotas could be used to offset inequalities as part of settlements in instances where previous discrimination was shown (*Bakke* v. *Regents of the University of California*; Buchholz 1990, 326; *Time* July 10, 1978, 8–20).

The Weber Case Brian Weber, a white male, sued his employer, Kaiser Aluminum and Chemical Corporation, and the Steelworkers Union on the basis that he had been discriminated against by being excluded from a quota-regulated training program. Weber won the case at the lower District Court and at the Court of Appeals. However, in 1979, the Supreme Court, in a 5–2 vote, overturned these decisions (*Weber* v. *Kaiser Aluminum Corporation*). The Court ruled that Afro-Americans can be given special consideration for what have been white-dominated jobs and that affirmative action programs are legal in order to rectify "manifest racial imbalances." The message the Supreme Court sent to employers was that reverse discrimination charges should not prevent them from implementing affirmative action programs. In this case, whites were not displaced or hurt because of the quota-based training program. The court confirmed the majority decision that affirmative action programs were a way of correcting "manifest racial imbalances."

The Stotts Case Carl Stotts, a black district fire chief in Memphis, sued the Memphis Fire Department in a class action suit in 1977, charging that the department discriminated against him and other blacks in its policy of "last hired, first fired" (or LIFO, "last in, first out"). The city announced layoffs in 1981 because of a budget deficit. The layoffs were done according to a union-negotiated seniority policy. Stotts won at the District Court level but lost in an appeal by the city of Memphis and the labor union in the Supreme Court in 1984. The majority vote in the Supreme Court ruled that bona fide seniority systems are protected under the 1964 Civil Rights Act and could not be disrupted, especially during periods of layoffs. The ruling, in effect, sent a message to employers that bona fide seniority systems are blind to color.

These cases show that the Supreme Court enforces affirmative action and protects minority and women stakeholders in their business work environments. Nevertheless, the Court continues to interpret affirmative action on a case-by-case basis. The messages the Court has sent to employers indicate that (1) it is in the best interests of businesses to take a proactive approach in addressing affirmative action and Equal Employment Opportunity goals, time tables, and guidelines in their minority and disability members' recruitment, hiring, promotion, and termination policies; and (2) bona fide seniority systems are still generally protected under civil rights laws. For employer and employee stakeholders, moral reasoning and legal guidelines regarding affirmative action go hand in hand in making employment-related decisions.

6.5 SEXUAL HARASSMENT IN THE WORKPLACE

Sexual harassment was not a specific violation of federal law before 1981. It may now be difficult to imagine such flagrant acts of sexual violation against women, as recent as 20 years ago, when they entered the mines and, like their male counterparts, were stripped and soaked in axle grease in a primitive hazing ritual; and then, unlike the male employees, the women were tied to wooden supports in spread-eagle positions (Strom 1991, 22). More recently, the Senate hearings on sexual harassment charges against the Supreme Court nominee Clarence Thomas awakened public and corporate concern about sexual harassment in society and the workplace. In addition, the overt sexual harassment of female naval professionals also brought attention to this issue. Although sexual harassment can be and is committed by both men and women, it is more often women who are the unwilling victims.

Is sexual harassment in the workplace widespread or isolated? In a *National Law Journal* survey, 60% of 900 women in 250 top law firms indicated they had experienced sexual harassment (DeWitt 1991, 29). Moreover, sexual harassment was ruled in 6,342 job-discrimination cases filed in 1984, an increase over the 5,110 claims filed in 1983. By 1985, the number of complaints climbed to 7,273. Between 1979 and 1984, federal courts had dealt with 300 sexual harassment cases (*Business Week* March 31, 1986, 35). An AT&T spokesperson stated that 19 out of every 20 complaints about sexual harassment are valid (Strom 1991, 1).

What Is Sexual Harassment?

The Supreme Court ruled in 1986 that sexual harassment is illegal under Title VII of the 1964 Civil Rights Act, and that when a "hostile environment" is created through sexual harassment in the workplace, thereby interfering with an employee's performance, the law is violated—regardless of economic harm done or demands for sexual favors in exchange for raises, promotions, bonuses, and other employment-related opportunities (Machlowitz and Machlowitz 1986, 20; Wermiel and Trost 1986, 2).

Under Title VII, the EEOC guidelines (1980) define sexual harassment as follows:

> Unwelcome sexual advances, requests for sexual favors, and other verbal or physical conduct of a sexual nature constitute sexual harassment when (1) submission to such conduct is made either explicitly or implicitly a term or condition of an individual's employment, (2) submission to or rejection of such conduct by an individual is used as the basis for employment decisions affecting such individual, or (3) such conduct has the purpose or effect of unreasonably interfering with an individual's work performance or creating an intimidating, hostile, or offensive working environment.

The courts have defined sexual harassment as conduct ranging from blatant grabbing and touching to more subtle hints and suggestions about sex. Forms of sexual harassment include the following (from Hayes 1991, B1; Lublin 1991, B1):

- Unwelcome sexual advances
- Coercion
- Favoritism
- Indirect harassment
- Physical conduct
- Visual harassment (for example, courts have ruled that sexual harassment was committed when graffiti was written on men's bathroom walls about a female employee, and when pornographic pictures were displayed in the workplace)

Who Is Liable?

The EEOC guidelines place absolute liability on employers for actions and violations of the law by their managers and supervisors, whether or not the conduct was known, authorized, or forbidden by the employer. Employers are also be liable for coworkers' conduct if the employer knew, or should have known, of the actions in question, unless the employer shows—after learning of the problem—that it took immediate and appropriate action to correct the situation. Employers may also be liable for nonemployees under the same conditions as those stated for coworkers (Mastalli 1991, 157, 158).

Moreover, employers under EEOC guidelines are responsible for establishing programs (as well as standards) that develop, train, and inform employees about sanctions and procedures for dealing with sexual harass-

ment complaints. It is in the employer's economic as well as moral interest to institute such programs, since courts mitigate damages against companies that have harassment prevention and training programs.

Some of the leaders in establishing sexual harassment policies and
programs are AT&T (see Figure 6-1), Du Pont, Digital Equipment
Corporation, Corning Inc., and Honeywell, to mention only a few.

Individual Guidelines

While sexual harassment often occurs as part of a power issue—that is,
people in more powerful positions exert pressure over people in less
powerful posts—a frequent observation is that men and women tend to
see sexual harassment differently. This certainly does not justify legally
or morally unwelcomed sexual advances. It does suggest, however, that
employers need to provide adequate education, training, and role playing between the sexes so that gender differences in perceptions and feel-
ings on what constitutes sexual harassment can be understood. Some
practical guidelines that individual employees (men in this instance) can
use to check motives and behavior regarding sexual harassment include
the following (from Foreman and Lehman, 1991):

- If you are unsure whether you have offended a woman, ask her.
  If you did offend, apologize, and don't do it again.
- Talk over your behavior with noninvolved women and with men
  you can trust not to make a mockery of your concerns.
- Ask yourself how you would feel if a man behaved toward your
  daughter the way you feel you may be behaving toward women.
- Ask yourself also if you would act this way if the shoe were on
  the other foot—if the woman were your boss or if she were phys-
  ically stronger or more powerful than you.
- Most of all, don't interpret a woman's silence as consent. Silence,
  is at least, "a red light." Through silence, a woman may be trying
  to send you a signal of discomfort.
- Be very certain your comments or behaviors are welcome, and if
  they are not, stop them.

6.6 WHISTLE-BLOWING VERSUS ORGANIZATIONAL LOYALTY

Among all of the rights discussed in this chapter, one of the most valued of a U.S. citizen is the freedom of speech. But how far does this right

Figure 6-1 AT&T's Sexual Harassment Policy

SEXUAL HARASSMENT POLICY

It is Company policy that all employees have a right to work in an environment free of discrimination, which encompasses freedom from sexual harassment of its employees in any form.

Specifically, no supervisor shall threaten or insinuate, either explicitly or
implicitly, that an employee's submission to or rejection of sexual advances will
in any way influence any personnel decision regarding that employee's
employment, wages, advancement, assigned duties, shifts, or any other condition of employment or career development.

Other sexually harassing conduct in the workplace which may create an offensive work environment, whether it be in the form of physical or verbal harassment, and regardless of whether committed by supervisory or nonsupervisory
personnel, is also prohibited. This includes, but is not limited to: repeated
offensive or unwelcome sexual flirtations, advances, propositions; continual or
repeated verbal abuse of a sexual nature; graphic verbal commentaries about
an individual's body; sexually degrading words used to describe an individual; and the display in the workplace of sexually suggestive objects or pictures.

An employee who believes that he or she is being harassed should:

- Consider carefully whether the conduct in question is harassment

- Confront the person responsible and request that the conduct cease

- If the problem is not resolved, take the complaint through lines of supervision, beginning with the employee's own supervisor

- If this is not desirable, appropriate, or possible, discuss the complaint with
  the applicable AT&T EO/AA representative.

Sexual harassment in the workplace by any employee:

- Will result in disciplinary action up to and including dismissal and

- May lead to personal legal and financial liability.

Source: AT&T.

extend into the corporation, especially if an employee observes an
employer committing an illegal or immoral activity that could harm others? What are the obligations and limits of employee loyalty to the
employer? Under what, if any, circumstances should employees blow
the whistle on their supervisors, managers, or firms?

Whistle-blowing is "the attempt of an employee or former employee of an organization to disclose what he or she believes to be wrongdoing in or by the organization" (James 1990, 332). Whistle-blowing can be internal (reported to a higher up in the organization), external (reported to external public interest groups, the media, or enforcement agencies), personal (harm reportedly done only to the whistle-blower), and/or impersonal (harm observed as done to another) (James 1990, 333). Whistle-blowing goes against a strong American cultural norm of showing loyalty toward one's employer and compatriots. On the other hand, there are strong cultural norms regarding fairness, justice, a sense of duty, and obedience to the law and to one's conscience. A moral dilemma occurs when a loyal employee observes the employer committing or assisting in an illegal or immoral act and must decide what to do.

For example, Roland LeBlanc of Natick, Massachusetts, and a former inspector for the Defense Department's contract administration service, has charged Raytheon with knowingly shipping defective missile and radar parts to the army and navy and fraudulently fabricating data to hide the problems. LeBlanc sued Raytheon under the Federal False Claims Act, which was intended to encourage citizens to report fraud by awarding whistle-blowers 25% of any damages awarded to the government. The issue perplexing the courts in this case is whether government employees can bring a case under this statute given their knowledge of alleged wrongdoing acquired in the course of their work. The First U.S. Circuit Court of Appeals ruled in 1990 that LeBlanc, as a federal employee, could not sue his employer, Raytheon. The U.S. Supreme Court in 1991 declined to hear an appeal of that decision by LeBlanc. Since that decision, the Eleventh and Ninth Courts of Appeals have contradicted the First Court's decision and ruled that a federal employee is not barred from issuing a lawsuit under the act. LeBlanc is suing Raytheon in the U.S. District Court in Orlando, Florida. He has been fighting the case for 3 1/2 years (Hemp 1992).

Under what conditions, then, is whistle-blowing morally justified? DeGeorge (1990, 208–214) discusses five conditions:

1. When the firm through a product or policy will commit serious and considerable harm to the public (as consumers or bystanders), the employee should report the firm.

2. When the employee identifies a serious threat to those who may be harmed, he or she should report it and state his or her moral concern.

3. When the employee's immediate supervisor does not act, the employee should exhaust the internal procedures and chain of command to the board of directors.

4. The employee must have documented evidence that is convincing to a reasonable, impartial observer that his or her view of the situation is accurate, and that the firm's practice, product, or policy seriously threatens and puts in danger the public and/or product user.

5. The employee must have valid reasons to believe that revealing the wrongdoing to the pubic will result in the necessary changes to remedy the situation. The chance of succeeding must be equal to the risk and danger the employee takes to blow the whistle.

The risks to whistle-blowers can range from outright termination to more subtle pressures such as strong and hidden criticisms, undesirable and burdensome work assignments, lost perks, and exclusion from communication loops and social invitations (Near, Miceli, and Jensen 1983). While 21 states have laws protecting corporate and governmental whistle-blowers from reprisal, experience shows that the government's actual protection to whistle-blowers, even if they are reinstated with back pay and compensation for physical suffering, is weak because of the many subtle forms of retaliation, as those listed above (Carroll 1989, 356).

When Whistle-Blowers Should Not Be Protected

The most obvious conditions when whistle-blowers should not be protected are when their accusations are false and/or when their motives are not justifiable or accurate.

David Ewing (1977) states the following instances when whistle-blowers should not have freedom of speech against their employers:

- When divulging information about legal and ethical plans, practices, operations, inventions, and other matters that should remain confidential and that are necessary for the organization to perform its work efficiently

- When an employee's personal accusations or slurs are irrelevant to questions about policies and practices that appear illegal or irresponsible

- When an employee's accusations do not show a conviction that a wrongdoing is being committed and when such accusations disrupt or damage the organization's morale

- When employees complain against a manager's competence to make daily work decisions that are irrelevant to the legality, morality, or responsibility of management actions

- When employees object to discharge, transfer, or demotion if management can show that unsatisfactory performance or violation of a code of conduct was the reason for its decision

Factors to Consider Before Blowing the Whistle

Whistle-blowing is a serious action with real consequences. Whistle-blowing often involves a decision to be made among conflicting moral, legal, economic, personal, family, and career demands and choices. No single answer may appear. Using a stakeholder analysis and questions can help identify the groups and individuals, stakes, priorities, and trade-offs in selecting among different strategies and courses of action.

The following 12 factors (from James 1990) can also assist in deciding whether to blow the whistle on an employer:

1. Make sure the situation warrants whistle-blowing. If more serious trade secrets or confidential company property is exposed, know the harm and calculated risks.

2. Examine your motives.

3. Verify and document your information. Can your information stand up in a hearing and/or court?

4. Determine the type of wrongdoing and to whom it should be reported. Knowing this will assist in gathering the type of evidence to obtain.

5. State your allegations specifically and appropriately. Obtain and state the type of data to substantiate your claim.

6. Stay with the facts. This minimizes retaliation and avoids irrelevant mud-slinging, name-calling, and stereotyping.

7. Decide whether to report to internal contacts or external contacts. Select the internal channel first if that route has proved effective and less damaging to whistle-blowers. Otherwise, select the appropriate external contacts.

8. Decide whether to be open or anonymous. Should you choose to remain anonymous, document the wrongdoing and anticipate what you will do if your identity is revealed.

9. Decide whether current or alumni whistle-blowing is the best alternative. Should you blow the whistle while you are an

employee or resign first? Resigning should not be an automatic option. If the wrongdoing affects others, your decision is not only a personal one, and you are fulfilling moral obligations beyond your own welfare.

10. Follow proper guidelines in reporting the wrongdoing. Check forms, meeting deadlines, and other technicalities.

11. Consult a lawyer at every step of the way.

12. Anticipate and document retaliation. This assists your effectiveness with courts and regulatory agencies.

Managerial Steps to Prevent Whistle-Blowing

Management has a responsibility to listen and respond to its employees, especially regarding the observations and reporting of illegal and immoral acts. In Chapter 4, we discussed such mechanisms as "ethics offices," ombudsman programs, and peer review programs. These procedures and processes are part of a corporation's responsibility to provide due process for employees to report and obtain effective and just resolution of their own grievances and also to report wrongdoings of others, including the employers. Four straightforward and simple steps management can use to prevent whistle-blowing are as follows (from James 1990; see also Ezorsky 1987; Grosman 1989; Walters 1975):

1. Develop effective internal grievance procedures and processes that employees can use to report wrongdoings.

2. Reward people for using these channels.

3. Appoint senior executives and others whose primary responsibilities are to investigate and report wrongdoing.

4. Assess larger fines for illegal actions. Include executives and professionals who file false and/or illegal reports, who knowingly market dangerous products, or who offer bribes or take kickbacks.

Preventing, reporting, and effectively and fairly correcting illegal and immoral actions, policies, and procedures are the responsibilities of employers and employees. Management cannot expect employees to be loyal to a company that promotes or allows wrongdoing to its stakeholders. Whistle-blowing should be a last resort. A more active goal is to hire, train, and promote morally and legally sensitive and responsive managers who communicate and work toward the welfare of all stakeholders.

SUMMARY

The demographics of work force 2000 are changing and will continue to change. These changes include the aging of employees and thus the "shrinking" of the work force, an increasing number of women and minority entrants, the growing gap in educational levels, and a greater demand for the skills of disabled workers. These changes in the composition of the work force signal changes in work-related values and motivations. Corporations and managers can expect moral tensions to rise regarding such issues as age discrimination, health care demands, conflicting communication, and requests for flexible as well as more structured work schedules. "One size fits all" management techniques will not work.

The "social contract" between corporations and employees has changed and will continue to do so. The original employment-at-will doctrine has been replaced by the doctrine of implied employee rights. The three underlying concepts of employee rights are balance, governmental rights, and moral entitlement.

The nature of legal and moral relationships between employers and employees is also changing. Recent court decisions have supported affirmative action and antidiscriminatory business practices. Current and future issues related to sexual harassment and reverse discrimination will continue to shape legal and moral guidelines for corporations. Conflicts regarding due process, privacy, and other employee rights issues will continue to be resolved through court cases and legislation; resolution of these conflicts will influence corporate policies in the future.

Sexual harassment laws and guidelines for employers and employees are presented and discussed. The moral dilemma of organizational loyalty versus personal ethics is presented. The justification of and alternatives to whistle-blowing are discussed in the chapter. Guidelines are offered for corporations to prevent whistle-blowing and for employees to consider before blowing the whistle.

Questions

1. Identify five major trends in the changing demographics of the work force. Can you think of other changes now occurring in the work force?

2. Identify moral tensions and conflicts associated with these changes in question 1.

3. What are major factors an employer should consider to avoid arbitrarily terminating an employee?

4. What does the term *moral entitlement* mean as it relates to employee rights? Give an example. Do you agree that employees have moral entitlement to some rights in the workplace? Explain.

5. According to Patricia Werhane, what are some procedural mechanisms that ensure an employee's right to due process?

6. What are the changes/effects of the Civil Rights Act of 1991?

7. Do you believe that members of groups in the United States that have been historically discriminated against should be protected and compensated under affirmative action now? Explain.

8. What are some arguments for and against "reverse discrimination"? What is your view on this topic?

9. Describe criteria used to determine whether verbal or physical actions constitute sexual harassment. What are some specific types of sexual harassment? Have you been sexually harassed in a work setting? Can you describe what happened and the outcome?

10. Are employees more or less loyal to employers and their companies now? Explain. Should employees be more loyal to their employers? Why or why not?

11. Do you believe whistle-blowing is justifiable in corporations? Why or why not?

12. How can corporate managers prevent whistle-blowing? Explain.

Exercises

1. Identify an example in the recent news of a court decision relating to an issue of discrimination or reverse discrimination. Briefly describe the case and the outcome. What are the implications of this decision for employers and other stakeholders? Do you agree with the outcome? Explain.

2. Select an employee right in the workplace from the chapter. Give an example, based on your own outside reading or experience, of a case involving this right. Was this right violated? How? What was the outcome? What should the outcome have been? Why?

3. Identify an example from your own experience of discrimination or sexual harassment. Did this experience influence your view of affirmative action or employee protection programs? If so, how?

4. Write a paragraph or two describing a situation from your experience in which you felt justified in blowing the whistle. Did you? Why or why not? Under what circumstances do you feel whistle-blowing is justified? Use this justification to support your opinion of the case of Roland LeBlanc.

References and Suggested Readings

Bakke v. *Regents of the University of California.* 553 p. 2d 1152 (1976).

Beauchamp, Tom L. and Norman E. Bowie. *Ethical Theory and Business.* 3d ed. Englewood Cliffs, NJ: Prentice Hall, 1988).

Bjork, Lars. "An Experiment in Work Satisfaction." *Scientific American* (March 1975): 17–23.

Boston Globe. "U.S. AIDS Cases Hit 206,392; Quicker Spread Is Feared," January 17, 1992, 10.

Buchholz, Rogene A. *Essentials of Public Policy for Management.* 2d ed. Englewood Cliffs, NJ: Prentice Hall, 1990.

Bunzel, John H. "AIDS Risks in Black and White." *The Wall Street Journal,* December 17, 1991.

Business Week. "Human Capital: The Decline of America's Work Force," September 19, 1988, 129.

———. "Sexual Harassment: Companies Could Be Liable," March 31, 1986, 35.

Carroll, Archie B. *Business and Society: Ethics and Stakeholder Management.* 1st and 3d eds. Cincinnati: South Western Publishing, 1989 and 1993.

Curfman, Gregory. "Patients vs. Physicians." *Boston Globe,* October 1, 1991, 17.

DeGeorge, Richard T. *Business Ethics.* 3d ed. New York: McMillan Publishing, 1990.

Des Jardins, Joseph R. and John J. McCall. *Contemporary Issues in Business Ethics.* 2d ed. Belmont, CA: Wadsworth, 1990.

———. "A Defense of Employee Rights." *Journal of Business Ethics* 4 (1985): 367–376.

DeWitt, Karen. "As Harassment Drama Plays, Many U.S. Employees Live It." *The New York Times,* October 1991, 29.

Equal Employment Opportunity Commission. "Guidelines on Discrimination on the Basis of Sex." Washington D.C., November 10, 1980.

Ewing, David. *Freedom Inside the Organization: Bringing Civil Liberties to the Workplace.* New York: McGraw-Hill, 1977.

Ezorsky, Gertrude, ed. *Moral Rights in the Workplace.* New York: State University of New York Press, 1987.

Fehrenbacher, Don. *The Dred Scott Case.* New York: Oxford University Press, 1978.

Foreman, Judy, and Betsy Lehman. "What to Do if You Think You May Be Guilty of Sex Harassment." *Boston Globe,* October 21, 1991.

Fulmer, William, and Ann Casey. "Employment at Will: Options for Managers." *Academy of Management Review* 4, no. 2 (1990): 102.

Galen, Michele. "Is Big Blue Hostile to Gray Hairs?" *Business Week,* October 21, 1991, 33.

Goldstein, Robert, and Richard Nolan. "Personal Privacy Versus the Corporate Computer." *Harvard Business Review* (March/April 1975): 62–70.

Griswold et al. v. *Connecticut,* No. 496, Supreme Court of the United States, 85 S. Ct. 1678 (1965).

Grosman, Brian. "Corporate Loyalty: Does It Have a Future?" *Journal of Business Ethics* 8 (1989): 565–568.

Hayes, Arthur. "How the Courts Define Harassment." *The Wall Street Journal,* October 11, 1991, B1.

Hemp, Paul. "Whistle-Blower Suing Raytheon." *Boston Globe,* February 21, 1992, 59, 65.

James, Gene. "Whistle Blowing: Its Moral Justification." In *Business Ethics: Readings and Cases in Corporate Morality.* 2d ed. Edited by Michael Hoffman and Jennifer Moore, 332. New York: McGraw-Hill, 1990.

Jamieson, David, and Julie O'Mara. *Managing Workforce 2000: Gaining the Diversity Advantage.* San Francisco, Calif.: Jossey-Bass, 1991.

Kanowitz, Leo. *Women and the Law.* Albuquerque, N. Mex.: University of New Mexico Press, 1969.

Karr, Albert, and Rose Guthfield. "OSHA Inches Toward Limiting Smoking." *The Wall Street Journal,* January 16, 1992, B1.

Lambert, Wade. "Discrimination Afflicts People with HIV." *The Wall Street Journal,* November 19, 1991, B1, B6.

Leary, Warren. "A.M.A. Backs Off of an AIDS Risk List." *The New York Times,* Sunday, December 15, 1991, 38.

Lublin, Joann. "Companies Try a Variety of Approaches to Halt Sexual Harassment on the Job." *The Wall Street Journal,* October 11, 1991, B1.

Machlowitz, Marilyn and David Machlowitz, "Hug by the Boss Could Lead to a Slap from the Judge," *The Wall Street Journal,* September 25, 1986, 20.

Mastalli, Grace. "Appendix: The Legal Context." In *Policies and Reasons: A Casebook in Business Ethics.* 2d ed. Edited by John Matthews, Kenneth Goodpaster, and Laura Nash, 157, 158. New York: McGraw-Hill, 1991.

Meyers, Diana, "Work and Self-Respect." In *Ethical Theory and Business,* 3d ed., by Tom L. Beauchamp and Norman E. Bowie, 275–279. Englewood Cliffs, NJ: Prentice Hall, 1988.

Monge v. *Beebe Rubber Co.* 114 N. H. 130, 316 A. 2nd 549, 1974.

Near, Janet, Marcia Miceli, Ramila Jensen. "Variables Associated with the Whistle-Blowing Process" Columbus, Ohio: Ohio State University, College of Administrative Science. Working Paper Series 83–111 (March 1983): 5. Cited in Carroll (1989), 354, 355.

Noah, Timothy, and Albert Karr. "What New Civil Rights Law Will Mean: Charges of Sex, Disability Bias Will Multiply." *The Wall Street Journal,* November 4, 1991, 31.

Payne v. *Western A.R.R. Co.* 81. Tenn 507 (1884). Also cited in Steiner and Steiner (1991), 625.

Pugh v. *See's Candies, Inc.* 161 Cal. App. 3rd 311, 171 Cal. Rqtr. 917 (1981).

Simmons, John, and William Mares. *Working Together.* New York: Knopf, 1983.

Sitomer, Curtis J. "Privacy and Personal Freedoms: The Impact of Technology." *Christian Science Monitor,* December 5, 1986, 1.

Steiner, George A. and John F. Steiner. *Business, Government and Society: A Managerial Perspective.* 6th ed. New York: McGraw-Hill, 1991.

Strom, Stephanie. "Harassment Rules Often Not Posted." *The New York Times,* October 20, 1991, 1, 22.

Tannen, Deborah. *You Just Don't Understand.* New York: Morrow, 1990.

Time. "Bakke Wins, Quotas Lose," July 10, 1978, 8–20.

Velasquez, Manuel G. *Business Ethics: Concepts and Cases.* 2d and 3d eds. Englewood Cliffs, NJ: Prentice Hall, 1988 and 1992.

Walters, Kenneth. "Your Employees' Right to Blow the Whistle." *Harvard Business Review,* (July/August 1975): 160–162.

Weber v. *Kaiser Aluminum and Chemical Corporation.* 563 F. 2nd 216 (5th Cir. 1977).

Werhane, Patricia. *Persons, Rights and Corporations.* Englewood Cliffs, N.J.: Prentice-Hall, 1985.

Wermiel, Stephen, and Cathy Trost. "Justices Say Hostile Job Environment Due to Sex Harassment Violates Rights." *The Wall Street Journal,* June 20, 1986, 2.

7

Nations and Multinational Stakeholders

The year is 1953. (Engine) Charlie Wilson, president of General Motors (GM) is testifying at his confirmation hearings to become secretary of defense. The question is put to him by Senator Robert Hendrickson (Republican from New Jersey): If he had to make a decision adverse to the interests of General Motors but in the interests of the United States, could he make that decision? Says Wilson, "Yes sir. I could. I cannot conceive of one, because for years I have thought that what was good for our country was good for General Motors—and vice versa. . . . Our company is too big. It goes with the welfare of the country. Our contribution to the nation is quite considerable."

Fast forward to 1992. General Motors is busily getting smaller, as is its contribution to the nation. GM's [former] chairman, Robert Stempel, has just announced a $4.45 billion loss for 1991, the largest loss in American business history. The company will close 21 plants over the next several years, lay off tens of thousands of workers, and undo the massive reorganization it undertook just a few years ago. You can practically hear the logical follow-up question being put to Stempel, almost 40 years after Wilson's testimony: "Is what's *bad* for GM also bad for America?" *(Webber and Taylor 1992, 73, 76)*

7.1 **THE COMPETITIVE GLOBAL BUSINESS ENVIRONMENT**

The question, "Is what's bad for GM also bad for America?" raises the following debated and controversial issues that we address in this chapter: (1) Does a large U.S.-based multinational corporation that is losing marketshare to the Japanese and other foreign firms represent and reflect the state of American domestic and global competitiveness? (2) Why is a former corporate leader like GM losing marketshare to Japanese competitors? (3) What could or should the U.S. government do to help GM and other industries and companies to compete in the global market? (4) Should U.S. corporations and the government in an egalitarian democratic society change moral codes and laws to compete with Japan and other nations that have less egalitarian institutional values and corporate practices?

These questions are the basis of ongoing debates over the nature of global competitiveness and what the U.S. response to it should be, topics that we will address in this chapter. We begin by summarizing the response to the question posed about GM by Alan Webber and William Taylor (1992) at the *Harvard Business Review*. Following this, we will discuss characteristics of the competitive global environment and the strategies and ethics of the major stakeholders.

Webber and Taylor's response to their own question is "yes and no." First, they argue, GM's (and Chrysler's and Ford's) loss of competitiveness is not bad for the United States because it does not mean the auto industry in America will end. Instead of Detroit's Big Three, there will be a "North American" auto industry producing "high quality, technologically advanced, affordable cars." Toyota, Nissan, and Honda will probably be the major auto producers. They already have captured over 30% of the U.S. market. Again, the dominance of their firms in the United States is not "bad," according to Webber and Taylor, since there will be substantial employment in the auto industry in the United States. The Japanese are shifting component manufacturing, research and development, and design and engineering to the United States. These authors conclude that "what's bad for General Motors is bad for General Motors—period. It has little to do with the rest of America's competitive standing."

However, what is bad for America, the authors argue, are the older corporate habits based on bureaucratic management, which giants like GM, Kodak, ITT, Aetna, and Sears have represented. These older corporate giants must change business practices to meet competitive requirements based on speed, simplicity, and service or else, "the handwriting is on the wall."

This response represents a critique and growing sentiment in the United States about the lack of competitiveness of some of the larger, older American industries and firms. However, this is only a partial, although important, response to the issue of U.S. competitiveness vis à vis Japan and the global competitors. We must also address unfair trade practices between countries like Japan and the United States, the role of the U.S. government in industrial competitiveness, and the way in which national culture influences these issues. We turn first to a discussion of the competitive global business environment as it has evolved since the late 1970s.

Evolution of the Competitive Global Business Environment

The competitive global environment of the 1990s began evolving after World War II and started to change rapidly in the late 1970s when global firms were organizing (Porter 1986). International forces that contributed to the emergence of global firms and the present competitive business environment include:

1. The rise of Japan's and Germany's dominant economies, which supported many of the non-U.S. multinational corporations now responsible for ending American dominance in several world markets.

2. The entrance of newly industrialized countries (NICs) such as Spain, Taiwan, and Korea, which produce and push low-cost, high-quality commercial products into markets faster than U.S. firms.

3. The convergence of consumer needs and preferences in what Kinichi Ohmae (1985) termed the "Triad," which includes the economies of Japan, Europe, and North America—a combined market of 640 million people with purchasing power. The firms that penetrate and control these markets dominate their global competition. Since 50% of free-world trade is concentrated in the Triad, global firms that can mass produce consumer products ahead of the competition will win marketshare (Ohmae 1985).

4. The emergence of other new market economies and blocs in addition to the Triad, such as eastern Europe, the C.I.S. (or former U.S.S.R.), and Canada/United States/Mexico, are also dropping trade barriers, expanding the competitive playing field, and providing new opportunities, rules, and success criteria for competing (Daft 1992).

Some of the major competitive success factors of global firms in this emerging global economy include (1) the capability to design, manufacture, and deliver higher quality, innovative products to world markets at lower costs; (2) the ability to deliver products that compete in service and price; (3) just-in-time manufacturing capability to transform innovative ideas into commodities backed up by service; and (4) the ability to be flexibly organized around customers and end-users in order to close the gap between product idea and delivery. The key to global competitiveness is integrated companies that operate on the imperatives of continuous quality improvement, responsiveness, speed, and loose-knit and entrepreneurial structures that collaborate and link the firm to suppliers, competitors, venture capitals, and other resources to focus on targeted markets. These success factors are different from the assembly line, top-down control and manufacturing processes that U.S. firms used right after World War II to dominate markets.

Competitiveness and Competition

In a survey of 4,000 *Harvard Business Review* readers in the 50 states, the District of Columbia, Puerto Rico, and 34 other countries, participants responded to the question, "Do you think there is a competitiveness problem?" Their responses showed that 92% believe U.S. competitiveness is deteriorating; 87% believe the problem predates the overvalued 1980s dollar; 95% believe that lowered competitiveness will harm the economic performance of the United States for the foreseeable future; and 89% think the problem is a threat to our standard of living and economic power (*Harvard Business Review* September/ October 1987).

Competitiveness is measured by the four indexes of the Council on Competitiveness (1988): standard of living, productivity, trade, and investment. The annual growth rate (as measured by the ratio of the rate of real gross domestic product [GDP] to workers) from 1982 to 1991 is as follows: Japan 3%, France 2.2%, Germany 1.8%, Britain 1.5%, and the United States 1.1% (*Business Week* April 6, 1992, 72). The United States has lagged in growth compared with Japan, West Germany, and other major countries. U.S. capital investment as a percentage of gross domestic product dipped below 18% in the mid-1970s and has remained lower than that of Germany and Japan and flat throughout most of the 1980s. Spending on nonmilitary R&D as a percentage of gross national product has also lagged behind Germany and Japan and has been flat since the 1980s (Greenhouse 1992).

The changing U.S. trade ($3 trillion) and budget ($150 billion) deficits are partly responsible for our lack of global competitiveness since these deficits (1) raise interest rates (to draw foreign lenders), which in turn increase the costs of doing business; and, (2) pull investment dollars away from R&D and plant renovations (Steiner and Steiner 1991, 434–435). The cycle becomes vicious: U.S. companies must pay higher costs to operate because of poor domestic economic conditions, which, in turn, constrain U.S. firms from succeeding at global competition. This is, of course, an oversimplification of a complex problem. Other documented factors that critics argue contribute to this country's low competitive global standing include stodgy managerial habits and organizational structures, and unfocused work cultures; the fixation of American business on short-term profits; pluralistic and antagonistic U.S. systems of government, law, and unions that create a "divide and conquer" environment for American businesses that face united, powerful national industrial strategies of countries like Japan; aging industrial plants and equipment; uncompetitive school systems; and an equalitarian cultural system of values and ideologies that treat foreign competitors on an equal footing with U.S. businesses. These factors are discussed in the following section because they influence the values and practices that govern stakeholder relationships.

7.2 **MULTINATIONAL COMPETITION: JAPAN AND THE UNITED STATES**

Successful multinational competition in world markets has demonstrated several important lessons: First, corporate competitiveness, as the Japanese have shown, is based on focused and coordinated, government-supported, long-term capitalized blueprint strategies. Second, global competitors focus less on piecemeal, random market approaches and more on domination of targeted critical industries and technologies to capture mass markets. Third, there has been an emphasis on low-cost, high-quality products backed by a work force committed to continuous improvement. In this section we compare Japanese with American competitiveness. We focus the discussion on how corporate competitiveness relates to national culture, the government system, and human resources as part of two very different uses of capital. (This is, intentionally, an abbreviated and summarized overview of this topic. Sources in the Reference section can be used for a more in-depth analysis.) Some Japanese scholars argue that their system of **capitalism (neocapitalism)** is unique and different from that of the West (Matsumoto 1991; Sakakibara 1990). The components of this system are explained below.

Japan, Inc.

Interest and debate continue to surround Japan's industrial strategies in winning markets and overtaking U.S. competitors. Since World War II, Japanese companies have leveled, and in some cases dominated, the current playing field in the following industries: consumer electronics, automobiles, semiconductors, machine tools, steel, textiles, and flat-screen computer panels (Dertouros, Lester, and Solow 1989; Steiner and Steiner 1991, 435). However, the United States presently maintains its competitive edge in university education, supercomputers, software engineering, artificial intelligence, computer-aided design and engineering, telecommunications, genetic engineering, laser and fiber optics, and high-performance materials (see Sethi, Namiki, and Swanson [1984], Chapter 2, pages 7–32, on which this discussion is based). The question that has gained the attention of the media, the White House, Congress, U.S. corporate presidents, and business schools is, "Why are the Japanese so successful?" Less attention has been given to the question, "At what and at whose costs?" We look at the success factors first.

The success factors behind "Japan, Inc.," as it has been called, are a mix among national cultural values and practices, business/government/political institutional relationships, corporate structures **(keiretsu),** human resource strategies and uses of capital, and human resource management. The nature and results of these combined relationships make up Japan's unique system of capitalism.

Cultural Characteristics Japan is a homogeneous culture. Maintaining the purity of its race is a valued cultural priority. This entails keeping foreign elements out (Sethi, Namiki, and Swanson 1984). The principal values of the Japanese society include: *amae* (dependence), *on* (duty), *giri* (social obligation), and *ninjo* (human feeling). *Amae* begins early in human development and continues throughout adulthood. It is this feeling that underlies adults' emotional attachment to each other, the group, the corporation, and even the state. *On* involves obligations that the recipient is indebted to repay. *Giri* relates to moral obligations that are mutual within a collectivity. *Ninjo* refers to what people prefer to do as well as what they believe they must avoid doing because of status or group membership. Maintaining harmony in the family, the group, the work organization, and the state is the theme around which these values revolve.

The family, household, and group form the center of the Japanese social structure. Individualism and standing out from the group are not valued. Respect and veneration for authority and interpersonal relationships are also highly valued. All of the above values and characteristics are shared by the society and are reflected in all major Japanese institutions, including corporations. Teamwork, consensus decision making, and a holistic concern for employees are all based and supported in these cultural values.

The veneration of authority in vertical relationships is also a central part of the Japanese culture. This relationship begins at home and is found in informal and work groups. Authority and respect in such relationships is absolute. Leaders are expected to show leadership characteristics, such as wisdom, vision, sympathy, and unselfishness. This tradition is based on the Confucian system of ethical conduct and was passed on in the ideologies and practices of the Samurai.

Sociopolitical Context The sociopolitical context of Japanese institutions can be summarized as an interdependent network of shared values, strategies, and traditions. Economic power has historically been—and continues to be—shared by government and business. This relationship was further cemented after World War II when the government actively sought to rebuild and support business growth. Government, unlike in the United States, coordinates business activities through long-term planning and industrial policy and manages businesses that are in trouble. Also, top-level government officials are generally well educated and respected and exercise powerful decisions in business activities. One of the most powerful agencies of Japan's six "economic bureaucracies" is MITI, the Ministry of International Trade and Industry. This agency shares significant power with private enterprises. This is especially the case, since MITI, like the other ministries, provides financial assistance and guidance to corporations. It is a working partnership.

Even though Japan's political system is a democracy, it is best characterized as semifeudal in nature. Because Japan never experienced a "people's revolution," the political system has few shared traditions with the public. Political parties compete for power and privileges, status, and positions within the ministries. Consequently, "Wheeling and dealing, bribery, coercion, collusion, threats and violence (including assassination) are as much a part of Japanese politics as they are of Japanese life" (Sethi, Namiki, and Swanson 1984; Yanaga 1965). In effect, the power and authority of the political system is ineffective in controlling business activity to protect the public. Scandals are discovered after the fact, and attempts are made to have business and political crises quickly resolved.

It should also be noted that Japan's social system focuses on the commercialization of knowledge. Japan's industries and companies are interweaved with government to the extent that business activities are rewarded, as these bring returns on investment to the society—more so than to any single individuals.

Industrial Groups: *Keiretsu* Against this cultural and political background are imbedded the powerful *keiretsu*, oligopolistic firms networked together in industrial cartels (Peck 1988). To understand the success of the Japanese competitive enterprise is to understand the *keiretsu* and its strategies and use of capital. The *keiretsu* are the inheritors of the post-World War II **zaibatsus,** economic monopolies started by powerful families and broken up by the American occupation. *Zaibatsus* were holding companies with large stock ownership in core companies. Each *zaibatsu* was controlled by a family trust. The core companies included manufacturing enterprises, a bank, a trust company, an insurance firm, and several smaller companies. *Keiretsu* are organized around the former *zaibatsu*.

The six dominant *keiretsu* include Mitsubishi (101 companies), Sumitomo (87 companies), Mitsui (65 companies), Fuji (87 companies), Sanwa (61 companies), and DKB (43 companies) (Klein 1987). As of 1980, these six groups accounted for 18% sales, 14% corporate profits, and 6%

employment in Japan. By 1992, the *keiretsu* accounted for almost a quarter of Japan's total business assets and revenues (Kelly et al. 1992). The *keiretsu* share stock ownership with the large firm holding equity, its suppliers, and the suppliers holding equity in the main company. They are interlocking partnerships and allies.

At the center of each *keiretsu* is a bank or cash-rich company that offers low-cost capital. Stocks are held mostly by other companies, therefore allowing managers to plan and operate on long-term market domination goals.

The largest manufacturer in the *keiretsu* dictates everything from prices to terms of delivery to the hundreds of suppliers that are bound to it. These cartels, then, have ready available capital from their member companies, from the bank in their group, and from government funds to target and exploit any market or technology on the globe.

Japanese Capitalism The *keiretsu* make up the industrial or business segment of Japan's unique system of communal capitalism, as depicted in Figure 7-1. This system is summarized as follows: (1) There are close alliances between government and business. These intimate relationships allow prices to be controlled, strategic industries to be targeted for growth, and the regulation of industry through fuzzy guidelines instead of rules, which also serve to keep outsiders out. If you do not understand the rules, you cannot play in the game. (2) The *keiretsu* control Japan's business interests. Cartels enable business groups to coordinate and focus capital from banks, the government, and other sources to obtain strategic global marketshare. (3) In the *keiretsu* system, the role of independent shareholder is, as stated above, weakened, since three quarters of Japanese companies' stocks are held by other firms. Consequently, Japanese managers concentrate on investing in long-term R&D projects and in competing for long-term marketshare instead of meeting short-term quarterly profits. (4) The relationship between Japanese workers and their firms is also different in this capitalist system (Neff 1992). Lifetime employment, consensual decision making, collective implementation of responsibilities, a slow evaluation and promotion system, informal and implicit control by peer groups and cultural norms, nonspecialized career paths, and a holistic concern for employees all mark different human resource practices than those found in the West (Ouchi and Jaeger 1978). Taken together, these four components of the Japanese capitalistic system present a formidable force in competing against countries and companies that are less organized and that have less infrastructural support.

Figure 7-1 *Capitalism Japanese-Style*

GOVERNMENT-INDUSTRY TIES

Benefits: Protects failing industries, nurtures growth industries
Drawbacks: Distorts market prices, hinders newcomers' entry

KEIRETSU

Benefits: Relationships between companies allow high-risk sharing,
              access to capital and technology
Drawbacks: Excluded companies have trouble competing

CORPORATE LOYALTY

Benefits: High productivity and quality, stable work force and top
              management team
Drawbacks: Excessive employee obedience and dependence limits time for
              socializing and leisure

FEW OUTSIDE SHAREHOLDERS

Benefits: Managers don't need to focus on short-term results
Drawbacks: Managers don't feel shareholder accountability

Source: Robert Neff. "Japan Takes a Good Hard Look at Itself." *Business Week*, February 17, 1992, 33.

Ethical Issues with Japanese Management and Capitalism The Japanese management system (based on lifetime employment, consensual group decision making, slow evaluation and promotion, informal peer group control, horizontal career paths, and a holistic focus on employees) has demonstrated superior performance in global markets. As with other countries, the management is embedded in the culture and in the capitalist system. At a closer view, this system does have problems. Workers lack individual freedom in the militaristic, rigid systems of control. Substandard wages, unsafe working conditions, and discrimination against women and temporary workers are also some of the more prominent moral issues in the Japanese management system (Sethi, Namiki, and Swanson 1984, 48–52). Lack of incentives for creativity and innovation are also a result of the consensus-oriented, conformist work group structure.

Lifetime employment is not a benefit shared equally by all; it is, in practice, more a function of the prosperity of the industry and firm. Most employees retire at age 55; in firms that are more successful, 58 is the retirement age. Moreover, retirement benefits are minimal. When forced into retirement, as is more often the case in larger firms, many retirees have financial difficulties.

Lifetime employment is believed to be given to 35% to 40% of the work force; that number is 40% to 60% in larger manufacturing firms and trading houses. Recession and other economic downturns are also affecting lifetime employment practices. Layoffs have occurred and are occurring in Japanese firms. It is also important to note that women are excluded from the lifetime employment benefit. Moreover, women often take more menial jobs than do men.

Long and exhausting working hours with little leisure or time off is another problem in the Japanese management system. Quality of work life has been a foreign concept to Japanese workers. Government agencies are studying how to maintain high performance while building more leisure attitudes and time into the work force.

Problems with Japanese Capitalism As recent stock market upheavals have shown, Japanese capitalism is not immune from the risky investments of the 1980s or from economic downturns. Institutional ownership of stocks does not protect falling value of investments.

At a system level, problems have evolved with Japanese capitalism from an international perspective. Japan's $1 trillion current-account surplus has caused critics to question Japan's trade policies and practices. Japanese companies, for example, have been caught and fined for price fixing and dumping products in the computer and electronic consumer products industries in the United States.

Critics also claim that the *keiretsu* oligopolies do not go after market-share only; they strategically target U.S. industries to dominate and ultimately put them out of business. Critics have accused Japan of practicing "predatory capitalism" in a military, warlike fashion. Japanese automobile and computer firms, for example, surround designated U.S. companies and deliberately seek to dominate and control these industries and firms by moving in the *keiretsu* manufacturing, finance, technology, and component suppliers with the aim of lowering prices until the competitors cannot compete on price or quality. The U.S. auto parts industry is one example. Although U.S. auto parts are world-class leaders in price and quality, the industry has failed in selling parts to Japanese automakers in Japan and in the United States. Why? One response follows:

> A number of academic studies have demonstrated that Japanese multinational companies don't act like other multinational companies when they go overseas. They are far less likely to buy local parts and equipment and to hire local people for high management positions than are European and

American multinationals, and they are far more likely to give most of their business to other Japanese companies. (*Murray 1992,* A1)

Former President Bush's now-memorable trip to Japan was an attempt to convince Japanese automakers in the United States to double their purchases from U.S. suppliers from $7 billion in 1990 to $15 billion by 1994 (Holbrook 1991–1992). Some have argued that this agreement represents "managed trade" and shows that Japan must be pressured to act more fairly. Still, critics argue that Japan's markets for critical technologies and products remain closed.

Some of the criticisms of Japan's industrial and trade practices may be unfounded. Defenders of Japanese capitalism and competitiveness claim that U.S. industries and companies are not accustomed to being second best or less successful than the Japanese. Holbrooke stated that, "accepting a more assertive and independent Japan will prove difficult for many Americans, who have come to regard Japan as a junior partner on most important foreign policy issues." It is also argued that American industries that are conservative and unwilling to change management practices are to blame for lack of competitiveness, not Japan. It is also pointed out that without Japanese investment and manufacturing operations in the United States, Americans would suffer even more, since competitors from other countries would pose similar threats to our standard of living and industrial weaknesses.

The debate continues over whether and to what extent Japan is competing fairly in international markets. Is Japan combining protectionist trade practices, price fixing, and predatory tactics with legitimate *keiretsu* strategies to dominate U.S. and other global prize industries such as auto, electronics, and semiconductors? Is Japan simply playing by the rules of the countries in which it does business and capitalizing on industry and corporate weaknesses and trade loopholes? The moral and industrial challenge for Japan will be its ability to maintain its productivity while competing in other countries in ways that are politically and legally compatible with other capitalist systems.

American Capitalism and Management

The American capitalist and management systems differ significantly from those in Japan. In this section we summarize some of the major themes already alluded to in other parts of the book, namely, dominant characteristics of American national culture, government, and the corporate management system. Our aim is to compare U.S. uses of capitalism with Japanese uses and to discuss the problems of American capitalism in the global arena.

Cultural Context America is a country of countries. Garreau (1981) argued that historically and culturally there are nine nations in North America (see also Kahle 1988). As such, America is an ethnically diverse society in which distinctive traditions and customs coexist and share the following common values: individualism, self-reliance, self-discipline, a Protestant-influenced work ethic, the value of private property, and the belief in fairness and individual rights. Some argue that the Protestant work ethic has undergone significant change. Preoccupation with self has developed into narcissism, and justice is being defined as fairness (Sethi, Namiki, and Swanson 1984, 104).

Individual rights and ownership of private property are at the center of the American value system. The Declaration of Independence focuses on rights as *inalienable*. Ownership of private property reinforces individualism in the social fabric. Americans also value family and collective group membership. Group membership, however, is based more on voluntarism than cultural norms. (This section draws on Sethi, Namiki, and Swanson [1984], Chapters 5 and 6.) The distinction between American and Japanese values is apparent. Japan is essentially a collective, group-oriented culture, whereas American values center on self and individualism. These value differences are reflected in the way American businesses reward and recognize individual entrepreneurs and inventors. Knowledge as it is patented and protected legally is the private property of the individual, not of the society, as is the case with Japan. In Japan the individual is not considered the focal point of industrial innovation or success.

Sociopolitical and Government Context The United States is a pluralistic political and government system. The Constitution grounds ultimate authority in the people and separates power among the executive, legislative, and judicial branches of government. Within this pluralistic system, government, business, and unions share power and solve problems through an adversarial relationship. Cooperation must continually be negotiated through advocacy, argument, and special interest and political action group lobbying.

Competition and fragmentation are built into the system, the very infrastructure of government and politics. Federal and state governments compete over the power of budgets, policies, and resources. For example, the national government lacks an industrial policy for the country, and the states develop their own and compete with each other for domestic and foreign investment. Iowa has used handsome tax incentives to convince Japanese auto manufacturers to build and operate along Interstate I–75. At the same time, Detroit automakers have unsuccessfully lobbied the president to adopt some form of a broad national industrial policy to limit Japanese auto imports and manufacturing in the United States. While Japan operates in global markets as a united front through combined government, unions, and *keiretsu* cooperation and strategies, the United States operates in a piecemeal, state-by-state, corporation-by-corporation manner. As one U.S. auto parts manufacturer commented on the comparison of American and Japanese business practices, "Japan is blueprint; the United States is an event."

American Capitalism American capitalism is based on the ideology of "free-market enterprise." Large business corporations have in the past embodied and modeled the wealth and success of the American business enterprise and therefore have defined the rules of the capitalist system. Larger corporations obtain equity capital from private investors and capital markets. These institutions compete among themselves and with the government for funds. Unlike the Japanese example, U.S. banks are not permitted to buy stock in corporations; this helps to prevent conflicts of interest. Also unlike Japanese *keiretsu*, the government is more often than not the watchdog and regulator of business growth and activity—not the strategic partner. The U.S. corporation, then, must depend on the attractiveness of its stock on the open market to survive and succeed (Meyer and Gustafson 1988; Sethi, Namiki, and Swanson 1984).

Because most of the larger corporations sell shares to the public, the stock market defines the health of a firm. The trading price of a company's shares also determines the firm's ability to obtain capital and resources to grow and innovate. Corporations, then, walk a tightrope between their debt and equity in their capital structure. "A highly leveraged company is more risk prone and must pay a higher cost for funds unless its growth prospects are phenomenal and investors are willing to assume above-average risks" (Sethi, Namiki, and Swanson 1984, 115–116).

Consequently, U.S. corporations are continuously monitored by the public and shareholders. The trading price of a company's stock, the quarterly earnings reports, its profit and loss statements, and the perception of a firm by financial markets all define American capital as a short-term, price-sensitive enterprise. For American managers, unlike their Japanese counterparts, this means that short-term planning, investing, and strategies are the rules and boundaries by which managers can operate. This system is currently being pressured by global competition and the changing nature of international markets to change.

American Management Practices In practice, the American management system is not a single system. American entrepreneurs have not followed—and probably will not follow—any single set of rules for borrowing, inventing, investing, or doing business. However, there is a historical background of management systems and thought that, again, larger and more traditional corporations have embodied and followed.

Although entrepreneurial firms differ from larger, older ones, and although there are a variety of management systems and changing styles in the United States, we can still make certain generalizations about American management practices, as these have been historically grounded in the dominant value system, the sociocultural context, the business/government relationship, and the American form of capitalism. These generalizations include an emphasis on (1) short-term time, profit, planning, and strategy horizons based on some of the cultural and sociosystem background factors explained above; (2) individual decision making, responsibility, performance, and rewards; (3) the manager having been understood, trained, and treated as a professional separate from any specific knowledge base; (4) outcomes over process, measured and monitored by short-term financial tools; (5) specialized and vertical career paths; and (6) individual career development. These characteristics are familiar, since they have been addressed in management literature and journals (see Ouchi and Jaeger 1978).

American management practices have also been greatly influenced by the school of **scientific management,** proposed by Frederick Taylor (1947) at the turn of the century. Taylor separated managers from workers and viewed managers as having a professional status; he articulated a logic for making and maintaining a division of labor and a chain of command; he laid the basis of building organizational structures to carry out separate tasks; and he defined work and management so that both could be measured and executed "scientifically," in a cost–benefit, compartmentalized, individualistic, and piecemeal way.

The legacy of scientific management left us with the stovepipe organization and isolated, specialized management functions. The artificial division of worker from manager, top-down decision making, and the eventual need for unions to advocate benefits for alienated and economically disadvantaged workers from management were also set in motion. Productivity was defined apart from the enterprise's mission and more on an individual piece-rate basis. Attention to process was lost. These are components of American management that are being ripped apart by global competition and the changing rules of knowledge technology as it replaces the linear assembly line.

Problems with American Capitalism and Management The American capitalist system's short-term overemphasis on financially measured corporate growth and returns has not been successful when compared with the Japanese *keiretsu* system. Not only have the Japanese mastered process technology, total quality, continuous improvement, and just-in-time inventory and management techniques for getting product ideas to market in one-third less time than U.S. competitors, but they have a head start of several decades in doing so. Moreover, our adversarial system of pluralistic competition and governance is still intact. The relationship among government, business, and unions is still politically divisive.

Among the most prominent problems with America's lagging competitiveness have been the blindspots—the inability of American managers to recognize the importance and prowess of international competition. The results of the 1989 Korn/Ferry–Columbia study, "Reinventing the CEO," stated,

> . . . it is troubling that the executives of most U.S. corporations, perhaps by virtue of minimal international exposure, discount the importance of an international outlook. What is most disturbing is that they do not acknowledge this liability, and so risk selecting a successor with the same narrow vision.

The U.S. legal system may also be part of the problem of America's competitiveness. While antitrust and other regulatory laws effectively controlled monopolies in this country at the turn of the century, these same laws are impeding the ability of American firms to form *keiretsu*-like coalitions to compete with the Japanese. Like professional managers, lawyers have mushroomed. The United States has 307.4 lawyers per 100,000 people, compared with Britain's 102.7, Germany's 82, and Japan's 12.1. In 1971, the United States had 355,242 lawyers compared with 750,000 in 1990 and a projected 1 million by 2000. In 1984, there were 14.1 million state court filings (lawsuits); by 1990, that number reached 18.4 million. Moreover, the legal costs U.S. companies pay could be spent in R&D and other competitive pursuits. For example, Dow Chemical spends more than $100 million a year on legal services and liability insurance (*Business Week* April 13, 1992, 61). The question arises, How much law and how many lawyers are necessary in the United

States to do what, for whom, at what and at whose costs? Presently, many companies are hiring dispute settlement professionals to lower legal costs.

Given these observations, it is important to note that the global competitive game is just beginning. The European Community market is just beginning to take off. U.S.-based multinationals are also competing with German, French, Italian, Swiss, and other European multinational competitors in the new global marketplace.

Because many larger corporations and traditional industries are losing competitiveness in the emerging global market, traditional and questionable U.S. management practices of governance and leadership have also come under scrutiny. The public is morally as well as economically concerned because Americans are losing jobs, community tax bases are eroding, the effectiveness of our school system is challenged, the role of government and politicians is questioned, our standard of living is deteriorating, and there is uncertainty about whether America will be a technology and manufacturing leader in the future or an assembler and distributor of other nations' innovative products. The effectiveness of our entire system of business, government, education, research and development, and production has been challenged. Immoral conduct and practices in government, business, education, and other American institutions are likely to be less tolerated by the public in such a deteriorating economic and competitive environment.

Steps to Regaining Competitiveness

Not all U.S. companies are stodgy and uncompetitive. Some of the more entrepreneurial flagship American firms include Sun Microsystems, Intel, Angen, Wal-Mart, Federal Express, and Microsoft, to name a few. While there are no magical formulas for reinventing U.S. competitiveness, there are many guidelines suggested and changes already occurring. This section summarizes some of the suggested directions the U.S. corporate enterprise and governance system should take.

Changes in Corporate Governance As we discussed in Chapter 5, the unusually high salaries, benefits, and perks of CEOs and the role of corporate boards of directors, shareholders, and top-level managers are being questioned, especially in companies that are not performing. Changes are being made. The General Motors board of directors startled the corporate world by cutting former CEO Stempel's salary by one third (down to $1 million) and by closing plants and shedding thousands of workers. This move may shake up other corporate boards and move them to action against waste and corruption, toward more entrepreneurial policies and practices.

American *Keiretsu* U.S. firms in industries that have been competing head-on with Japanese *keiretsu* have realized that the competition is too great to go it alone. As a result, U.S. firms have been forming their own kind of *keiretsu*. Ford has been focusing on its automotive and financial-services businesses through the strategies of acquisitions, equity holdings, international linkages, and research consortiums. In its vehicle assembly business, for example, Ford has a 25% equity stake in Mazda, 10% in KIA Motors in Korea, 75% in Aston Martin Lagonda and 48% in Iveco Ford Truck of Britain, and 49% in Autolatina in Brazil and Argentina. Ford also is a member of eight R&D consortiums that investigate environmental issues and other innovative projects. Ford also has partners in its parts, production, financial services, and marketing businesses (Kelly et al. 1992, 52–60). IBM also is becoming a kind of American *keiretsu*.

In the 1980s U.S. industries created over 250 R&D consortiums. The federal government has funded $120 million to Detroit's automakers to work jointly on a new battery technology for electric cars (Kelly et al. 1992, 53). Finally, U.S. firms are following the strategy, "If you can't beat them, join them." Detroit's auto manufacturers and U.S. computer firms have several strategic alliances and joint ventures with their Japanese counterparts. Ford has aligned with Mazda, Mitsubishi in Japan. Chrysler also is aligned with Mitsubishi. GM is in an alliance with Suzuki. Honeywell and Nippon Electric of Japan share business dealings, and IBM and Matsushita are partners.

Reinventing American Management Practices A number of books and studies have offered suggestions for improving U.S. productivity and competitiveness. Among the most notable is Dertouros, Lester, and Solow's (1989) *Made in America: Regaining the Productive Edge.* Steiner and Steiner (1991) use this source, among others, to summarize the following points offered for U.S. firms: (1) Think globally; (2) balance short-term and long-term thinking; (3) implement global strategy; (4) give high priority to the improvement of production processes; and (5) improve human resource management (Steiner and Steiner 1991, 451–454). Also, government should focus on public policies that strengthen science and technology advantages and increase tax credit for R&D projects.

W. Edwards Deming, the American management guru who, when shunned by the U.S. corporate establishment after World War II,

Figure 7-2 Deming's 14 Points for Improving Management's Productivity

1. Plan for the long-term future, not for the next month or year.
2. Never be complacent concerning the quality of your product.
3. Establish statistical control over your production processes and require your suppliers to do so as well.
4. Deal with the fewest number of suppliers—the best ones, of course.
5. Find out whether your problems are confined to particular parts of the production process or stem from the overall process itself.
6. Train workers for the job you are asking them to perform.
7. Raise the quality of your line supervisors.
8. Drive out fear.
9. Encourage departments to work closely together rather than to concentrate on departmental or divisional distinctions.
10. Do not be sucked into adopting strictly numerical goals, including the widely-popular formula of "zero deficit."
11. Require your workers to do quality work, not just to be at their stations from 9 to 5.
12. Train your employees to understand statistical methods.
13. Train your employees in new skills as the need arises.
14. Make top managers responsible for implementing these principles.

Source: W. Edwards Deming. "Improvement of Quality and Productivity Through Action by Management." *National Productivity Review* (Winter 1981–1982): 12–22.

turned to Japan to impart total quality management, continuous productivity improvement, and statistical system control methods. Deming is, after the last four decades, welcomed back by American firms. His 14 points for improving management's productivity are summarized in Figure 7-2.

American entrepreneurship is also a driving force that our industrial leaders are striving to reward and maintain in the midst of changing corporate structures and manufacturing techniques. The challenge is not how to become like the Japanese or any other management system. We cannot. The challenge is how to adopt successful elements from world-class management systems to our entrepreneurial business practices. Figure 7-3 illustrates a modified American management system (Type Z) based on the integration of successful Japanese practices (Type J) into our existing dominant practices (Type A).

There are no quick fixes that will turn the U.S. economy and corporations back to global competitiveness. Some argue that the United States will never again command the scope and extent of global control of manufacturing and production power it had after World War II; the world economy and politics are too complex and competitive. The United

Figure 7-3 Modified American Management System Based on Integration of American and Japanese Practices

	TYPE A (AMERICAN)	TYPE J (JAPANESE)	TYPE Z (MODIFIED AMERICAN)
Employment	Short-Term	Lifetime	Long-Term
Decision making	Individual	Consensual	Consensual
Responsibility	Individual	Collective	Individual
Evaluation	Rapid evaluation and promotion	Slow evaluation and promotion	Slow evaluation and promotion
Control	Explicit, formulized	Implicit, informal	Implicit, informal with explicit, formalized measures
Career path	Specialized	Nonspecialized	Moderately specialized
Concern for employees	Segmented	Holistic	Holistic

Source: William G. Ouchi and Alfred M. Jaeger. "Type Z Organizations: Stability in the Midst of Mobility." *Academy of Management Review* 3 (1978): 308.

States should, therefore, assume its competitive and cooperative place within this new economic system. Still, to do so requires the momentous changes, many of which are occurring now, and a major question remains: "Can the U.S. afford to maintain its democratic and Constitutional principles in the face of less-principled international business practices?"

7.3 MULTINATIONAL ENTERPRISES AS STAKEHOLDERS

Multinational enterprises (MNEs) are corporations that "own or control production or service facilities outside the country in which they are based" (United Nations 1973, 23). MNEs are also referred to as global, transnational, and international companies (Czinkotz and Ilkka 1987, 338).

While MNEs often reflect and extend their home nation's culture and resources, many act as independent nations. This section focuses on MNEs as independent, powerful stakeholders, using their power across national boundaries to gain comparative advantages, with or without home country support. Common characteristics that MNEs share include (1) operating a sales organization, manufacturing, distribution center, licensing, and/or subsidiary in at least two countries; (2) earning an estimated 25% to 45% of revenue from foreign markets; and (3) having common ownership, resources, and global strategies (Sturdivant and Vernon-Wortzel 1990, 189–190). Since MNEs often span nations, governments, and different types of businesses and markets, their operations are based on a shared network of strategies, information and data, expertise, capital, and resources (Vernon and Wells 1986, 2). MNEs have become the most strategically powerful stakeholders in the race to compete and dominate global industry marketshares.

Many MNEs are more economically powerful than the nations in which they do business. For example, IBM operates in over 126 countries, communicates in 30 languages, runs 23 foreign plants, and obtains over one half its total net income from its foreign business (Donaldson 1989, 31, 32). The 10 largest U.S.-based MNEs in terms of export sales dollars are shown in Figure 7-4. Figure 7-5 lists the 10 largest MNEs headquartered outside the United States. Of these foreign-based multinationals, seven are located in Western Europe and three are located in Japan. America's largest international exporters, as shown in Figure 7-4, include Boeing, GM, GE, Ford, IBM, Chrysler, E.I. Du Pont, United Technologies, McDonnell Douglas, and Caterpillar. The foreign-sales share of total sales for the world's largest MNEs, once estimated at one fourth (Dunning and Pearce 1981), is now closer to 40%.

The dominant goal of MNEs is to make a profit. Corporations expand and do business across national boundaries to take comparative advantage of marketing, trade, cost, investment, labor, and other factors. At the same time, MNEs assist local economies in many ways, as will be explained below. The ethical questions that critics of MNEs have raised are reflected in the following statement by the noted Harvard professor, Raymond Vernon (1971): "Is the multinational enterprise undermining the capacity of nations to work for the welfare of their people? Is the multinational enterprise being used by a dominant power . . . as a means of penetrating and controlling the economies of other countries?" We address these questions in the following discussion of mutual responsibilities and expectations of MNEs and their host countries.

Recent crises since the birth of the multinational corporation after World War II have raised international concern over the ethical conduct of MNEs in host and other countries. For example, Union Carbide's chemical spill in Bhopal, India, which resulted in thousands of deaths

Figure 7-4 America's Biggest Exporters

		EXPORT SALES		TOTAL SALES	
RANK 1990	COMPANY	$MIL	% CHANGE 1989–1990	$MIL	FORTUNE 500 RANK
1	Boeing, Seattle	16093.0	46.0	27595.0	13
2	General Motors, Detroit	10315.9	1.3	126017.0	1
3	General Electric, Fairfield, Conn.	7128.0	(1.9)	58414.0	6
4	Ford Motor, Dearborn, Mich.	7098.0	14.0	98274.0	6
5	International Business Machines, Armonk, NY	6195.0	13.1	69018.0	4
6	Chrysler, Highland Park, Mich.	5004.0	(7.1)	30868.0	11
7	E.I. DuPont de Nemours, Wilmington, Del.	4352.0	(10.2)	39839.0	9
8	United Technologies, Hartford	3606.0	9.0	21783.2	17
9	McDonnell Douglas, St. Louis	3538.0	22.2	16351.0	24
10	Caterpillar, Peoria, Ill.	3425.0	4.4	11540.0	39

Source: Excerpted from *Fortune*'s annual special issue (Spring/Summer 1991): 58. ©1991 Time Inc. All rights reserved. Reprinted with permission.

and injuries, alarmed other nations over questionable safety standards and controls of MNE foreign operations. Nestlé's marketing of its powdered infant milk formula that resulted in disease and death of a large number of infants in underdeveloped countries raised questions over the lack of proper product instructions issued to poorer, less-educated consumers. (Nestlé's practice resulted in a boycott of the company from 1976 to 1984.) Also, the presence of MNEs in South Africa raises criticisms over the role of large corporations in actively supporting apartheid or government-supported racism. Because MNEs have to pay taxes to the South African government, and because apartheid is a government-supported policy, MNEs—it is argued—support racism. Several U.S.-based MNEs that operated in South Africa witnessed boycotts and disinvestments by many shareholders. Many MNEs, including IBM and Polaroid, withdrew. Another long-standing moral issue is the practice of MNEs not paying their fair share of taxes in countries where they do business and in their home countries. Through the process of transfer pricing and other creative accounting techniques,

Figure 7-5 The Ten Largest Non-U.S. Multinational Companies

RANK 1990	COMPANY	SALES		PROFITS		
		$MIL.	% CHANGE FROM 1989	$MIL.	RANK	% CHANGE FROM 1989
1	Royal Dutch/Shell Group, Britain/Neth.	107203.5	25.3	6442.1	1	(.06)
2	Toyota Motor, Japan	64516.1	6.7	2993.3	7	60.2
3	IRI, Italy	61433.0	25.2	926.5	53	(21.3)
4	British Petroleum, Britain	59540.5	20.3	3013.1	6	(13.9)
5	Daimler–Benz, Germany	54259.2	33.6	1041.6	46	(70.9)
6	Hitachi, Japan	50685.8	(0.4)	1476.9	28	2.1
7	Fiat, Italy	47751.6	30.0	1346.4	34	(44.2)
8	Samsung, South Korea	45042.0	28.0	N/A	N/A	—
9	Volkswagen, Germany	43710.2	25.8	651.6	78	24.5
10	Matsushita Electrical Industrial, Japan	43516.1	1.0	1649.1	21	(0.9)

Source: Adapted from *Fortune* (July 28, 1991): 245. ©1991 Time Inc. All rights reserved. Reprinted with permission.

many MNEs have shown paper losses—thereby enabling them to avoid paying any taxes. We discuss the ethical concerns that surround MNEs in the following overview of two perspectives (that of the MNE and of the host country) relating to the arguments for and the criticisms of MNE presence in host countries.

MNE Perspective

The MNE enters a foreign country primarily to make a profit. MNEs expand globally for a number of reasons; for example, they seek to benefit from currency fluctuations, more available and cheaper labor costs, tax and trade incentives, and use of natural resources. They also hope to gain access to more foreign markets and to create or maintain competitiveness.

MNEs benefit their host countries through foreign direct investment (FDI). Through their direct investment and presence, MNEs (1) attract local capital to projects; (2) provide for and enhance technology transfer;

Figure 7-6 MNE Stakeholder Environmental Issues and Ethical Concerns

Economic Environmental Stakeholder Issues:

exchange rates; wages; income distribution; balance of payments; import/export levels; taxes; interest rates; GNPs; transfer pricing

Political Environmental Stakeholder Issues:

governments; media; instability; local laws; antitrust laws; military; foreign policy and treaties; corruption; local competition

MNEs Managing Ethical Concerns:

observing home and host countries' legal and moral codes e.g., Foreign Corrupt Practices Act; workplace safety; product safety; responsible marketing and advertising standards; moral ecological practices

Ecological Environmental Stakeholder Issues:

air, water, land pollution; toxic wastes and dumping; industrial accidents; use/misuse of natural resources; restoring national environment

Technology Environmental Stakeholder Issues:

intellectual property protection; licensing; agreement fees; technical resources; alliances and sharing of technology

Social and Labor Environmental Stakeholder Issues:

values, attitudes, customs; religious, political, social class practices and norms; labor unions; availability of skills; expatriate requirements, needs; workplace safety

(3) develop particular industry sectors; (4) intensify competition in the country by introducing new products, services, and ideas; and (5) help decrease the country's debt and improve its balance of payments and standard of living. Moreover, MNEs open less developed countries (LDCs) to international markets, thereby helping the local economy to attract greatly desired hard currencies. Also, new technical and managerial skills are brought in and local workers receive training and knowledge. Job and social class mobility is provided to inhabitants (Czinkota and Ilkka 1987, 346–347). Some MNEs also introduce schools, colleges, and hospitals to their host countries.

The MNE must manage overlapping and often conflicting multiple constituencies between and in its home and host country operations. Figure 7-6 illustrates some of the major environments and stakeholder issues that must be technically and ethically balanced and managed by the MNE in its foreign location. From the MNE's perspective, managing these stakeholder issues is difficult and challenging, especially as the global economy presents new problems.

MNE executives and managers also complain of what they consider unethical practices and arbitrary control of host country governments. For example, local governments can and sometimes do (1) limit repatriation of assets and earnings of MNEs; (2) pressure and require MNEs to buy component parts and other materials from local suppliers; (3) require MNEs to use local nationals in upper-level management positions; (4) require MNEs to produce and/or sell selected products in order to enter the country; (5) limit imports and pressure exports; and (6) require a certain amount or percentage of profit to remain or be invested in the country. Finally, MNEs always face the threat of expropriation or nationalization of their operations by the host government (Steiner and Steiner 1991, 397–399).

Host Country Perspective

Arguments critical of the presence and practices of MNEs in host and other foreign locations include the following (1) MNEs dominate and protect their core technology and research and development, thus keeping the host country as a consumer, not a partner or producer. For example, the Brazilian government has entry barriers and laws that have protected the complete control of its own electronics industries from foreign manufacturers since the 1970s. It is also argued (or feared) that Japan could in the long-term dominate certain critical industries (like electronics and perhaps automobiles) in the United States, and use American labor more as assemblers rather than technology R&D partners. (2) MNEs destabilize national sovereignty by limiting a country's access to critical capital and resources, thereby creating a dependency of governments and politics on the MNE. (3) MNEs create a "brain drain" by attracting scientists, expertise, and talent from the host country. (4) MNEs create an imbalance of capital outflows over inflows. MNEs create production but emphasize exports over imports in the host country, thereby leaving local economies dependent on foreign control. (5) MNEs disturb and disrupt local government economic planning and business practices by exerting control over the development and capitalization of a country's infrastructure. Also, by providing higher wages and better working conditions, a country's traditions, values, and customs are influenced and changed. "Cultural imperialism" is imported through business practices.

(6) MNEs sometime destroy, pollute, and endanger host and underdeveloped countries' environments and the health of local populations. For example, the mining of and dangerous exposure to asbestos continues in some LDCs and in Canada.

Obviously, these criticisms do not apply to all MNEs. These criticisms represent concerns of host and underdeveloped country governments that have suffered abuses from multinationals over the decades. Tensions in the relationships between MNEs and host countries and other foreign governments, especially in more underdeveloped settings, endure. Whenever the stakes for both parties are high, so will be the pressures to negotiate the most profitable and equitable benefits for each stakeholder. Often, it is the uneducated, poorer inhabitants of underdeveloped nations who suffer the most from the operations of MNEs.

7.4 MNE GUIDELINES FOR MANAGING MORALITY

Guidelines for managing ethical conduct have received detailed attention and work over the past four decades in the areas of consumer protection, employment, environmental pollution, human rights, and political conduct. (This section is based on Frederick [1991, 165–177].) The driving forces behind the development of these published guidelines include the United Nations, the International Labor Office, and the Organization for Economic Cooperation and Development.

The underlying normative sources of the guidelines developed by these global organizations include the beliefs in (1) national sovereignty, (2) social equity, (3) market integrity, and (4) human rights and fundamental freedoms (Frederick 1991, 168–169).

The following MNE (referred to here as MNC—multinational corporation) guidelines are summarized under the categories of employment practices and policies, consumer protection, environmental protection, political payments and involvement, and basic human rights and fundamental freedoms (Frederick 1991, 166–167).

Employment Practices and Policies

- MNCs should not contravene the manpower policies of host nations.

- MNCs should respect the right of employees to join trade unions and to bargain collectively.

- MNCs should develop nondiscriminatory employment policies and promote equal job opportunities.

- MNCs should provide equal pay for equal work.

- MNCs should give advance notice of changes in operations, especially plant closings, and mitigate the adverse effects of these changes.

- MNCs should provide favorable work conditions, limited working hours, holidays with pay, and protection against unemployment.

- MNCs should promote job stability and job security, avoiding arbitrary dismissals and providing severance pay for those unemployed.

- MNCs should respect local host country job standards and upgrade the local labor force through training.

- MNCs should adopt adequate health and safety standards for employees and grant them the right to know about job-related health hazards.

- MNCs should, minimally, pay basic living wages to employees.

- MNCs' operations should benefit lower-income groups of the host nation.

- MNCs should balance job opportunities, work conditions, job training, and living conditions among emigrant workers and host country nationals.

Consumer Protection

- MNCs should respect host country laws and policies regarding the protection of consumers.

- MNCs should safeguard the health and safety of consumers by various disclosures, safe packaging, proper labeling, and accurate advertising.

Environmental Protection

- MNCs should respect host country laws, goals, and priorities concerning protection of the environment.

- MNCs should preserve ecological balance, protect the environment, adopt preventive measures to avoid environmental harm, and rehabilitate environments damaged by operations.

- MNCs should disclose likely environmental harms and minimize risks of accidents that could cause environmental damage.

- MNCs should promote the development of international environmental standards.

- MNCs should control specific operations that contribute to pollution of air, water, and soils.

- MNCs should develop and use technology that can monitor, protect, and enhance the environment.

Political Payments and Involvement

- MNCs should not pay bribes nor make improper payments to public officials.

- MNCs should avoid improper or illegal involvement or interference in the internal politics of host countries.

Basic Human Rights and Fundamental Freedoms

- MNCs should respect the rights of all persons to life, liberty, security of person, and privacy.

- MNCs should respect the rights of all persons to equal protection of the law, work, choice of job, just and favorable work conditions, and protection against unemployment and discrimination.

- MNCs should respect all persons' freedom of thought, conscience, religion, opinion and expression, communication, peaceful assembly and association, and movement and residence within each state.

- MNCs should promote a standard of living to support the health and well-being of workers and their families.

- MNCs should promote special care and assistance to motherhood and childhood.

Frederick (1991, 167) states that these guidelines should be viewed as a "collective phenomenon," since all do not appear in each of the six international pacts from which they originated (that is, the 1948 United Nations Universal Declaration of Human Rights; the 1975 Helsinki Final Act; the 1976 OECD Guidelines for Multinational Enterprises; the 1977 International Labor Organization Tripartite Declaration of Principles Concerning Multinational Enterprises and Social Policy; and the 1972 UN Code of Conduct on Transnational Corporations).

The guidelines serve as a broad basis on which all international organizations can design and apply specific corporate policies and procedures in such areas as:

... childcare, minimum wages, hours of work, employee training and education, adequate housing and healthcare, pollution control efforts, advertis-

ing and marketing activities, severance pay, privacy of employees and consumers, information concerning on-the-job hazards and . . . for those companies with operations in South Africa . . . as the place of residence and free
movement of employees (*Frederick 1991, 167*)

The problem remains: Who enforces these types of principles across geographic boundaries when complex situations involve competing interests and power demands?

7.5 ETHICS AND GLOBAL STAKEHOLDER DISPUTES

In the real world of trade and buying and selling, MNEs and host governments will continue to quarrel and litigate over control of high-stakes
technologies, intellectual patents, and controversial issues relating to
industrial abuses of health, physical environments, and cultural traditions. Governments will claim they have a right to, for example, their
apartheid laws, while other nations will boycott companies who do busi-
nessin such nations. Countries such as Brazil may attempt to continue
protecting their small to midsize computer firms by imposing laws and
regulations over foreign companies that attempt to overwhelm the R&D
ability of that nation's computer industry, while Western high-technol-
ogy producers threaten to leave Brazil if their control is jeopardized. The
Fujitsus of Japan and other countries and the IBMs of the United States
and Europe continue to debate over what constitutes "intellectual property," whose definition should be used, and what moral and legal criteria should be applied to settle alleged violations.

These examples, again, take us back to Chapters 1 and 3 of this book:
"Who is right and who is wrong in ethical dilemmas in which the stakes
are high for both parties who are both right? Whose morals and solutions should then be followed?"

These questions become even more difficult in international disputes
when both sides have valid, legitimate claims, according to their historical traditions, customs, and legal history and practices.

The summary of universally recognized rights of international firms
and countries in section 7.4 is a starting point for identifying conflicts of
interest. After that, advocating a specific ethic usually does not satisfy a
solution when cultural, religious, economic, and legal "rights" of two
disputing parties historically differ. The conflicting claims must be negotiated.

Thomas Donaldson (1989) offered an "ethical algorithm" to help
resolve difficult conflicts of interests between international parties.

However, this logic appears somewhat cumbersome and even mechanical in real-time experience.

We advocate a more practical exercise that business and legal professionals are accustomed to using, namely a stakeholder analysis (see Chapter 2 of this book). Once the issues, stakes, and priority ranking of stakes are identified, then the two parties should begin to discuss the differing legal, cultural, historical, and social value differences that underlie each party's claims and motivations. The different ethical value systems in Chapter 3 can be applied as a "first pass" to understand the moral nature of the claims, even though other moral traditions may also be relevant to the situation. Using the list of universal rights in section 7.4 provides a starting point for reviewing issues of justice, duty, and moral obligations of the parties, but beyond this exercise, negotiation techniques are required to thrash out assumptions and issues to settle disputes (see Chapter 8).

Again, there are no quick fixes for resolving high-stakes ethical and economic dilemmas between international players when both sides are "right." Sensitivity to communication and diligence with negotiation techniques that help us understand and consider the differences in cultural traditions, language, and assumptions are required in order to reach what Roger Fisher, in his influential book on negotiations, termed "getting to yes" (1983).

SUMMARY

The global business and economic environment has dramatically changed since the 1970s. The rise of Japan's and Germany's strong economies, the entrance of newly industrialized countries, and the convergence of consumer needs and preferences in the "Triad" (Europe, North America, and Asia) have created new global markets and competitive opportunities. In this new context, industrial competitiveness is no longer dominated by American firms. International forces that have supported and reflect the emergence of successful Japanese and European multinational firms are presented in this chapter. Also, the new industrial rules of global competition are identified and used to compare U.S. corporations' competitiveness.

Arguments regarding the "ethics" of U.S. versus Japanese uses of capital in the global environment are presented. Japanese *keiretsu* (corporate alliances) is discussed as a cultural and sociopolitical extension of that country's society. Elements of our dominant American management are compared to the Japanese management system. Steps for regaining U.S. competitiveness in the global economy are outlined.

Moral issues and practices that historically and currently pertain to multinational conduct are identified. Guidelines drawn from over four decades of international agreements and charters are summarized to illustrate a consensus of host country rights, which have been used to help multinationals design equity into their policies and procedures.

Finally, because of the complexity and differences of national stakeholders' cultural, legal, economic, and value systems, no single moral or ethical code will be sufficient for resolving business disputes over issues when both parties are right, such as the issue of infringement of intellectual property or technology transfer. Global negotiating skills with knowledge of and sensitivities to language and to national sociopolitical and legally different systems and assumptions are required. The stakeholder approach becomes an important method in this new global business arena for identifying the different ethical assumptions of issues and for establishing compatible bases to morally resolve disputes between parties who are both right.

Questions

1. Describe the emerging competitive global business environment and the forces that define it. What is different about the "new" global environment?

2. Define "competitiveness" as discussed in the chapter. Are U.S. corporations really becoming less competitive? Explain.

3. Characterize Japan's system of capitalism.

4. Characterize the American system of capitalism.

5. What are advantages and disadvantages of Japan's and America's systems of capitalism for doing business internationally?

6. Explain the differences in perception and experience of moral issues from (a) a host country toward an MNE and (b) an MNE toward a host country. Which perspective are you more inclined to support or sympathize with? Why?

7. Evaluate the practicality and use of the guidelines in section 7.4 from an MNE's perspective.

Exercises

1. Argue and defend your positions on the following statements:

   A. "What is bad for General Motors is bad for the United States."

B. "Japan is more globally competitive and has a large trade surplus because of unfair trade practices, not because of its system of capitalism and corporate practices."

C. "The American management system cannot become more competitive than the Japanese system because of the two capitalist systems' differences."

D. "MNEs cannot financially afford to follow the guidelines in section 7.4; it would be too costly for them."

E. "When two national MNEs are both right over a controversial issue—for example, violation of patent or intellectual property rights—ethics should be avoided and other, more concrete issues should be used to resolve the dispute."

2. Identify from the news or current press a dispute between (a) two multinational corporations and, (b) a multinational corporation and a nation.

3. Answer these questions from 2(a) and 2(b): Who is right and who is wrong? Why? How would you propose to resolve the dispute? Include a moral perspective in your answer.

References and Suggested Readings

Business Week. "Industrial Policy: Call It What You Will, The Nation Needs a Plan to Nurture Growth." April 6, 1992, 72.

———. "Guilty: Too Many Lawyers, Too Much Litigation." April 13, 1992, 61.

Council on Competitiveness. *Competitive Index,* May 1988.

Czinkota, Michael, and Ilkka Ronkainer. *International Business.* Chicago: Dryden Press, 1989.

Daft, Richard. "Contemporary Designs for Global Competition." In *Organization Theory and Design.* 4th ed., 218–241. St. Paul, Minn.: West Publishing Company, 1992.

Dertouros, Michael, Richard Lester, Robert Solow, and the MIT Commission on Industrial Productivity. *Made in America: Regaining the Productive Edge.* Cambridge, Mass.: MIT Press, 1989.

Donaldson, Thomas. *The Ethics of International Business.* New York: Oxford University Press, 1989.

Dunning, John, and R. D. Pearce. *The World's Largest Industrial Enterprises.* Farnborough, England: Gower, 1981.

Fischer, Roger. *Getting to Yes: Negotiating Agreement Without Giving In.* New York: Penguin, 1983.

Frederick, William. "The Moral Authority of Transnational Corporate Codes." *Journal of Business Ethics* 10 (1991): 165–177.

Garreau, Joel. *The Nine Nations of North America.* New York: Avon, 1981.

Greenhouse, Steven. "Attention America! Snap Out of It!" *The New York Times,* Section 3, February 9, 1992, 1, 2, 8.

Harvard Business Review. "Competitiveness Survey: HBR Readers Respond." (September/October 1987): 8–11.

Holbrook, Richard, "Japan and the United States: Ending the Unequal Partnership." *Foreign Affairs.* (Winter 1991–92): 52.

Kahle, Lynn R. "The Nine Nations of North America and the Value Basis of Geographic Segmentation." In *Regional Cultures, Managerial Behaviors, and Entrepreneurship: An International Perspective*, edited by Joseph Weiss, 43–60. New York: Quorum Books, 1988.

Kelly, Kevin, Otis Port, James Treece, Gail DeGeorge, and Zachary Schiller. "Learning from Japan." *Business Week*, January 27, 1992, 52–60.

Klein, Lisa. "The Impact of Group Structure on the Strategy of the Japanese Firm." Yale College Senior Essay, Yale University, 1987.

———. "Kigyo Keiretsu Soran, The Impact of Group Structure," *Oriental Economist*. 2.

Kochan, Thomas, Robert McKerie, and Henry Katz. *The Transformation of American Industrial Relations*. New York: Basic Books, 1986.

Korn/Ferry International and Columbia University Graduate School of Business. *21st Century Report: A Journal on Critical Issues Affecting Senior Executives and the Board of Directors, Reinventing the CEO*. A Global Study by Korn/Ferry International and Columbia University Graduate School of Management, 1989.

Matsumoto, Koji. *The Rise of the Japanese Corporate System*. 1991.

Meyer John, and J. Gustafson. *The U.S. Business Corporation: An Institution in Transition*. Cambridge, Mass.: Ballinger, 1988.

Morton, Michael S. Scott. *Corporations of the 1990s: Information Technology and Organizational Transformation*. New York: Oxford University Press, 1991.

Murray, Alan. "Managed Trade May Serve a Purpose." *The Wall Street Journal*, January 20, 1992, A1.

Nagayasu, Yukimasa. "Japanese Economic System and Business Ethics." Paper presented at the Ninth Bentley Conference on Business Ethics, March 31, 1992. Bentley College, Waltham, Massachusetts.

Neff, Robert. "Japan Takes a Good, Hard Look at Itself. Is Its Brand of Capitalism Simply Better?" *Business Week*, February 17, 1992, 32–34.

Ohmae, Kinichi. *Triad Power: The Coming Shape of Global Competition*. New York: Free Press, 1985.

Ouchi, William, and Alfred Jaeger. "Type Z Organizations: Stability in the Midst of Mobility." *Academy of Management Review* 3 (1978): 305–314.

Peck, Merton. "The Large Japanese Corporation." In *The U.S. Business Corporation: An Institution in Transition*, edited by John Meyer and J. Gustafson, 21–42. Cambridge, Mass.: Ballinger, 1988.

Piore, Michael, and Charles Sabel. *The Second Industrial Divide*. New York: Basic Books, 1984.

Porter, Michael, ed. *Competition in Global Industries*. Boston: Harvard Business School Press, 1986.

Rubner, Alex. *The Might of the Multinationals: The Rise and Fall of the Corporate Legend*. New York: Praeger, 1990.

Sakakibara, Eisuke. *The Japan That Surpassed Capitalism*. 1990.

Sethi, S., Nobuaki Namiki, and Carl Swanson. *The False Promise of the Japanese Miradi: Illusions and Realities of the Japanese Management System*. Boston: Pitman, 1984.

Steiner, George A., and John F. Steiner. *Business, Government & Society: A Managerial Perspective*. 6th ed. New York: McGraw-Hill, 1991.

Sturdivant, Frederick and Heidi Vernon-Wortzel. *Business and Society: A Managerial Approach.* Homewood, IL: Irwin, 1990.

Taylor, Frederick W. *Scientific Management.* New York: Harper & Row, 1947.

United Nations. *Multinational Corporations in World Development.* New York: United Nations, 1973.

Vernon, Raymond. *Sovereignty at Bay.* New York: Basic Books, 1971.

———. *Storm over the Multinationals.* Cambridge, Mass.: Harvard University Press, 1977.

Vernon, Raymond, and Louis Wells, Jr. *Manager in the International Economy.* 5th ed. Englewood Cliffs, N.J.: Prentice-Hall, 1986.

Webber, Alan, and William Taylor. "Is What's Bad for General Motors Bad for the U.S.A.?" *Boston Globe,* March 1, 1992, 73, 76.

Wilkins, Mora. *The Emergence of Multinational Enterprise: American Business Abroad from the Colonial Era to 1914.* Cambridge, Mass: Harvard University Press, 1970.

Yanaga, Chitoshi. *Japanese People and Politics.* New York: Wiley, 1965.

8

Business Ethics into the 21st Century

8.1 **A PERSPECTIVE ON THE FUTURE OF BUSINESS AND ETHICS**

The legitimacy of American business institutions was founded on the notion that the free-market system operated to provide value to society and to serve the public good. The historical role of business was initially believed to maximize profits in order to effect greater economic welfare for the general public. Business fulfilled its social and economic responsibilities through the "invisible hand" working in the market system (Weaver 1990). The underlying public support for business as a legitimate institution stems from that perception.

In recent decades, however, perceptions about the contributions of business to society have changed. The Savings and Loan scandal, oil spills, toxic dumping, and other business-related crises discussed earlier in this book have, to some degree, decreased public confidence in the legitimacy of business as an institution. The single goal of maximization of profits will no longer be sufficient to satisfy the legitimacy of business activities in promoting a good society. Increased public perception and experience that the free-market system alone does not adequately contribute to the general welfare has eroded the notion that corporate management's sole responsibility should be to its shareholders.

The stakeholder perspective taken in this book argues that businesses have both moral and economic obligations to their constituencies. Although there was a time when the moral obligations of corporations were taken for granted and were assumed to be fulfilled when economic functions were achieved, that time is past. A stakeholder perspective of the firm holds that the legitimacy, power, and long-term success of a company depends on the extent to which it serves the public through its economic competitiveness and innovation while meeting moral obligations to its stakeholders. These are not mutually exclusive goals. A firm, for example, should not destroy the environment while using it to produce short-term profits. A firm should not market dangerous products to its customers. The stakeholder view acknowledges the economic and competitive nature of the corporation while arguing that the moral imperative of serving the public good through the responsible design, manufacture, and distribution of products and services is essential to the firm's long-term survival and relationship to its buying public. Government as a consumer and partner of business also acts as a regulator when corporations overstep their legal and moral boundaries with consumers and stakeholders.

Issues that business must prioritize in the 21st century include economic, political, and moral obligations to a wide range of stakeholders. For example, some of the more predominant issues involve resolving national rivalries over trade wars and competing cross-cultural stereotyping, prioritizing consumer protection and product safety, preventing environmental pollution and depletion of the ozone layer and natural resources, actively using economic influence and investments to alleviate domestic and international social injustices, providing safe and healthy working environments, and providing policies and procedures that prevent discrimination within the organization. These issues are now global in scope.

Stakeholders that must be given increased importance in this decade include national trading partners and competitors, consumers (particularly those in underdeveloped nations who are unprotected by institutions and laws), public interest groups, employees, suppliers, end-users, and the media. As business alliances across national boundaries increase, nations and international alliances (e.g., trading blocs) become stakeholders of international businesses. Balancing national and international interests will continue to confront business leaders. Serving consumers in developed and underdeveloped nations through fair and just competitive practices must be a high moral priority for corporations that seek to uphold their reputations. Relationships between corporations and stakeholders are also changing, since end-users and suppliers are becoming strategic partners with businesses. Therefore, the value and intensity of these relationships will increase as economic and social exchanges are more frequent and strategic. Becoming more moral for businesses means valuing and attending to stakeholder relationships, inside and outside the firm.

The following sections summarize and extend what have been major themes throughout the book. Here, the emphasis is placed on the argument that the economic and moral responsibilities of business to the global environment, employee welfare, and the general public is increasing in urgency given the accelerated pace at which technology, industrial activity, and destruction to the environment are occurring.

Before turning to an overview of these social issues, we discuss some of the broader fundamental changes that affect the importance of ethics for business institutions.

8.2 **FUNDAMENTAL CHANGES FOR THE FUTURE OF BUSINESS ETHICS**

Changes in society's values and the resultant demands on business organizations affect the growing need for ethical standards as an integral part of corporate policy. Leonard Brooks (1989) discussed six reasons why corporations are increasing their present and future focus on business ethics: (1) the growing crisis of public confidence over corporate activities; (2) an increasing emphasis on quality of life (that is, health, leisure time, attention to family needs); (3) growing corporate expectations of the high penalties to be paid for unethical behavior; (4) increased ethical awareness through the growing power of special interest groups; (5) the degree of publicity the above four factors have generated; and (6) a change in corporate objectives that influence the control of business activities. Each of these themes is briefly summarized.

Public Crises of Confidence

Many corporations are currently facing a lack of confidence in their credibility and contribution to society by the general public. Scandals such as the Michael Milken junk bond ordeal and the Union Carbide disaster in India have contributed to the decline. A recent poll showed that 69% of those surveyed thought business has too much power over American life; 47% believed firms would damage the environment for profit (*Business Week* May 20, 1989, 29).

An increasing number of corporate executives now wish to formalize corporate ethical standards into their operations in order to control illegal behavior and to improve corporate competitiveness. Johnson & Johnson and Procter & Gamble are two firms that have effectively incorporated ethics into their operating procedures.

Emphasis on Quality of Work Life

The second driving force that has awakened executives' interest in business ethics is the increasing value the American society has placed on the **quality of work life (QWL).** General Motors, GTE, Digital Equipment Corporation, Xerox, and Packard Electric are a small sample of U.S. firms that have implemented QWL programs. Because of the increase in dual-career working couples, an increased national awareness of personal and family health, and a growing concern for balanced life-styles, employees and employers are seeking to increase their quality of life at work. Flex-time, emphasis on health and fitness, compressed work weeks, work-at-home programs, childcare centers in companies, and other programs are being implemented by employers who wish to attract and keep a productive work force.

Implementation of QWL programs along with quality circles—that is, increased worker involvement and participation in decision making—has been effective in improving employee morale, job interest, commitment, and satisfaction (Pearce and Ravlin 1987). Trends point to a greater use of QWL types of programs to effectively meet employees' social and employment needs.

Penalties for Unethical Behavior

Employment discrimination and violations of pollution standards, safe working conditions, and on-the-job health and right-to-know information requirements have all contributed to sizable legal and other economic penalties and costs for companies that have not prevented or curbed illegal activities in these areas. Federal and state governments have demonstrated their willingness in courts to enforce laws to protect the environment and employees from arbitrary and unjust management practices.

The increased expectation of stiffer penalties for companies engaging in unethical behavior also represents a fundamental change in society's views about the role of business. Corporations are expected to act responsibly not only to their shareholders but to all stakeholder groups and society in general. As a result, larger corporations, in particular, are implementing "ethics offices," discussed in Chapter 4, and other employee-related programs that encourage open discussion of complaints and observed wrongdoings before such actions lead to illegal activities.

Power of Special Interest Groups

Special interest groups continue to target and showcase corporations that threaten the public welfare in the media. Ralph Nader, for example, pioneered the consumer interest group movement, which has increased and diversified since the first organization, Public Citizen, in 1971. Other consumer interest groups include the Health Resources Group, the Citizen Action Group, the Litigation Group, and Congress Watch, to name a few (Frederick, Davis, and Post, 1988, 271).

Brooks (1989) also cites three groups in particular whose influence has been felt strongly in the capital markets, which has also drawn attention to corporate ethical performance. These groups include minority interests, institutional investors, and ethical investors (Brooks 1989, 31–38).

Role of Media and Publicity

Publicity through increased media attention has also become a major concern for companies today. The media as a major stakeholder will continue to significantly affect and shape public perceptions about business in the future. The *Exxon Valdez* incident, the Three Mile Island disaster, the Clarence Thomas sexual harassment hearings, and other publicized events and crises have brought instant and sometimes prolonged media coverage into the public living room. Corporations also need to "police" the media to ensure fair practices. For example, NBC overstepped its boundaries by fabricating stories of how dangerous GM vehicles were.

Corporations must continue to learn how to relate responsively to the media as a public stakeholder. Crisis management techniques, discussed in Chapter 5, will increase in importance as commercial accidents and incidents involve the public's welfare and interests.

Changing Corporate Forms and Ethics

As corporations outsource operations and evolve into geographically dispersed networks, alliances, partners, strategic business units (SBUs) and independent profit centers, the following ethical questions also arise: (1) How are individual and organizational control and accountability to be defined and maintained? (2) Who is the focus of responsibility in final decisions that are removed from any center of operations? (3) Who decides and what are the rules for resolving conflict in dispersed, changing business relationships? (4) Who will balance competing and contradictory moral interests between government and firms? Between manufacturer and customer? Between purchasing agent and supplier? (5) As individual and operational unit discretionary power increases and is independent from single government, legal system, and "headquarters" authority, who will intervene and resolve complaints involving consumers, the public interest, and corporate actors? (See Badaracco 1988, 67–91.)

Although there are no easy answers to these dilemmas, there are some clues. First, previous conceptions and definitions of business structure, efficiency, and social responsibility relationships must be revised and changed. Hierarchically based theories of corporations are inadequate to explain how to manage moral responsibility in networked organizations. Working and solving problems in networks and other dispersed, decentralized structures are current research themes in which more fieldwork is required, especially regarding the ethical questions posed above. Second, business ethics must also focus concepts, applications, and guidelines on individuals and teams working in these changing architectural organization structures. For example, the following topics will need to be explored: (1) articulating independent, responsible *choices* that are compatible with the corporation's and other stakeholders' values and missions; (2) understanding the uses and limits of responsible corporate power in autonomous business relationships; (3) maintaining responsibility in flexible business relationships while balancing profit with different ethical imperatives; (4) negotiating cross-cultural values, interest, and expectations while maintaining one's core values and business commitments; and (5) listening and assertively communicating with conflicting moral demands to reach consensus without sacrificing one's ethical position.

These are not new skills for managing morality in business transactions, but they increase in scale, importance, and risk as employees gain independence, autonomy, authority, and control in dispersed organizations. While the ethical principles discussed in Chapter 3 remain important moral guidelines for employees in networks and other independent organizational units, an added emphasis is placed on identifying ethical values that balance an individual's own sense of professional integrity and worth with the corporation's. This is and always has been a complex undertaking. International managers have experienced these challenges. Now, domestic managers and employees must learn these lessons.

Emphasis is now placed on understanding and identifying one's own ethical values, as well as the corporation's ethical imperatives, guidelines, and boundaries, and ensuring an understanding and psychological contract between these. The new ethical challenge is not choosing the "right" course of action; it is negotiating between two or more "right" alternatives, especially in dealing with other stakeholders' values and business priorities. Communicating and negotiating moral and business consensus without sacrificing one's own moral integrity with external stakeholders is a major task at hand.

Changing Corporate Objectives

The final factor, the nature of corporate objectives, has come under scrutiny as an important indication of a business's ethical directions and intentions. For example, short-term profit objectives, in particular, are under criticism as a primary goal of many larger corporations. A new emphasis is being placed on achieving long-term value and success by producing quality products and services that increase a firm's global and domestic competitiveness and add to a society's public welfare.

U.S. corporations are also pooling and sharing resources through strategic alliances and consortia to compete with Japanese *keiretsu*, discussed in Chapter 7. Ford, IBM, Digital Equipment Corporation, and a number of other American firms are pooling capital and resources to protect their industries against more focused, government-supported foreign competition. This collectivist type of corporate objective represents a significant change of individual and singularly pursued company objectives in the United States since the 1960s and 1970s.

"America's Most Admired Corporations" in 1991 (Merck, Rubbermaid, Wal-Mart, Liz Claiborne, Levi Strauss, Johnson & Johnson, Coca-Cola, 3M, PepsiCo, and Procter & Gamble) illustrate eight key attributes of successful company reputations, which reflect the changing nature of corporate objectives. These attributes are (1) quality of management; (2) financial soundness; (3) quality of products or services; (4) ability to attract, develop, and keep talented people; (5) use of corporate assets; (6) value as a long-term investment; (7) innovativeness; and (8) community and environmental responsibility (Ballou 1992). These attributes reflect a balance between marketplace competitiveness and public responsibility that corporations must strive to achieve to meet their stockholder and stakeholder responsibilities.

Concept of "Total Ethics"

A central concept that is evident in many successful and moral companies is termed **total ethics** (Evans 1991). This concept is similar to the "zero defects" theory of organizational behavior. The basic premise of the concept is that businesses must understand their ethical responsibilities not as responses to external pressures or threats, but rather as an integral component of their ongoing activities.

Evans (1991) questions the long-standing perception that business should *coexist* with society, rather than intentionally seek to be an active, concerned *participant* in society. If business organizations view themselves and are viewed as integral members of the society, then ethical concerns regarding the effects of business's actions on others will become priorities of corporate executives.

Since an increasing number of companies are becoming international, business decisions have far-reaching consequences on different populations and cultures. The "total ethics" concept calls for business decision makers to think beyond the maximization of profits and containment of damage, to decisions that will eliminate human and environmental damage. This proactive view advocates the use of the stakeholder model in order to examine whether the company is meeting its ethical responsibilities to a wider range of groups, such as creditors, employees, investors, consumers, and suppliers, and to the public at large.

Evans (1991) illustrates the "total ethics" concept by offering a practical example in the case of Traidcraft Plc. Traidcraft was founded in Bangladesh in 1979. The company began by selling craft items from Bangladesh. The underlying mission of the founders was to reform existing trading policies in order to help redistribute some of the wealth between poor Third World countries and rich industrialized nations.

In 1986, Traidcraft established a "Statement of Objectives," which was developed primarily by employees of the company. This document illustrates an effort to consider and involve all groups affected by the operation of Traidcraft. The company also published its purchasing policy and made it available to suppliers and the public. The policy attempts to protect the aims of all parties involved and provides the basis for a solid business relationship. The role of ethics in business practices is questioned in terms of whether ethical behavior helps to yield financial success. The case of Traidcraft offers an example for future corporations to act with a "total ethics" objective.

When the first prospectus of Traidcraft came out, the English newspaper *Guardian* stated:

> A Gateshead company called Traidcraft urgently needs a £300,000 cash injection from new shareholders—but it is offering them in return only "love, justice and equity." And equity to Traidcraft means putting a higher value on sharing the world's resources fairly than on its own share certificates. Investors must prefer goodness to greed, and should never expect "personal gain or profit" the prospectus warns. *(Evans 1991)*

The reaction in England was extremely favorable and demonstrated that consumers are often willing to pay higher prices in order to benefit from moral as well as economic business objectives.

We argue that successful corporations must include a "total ethics" perspective in their corporate and operating objectives in order to meet stakeholder obligations. Integrating ethical standards from the top executive down, through all levels, formally and informally, in corporations ensures a total ethics perspective. Corporations that depend only on ethics codes or formal statements of ethical intent and do not implement, reward, and discipline the use of ethical standards in daily operations will not realize a total ethics perspective.

8.3 GLOBAL ETHICS: INTERNATIONAL INTERDEPENDENCIES

The number of multinational firms operating in the global marketplace today has set the stage for increasing interdependencies. While further globalization of multinational corporations provides new business and economic opportunities, it also provides a background for conflict between cultures with differing values and moral codes of conduct. This is especially true given the opening of territorial and cultural boundaries in Europe and the Commonwealth of Independent States (formerly the U.S.S.R.). Corporate objectives, policies, and skills must effectively deal with cross-cultural and moral differences in doing business.

Buller, Kohls, and Anderson (1991) define ethics to include "both the moral codes and values used in the reasoning process as well as the decisions and the behaviors that result from them." Their goal is to determine and achieve a global *level of consensus* between different parties regarding the rightness or wrongness of particular acts, policies, and decisions. The authors suggest that four interrelated levels (the individual, corporate, societal, and global) strongly influence each other. The ethic of an individual, for example, is greatly influenced by ethical standards common to his or her society and corporate environment. While corporate ethics largely reflect the society in which the organization is operating, individuals within the organization also bring their own perspectives and ethical beliefs into the firm.

The concept of global ethics is even more complex as people and institutions reflecting different individual, corporate and societal ethical standards interact. The degree to which different nations, firms, or multinational enterprises share value, belief, and opinion consensus of ethical conduct on specific issues, the greater the ability to establish global ethical guidelines. The challenge is learning to (1) become aware of value and perception differences across cultures, at these different levels, and (2) become competent in negotiating differences into consensual agreements.

The strongest argument in support of the development of a global ethic is that it can be used to understand common moral goals that underlie cultural and national differences. For example, a global ethic that could possibly gain consensus across individual, corporate, and societal levels would be an ecology policy designed to protect natural forests and bodies of water. Such an ethic could help reduce conflicts in the increasingly diverse realm of environmentally harmful industrial activities. However, a danger in adopting a global ethic lies in consolidating a consensus of opinions that could later impede the search for improved methods in a particular policy area. Also, once a certain practice has attained a global ethical standard, it may be difficult to change behavior, even if it is later viewed as undesirable.

Nevertheless, the multinational corporation is in a unique position to promote global ethics. As more firms develop international ties, they will increase their interdependencies, and the need for cooperation between nations will become more important. This process may give rise to uniform ethical guidelines for conducting business on a global scale in the near future. The most realistic promise for the emergence of a global ethic lies in the mutual perception and negotiation of individuals and nations as members of an international community that shares joint goals and concerns. The resurgence of democratic principles in (what were once) Communist bloc and Third World countries, along with joint environmental concerns, is pressuring nations to adopt such a global ethic. However, until global ethics are defined for environmental and other critical areas, corporations and governments must continue to negotiate their competing interests—economic, political, and moral.

Cross-Cultural Conflict Negotiation

Negotiating cross-cultural value and business differences will be imperative in this and the next decade as corporations seek new alliances, partners, mergers, and acquisitions across geographies. We will not deal with this topic in depth here but will introduce some central concepts to illustrate the importance of negotiating for business in the global arena.

Nancy Adler (1991, 182) stated that "negotiation is one of the single most important international business skills." Since negotiation is the process in which one party attempts to persuade another to accept its ideas, plan, or behavior, it is obvious that a range of factors and options exist that can influence this goal. The following six factors (from Adler 1991)* influence how a corporation or party interprets a situation to determine whether to negotiate:

*Adapted from Ellen Raider. "Strategy Assessment." In *International Negotiations.* Plymouth, Mass.: Situation Management Systems, 1982, 4–16.

1. *Value of the Exchange:* The more beneficial a corporation views the exchange of resources with a foreign firm, the harder the corporation will pursue negotiations.

2. *Commitment:* The higher the level of commitment a company holds toward a particular issue, the greater the extent to which it is willing to negotiate. If an issue is of great importance to the firm, it will invest the time in negotiations.

3. *Relationship:* The more valuable a successful relationship with a foreign firm is regarded, the more a corporation is willing to negotiate.

4. *Time:* Since negotiation is a time-consuming process, the firm will pursue it as a strategy only if sufficient time exists to allow completion of the negotiation. The more urgent the situation, the less viable negotiation becomes as a strategy.

5. *Trust Level:* The higher the level of trust that exists between the two parties, the greater the possibility for successful negotiations. Serious, good-faith negotiation will also help to increase the level of trust that already exists.

6. *Power Distribution:* If a firm's power position is low relative to the other party, it will be more apt to negotiate as it is at a relative disadvantage in terms of being able to implement its own objectives. A firm in a greater relative power position would be more likely to possess a take-it-or-leave-it attitude. (See Adler [1991, 185–215] for a detailed discussion of these factors.)

The more successful negotiators tend to consider a greater number of possible outcomes and alternatives, talk more about mutually beneficial areas of interest, concentrate more on long-term issues, concentrate on discussion of issues versus following a set sequence of topics to be discussed, and set a range of possible outcomes instead of rigid expectations (Adler 1991).

Buller, Kohls, and Anderson (1991) also present seven approaches for dealing with cross-cultural conflicts. We summarize these as examples for managing ethical issues across cultures. While these approaches are not new, they illustrate a starting point for discussing several choices a corporation or party can use to persuade another to accept a goal, idea, or behavior. The seven approaches include avoidance, forcing, education–persuasion, infiltration, negotiation/compromise, accommodation, and collaboration. It is important to note that these approaches depend on individual characteristics, situational contingencies, and the process of the strategies. Although a win–win outcome is always desirable, it is not always feasible. These approaches suggest ways to minimize further conflict as well as to solve all conflicting demands:

1. *Avoidance:* When using this technique, the conflict is relegated to a background position and is not dealt with directly. If one party is in a significantly stronger bargaining position, avoidance as a negotiation and conflict resolution strategy may be used to prevent further or escalating ethical conflicts.

2. *Forcing:* This technique is used when one party imposes its will over another. Many multinational corporations have been accused of disrespecting and intruding on host country cultures. Host country governments—as in Brazil and Spain, for example—have responded in the past by forcing restrictions on MNEs' profits that must stay in the country and by limiting technology manufacturing. This is a higher risk strategy in the international arena and should be considered only when the situation, people, and interests require it. Some critics argue the U.S. government should use this tactic more with Japan regarding trade policies. The United States has, it is argued, negotiated with Japan from a position of weakness and has not identified what long-term stakes our government really needs in order to bargain.

3. *Education/Persuasion:* This technique employs the use of a specific means of relating the values of one party's perspectives in order to persuade the other to adopt its position. Multinationals have educated host country employees on the value and uses of new technologies, and MNEs have learned from host governments how to share resources and help develop local economies.

4. *Infiltration:* This technique is an often slow process of introducing others to your ethic. Infiltration can result in wide acceptance of particular ideas if they hold some appeal for these individuals. Infiltration is often used unintentionally rather than strategically. For example, many former Eastern bloc countries are pursuing market economies based on their interaction with and evolving desires for Western societal structures and values. As Western market-oriented nations penetrate these economies, infiltration of marketing concepts and methods will occur.

5. *Negotiation/Compromise:* This technique is used when the ethical conflict presents a severe obstacle to productivity. Resolution through negotiation will often lead to compromise on both sides. While this technique may allow the business transaction to occur, it can often leave both sides feeling that the underlying issue was never resolved.

6. *Accommodation:* In using this technique, either party may find it beneficial to adopt the ethic of the other and may do so with little, if any, resistance. This technique requires patience, "give and take," and listening.

7. *Collaboration:* In implementing this technique, both parties would discuss the conflict and attempt to reach a mutually beneficial solution. Willingness to learn, change attitudes, and renegotiate interests is vital with this technique. This is the most desired form of conflict resolution because it deals directly with the source of the conflict (Buller, Kohls, and Anderson 1991, 767–775)

It should be noted that negotiation is an art and a skill. Professor John Graham at the University of Southern California listed key individual characteristics of American, Japanese, Taiwanese, and Brazilian managers (see Adler 1991, 187). Some of the skills that overlapped cultures and countries included preparation and planning, listening, judgment and intelligence, integrity, thinking under pressure, product knowledge, and the ability to win and respect the other party's confidence. Other skills include the following: Know your strengths and start the process with these; do not be under time pressure to negotiate; be vague at first until all stakes of all parties are on the table; and be confident in your ability to win concessions.

Learning to read and understand cross-cultural cues, historical contexts, different systems of law, custom, and expectations based on past political, historical, and religious traditions will increase in importance as businesses become more global. Cross-cultural negotiation skills are essential for business professionals in the coming decade, especially when meeting moral obligations involves conflicting cultural values.

8.4 CHANGES IN THE WORK FORCE

The composition of the work force has been changing and will continue to change into the next century, as Chapter 6 indicated. The U.S. labor pool that will be available to employers in the year 2000 and beyond will require employers and managers to review their values and expectations toward work and workers. The following "Work Force 2000" changes discussed in Chapter 6 are briefly summarized here with ethical implications for the future of business.

The Aging Work Force

The aging of the "Baby Boom" generation combined with the relatively low supply of younger entrants to the labor market will have definite implications on the value system of many corporations. For example, health and wellness programs, retirement planning, and reward systems that provide more leisure time in place of financial benefits are likely to become more prevalent. Also, an increase in the demand for younger workers will lead to an increase in the demand for available employees: women, immigrants, retirees, and disabled workers. Companies will need to institute adequate training programs to develop necessary skills in a labor pool that will most likely be lacking in many skill areas. This change will also lead to increasing competition for entry-level workers. Restructured compensation packages will be required to respond to the needs and values of younger and other "nontraditional" workers (Jamieson and O'Mara 1991).

The clustering of employees at the middle and upper levels of the organization will also lead to a decline in the percentage of available promotions. This can lead to frustration and dissatisfaction with employees' careers. Many companies will be faced with the challenge of having to provide a stimulating and rewarding work environment for those who find promotions in scarce supply. Dependent care and family responsibilities will also appear as dominant concerns for a growing majority of the work force. These changes will put pressure on established values and stakeholder's rights.

Women in the Work Force

It is estimated that women will account for over 50% of the active work force by the year 2000 (Jamieson and O'Mara 1991). As a result, corporations hoping to attract and retain qualified female employees will need to address issues relevant to women in particular. Some of these will include changes in the measurements of success, as more females reach the executive level; changes in leave policies to accommodate family responsibilities; varying benefit requirements of single mothers, women in dual-career families, and women without children; emphasis on child care; and flexible or home-based positions. "Fairness" issues will increase.

Ethnic Diversity in the Work Force

The decline in the availability of younger entrants to the work force will also increase the demand for immigrants, thus creating greater cultural diversity within the labor pool. The challenge here will be to integrate varieties of values, norms, and ethical principles. Corporations will need to adopt many new policies and procedures in order to meet

this challenge. Some of these may include providing cultural awareness training; redesigning jobs and establishing training to compensate
for language barriers; establishing reward systems and promotion possibilities that correspond to different value systems; developing new
and improved methods for dealing with cultural diversity; and perhaps
formally recognizing managers who are successful at integrating a
diverse work force.

Disabled Workers

Once again, a diminishing traditional labor pool will precipitate the need
to tap into currently dormant resources. The disabled worker population
has remained largely underused, but, in the future, an increasing
demand is predicted for skills this group offers. Disabled workers have
typically had problems finding and maintaining jobs even though legislation has been enacted to protect their rights. This is due in large measure to distorted perceptions of the skills of the disabled and a lack of
support for those who attempt to fit into rigid corporate cultures.
Corporations will need to implement policies to assist and support both
disabled and nondisabled workers. Programs to provide education to
nondisabled coworkers, career development programs for the disabled,
flexible hours and working conditions, interaction with legislators and
health care providers, and effective employee assistance programs are
but a few of the necessary steps companies will need to adopt to deal
effectively with this unique human resource.

The Education Gap in the Work force

The concern here is with the growing segment of the population known
as the functionally illiterate. A smaller percentage of the U.S. population
is obtaining quality higher education, and more people are graduating
from high school without the basic skills necessary to function in a business environment. This disparity will divide the work force into two
segments: (1) the highly educated middle-aged employees who will
demand a challenging, semiautonomous, performance-based environment, and, (2) the less educated who require structured special training.
The company may need to sponsor programs within the community to
facilitate this training. Firms will also need to research appropriate motivations for success within this population.

The task of managing the wide range of employee needs, values,
and ethical standards will indeed be a primary challenge for corpora-

tions in the future. Managers need to be increasingly aware of the mix of values with which they are dealing. Accurate understanding of the diverse cultures and underlying value systems inherent in a particular work force can lead to the establishment of effective motivation and reward systems and can mean the difference between business success and failure.

8.5 ENVIRONMENTAL ISSUES

One estimate states that the developed world must provide the Third World with an additional $70 billion of new aid, in addition to the current $50 billion annually provided, to protect and sustain the physical global environment (Gutfeld 1992, A2). Global warming, acid rain, air and water pollution, and toxic waste are all environmental concerns discussed in Chapter 5. These are concerns in which business is both cause and effect. Industries that participate in polluting the environment must also help pay for the effects of this damage. Environmental destruction will have a growing impact on social, political, and business policies of the future. The environment is a concern that affects all people and all nations. Ethical decision making by business can play an important role in preserving and protecting the environment now and for future generations. The Earth Summit meeting in Rio de Janeiro in 1992 was a step toward defining international commitments to the environment.

Global warming was termed "the greatest crisis ever faced collectively by humans" (Stevensen 1991) at the Conference on Global Warming and Climate Change in 1989. A crisis of this magnitude demonstrates the need for an international business code of conduct aimed at protecting the environment and searching for alternative energy sources. A transnational global ethic is needed in this area.

The stakeholder approach to decision making can be implemented in this instance to address the variety of values and interests affected by a global energy policy. Developing countries have resisted suggestions of regulating CO_2 emissions. Many feel that they cannot restrict their emissions while they are in an economically industrial growth stage, and that they are being unjustly penalized as a result of pollution caused primarily by developed industrialized countries. Future generations also share a stake in current energy policies. More education, resource sharing, and economic cooperation between richer and poorer nations must occur to relieve environmental damage of the rain forests, the ozone layer, and bodies of water.

Alternatives to fossil fuels are beginning to be seriously researched around the world. Special interest groups and individual stakeholders will likely take strong positions on these issues and will press for viable solutions. For example, in 1989, Canada's environment minister indicated that he supported research into nuclear energy sources. This met with widespread opposition and concern. In decisions such as these, it is important for business and political leaders to monitor their stakeholders' concerns and to negotiate with the claims of all groups involved. The environment affects everyone.

Lucien Bouchard, Canadian environment minister in 1989, stated at the Symposium on the Arctic and Global Change: "We must change to development processes that are environmentally sustainable." This suggestion provides a basis for research and development, as well as an ethical guideline for future business operations that affect the global environment.

A recent study completed by the United Nations found that the most efficient way to combat global warming is to use private financial markets. The study suggests that a global Environmental Protection Agency be created. The agency would be responsible for distributing pollution allowances that could, in turn, be exchanged between polluters and with others. The study also proposes that an exchange-based, over-the-counter futures and options market for pollution rights be created.

The proposal would have to be reviewed by the governments of the Conference on Trade and Development and the United Nations. However, according to Frank Joshua, economic affairs officer for the U.N. Conference on Trade and Development, this plan could establish a global precedent for using financial markets as a means of cleaning up the environment (Taylor 1991).

8.6 INTEGRATING CODES OF CONDUCT INTO PRACTICE

Ethical principles and practices in business start with top leaders' expressed, shared, and implemented values. The corporate culture then embodies these values and practices. Development and implementation of these ethical values into codes, ethics training courses, ethics offices, sexual harassment programs, and ombudsman and peer review programs become operating initiatives that corporations pursue to remain competitive and responsible, to build and sustain trusting relationships with stakeholders. The implementation of these ethical values into operating programs requires commitment, time, and effort of a company's leaders in order to be structured to best serve all the relevant stakeholders. L. J. Brooks (1989) offers seven recommendations for realistically implementing ethical codes of conduct and practice into corporate strategy, culture, and values:

- Confidentiality should not be so restrictive that it prohibits employees from consulting with internal personnel regarding ethical questions.

- A fair and objective hearing process should follow any report of an ethical problem or conflict.

- Assurance should be given to all employees that their rights with respect to discrimination, and notice and compensation in the event of a layoff will be protected.

- A section on employer rights or terms of employment should follow the employee rights section, in order to facilitate open communication and clarify expectations.

- Executive support of the code of conduct should be demonstrated in the form of clear sanctions against those who violate it.

- Conflicts of interest revolving around ownership interest in related concerns need to be addressed, as these conflicts can cloud judgments.

- Consider any other ethical codes that influence employees in the corporation, and design the corporate code so as not to conflict with these external codes of conduct.

Ethical conduct in corporations must be a shared vision and practice that is actively communicated and modeled by executives, managers, and employees on an ongoing, daily basis. As shareholders become more informed and involved in the moral management of companies, CEOs and boards of directors must also work more cooperatively and responsively as partners with the firm's stakeholders to ensure that justice and fairness are exemplified by the firm's leadership and integrated into everyday operations of the organization.

SUMMARY

Business is a vital partner with its employees, stockholders, government, consumers, customers, suppliers, and the public. This network of relationships is based on trust as well as performance. As the 21st century approaches, the adversarial and segmented basis underlying these relationships must give way to cooperative alliances grounded on a win–win philosophy for all stakeholders. This must happen because global competitiveness has required it. Short-term objectives based on greed or self-interests of a few groups are proving fatal in the marketplace when faced with countries and companies that implement a holistic approach in their joint business, government, employee, and union alliances. Total quality management processes introduced by Dr. Deming have worked in Japan and are now being tried, after 40 years, by U.S. firms. Without a total quality, continuous improvement, team-oriented approach to doing business, companies will continue to fall behind.

Underlying this holistic approach to competition are moral imperatives of a stakeholder approach: Stakeholders should be respected and treated fairly and justly; stakeholder and stockholder relationships should be based on trust as well as performance criteria; society, customers, and consumers are strategic stakeholders and must be included in business strategies; and ethics is an integral part of doing business.

References and Suggested Readings

Adler, Nancy J. *International Dimensions of Organizational Behavior.* Boston, Mass.: PWS-Kent, 1991.

Badaracco, Joseph. "Changing Forms of the Corporation." In *The U.S. Business Corporation: An Industry in Transition,* edited by John Meyer and James Gustafson, 67–91. Cambridge, Mass.: Ballinger, 1988.

Ballou, Kate. "America's Most Admired Corporations." *Fortune,* February 10, 1992, 40–46.

Brooks, L. J. "Corporate Ethical Performance: Trends, Forecasts, and Outlooks." *Journal of Business Ethics* 8 (1989): 31–38.

Buller, Paul, John Kohls, and Kenneth Anderson. "The Challenge of Global Ethics." *Journal of Business Ethics* 10 (1991): 767–775.

Business Week. Results from a 1989 Harris Poll cited in "The Public Is Willing to Take Business On." May 20, 1989, 29.

Evans, Richard. "Business Ethics and Changes in Society." *Journal of Business Ethics* 10 (1991): 871–876.

Frederick, William, Keith Davis, and James Post. *Business and Society Corporate Strategy, Public Policy, Ethics.* 6th ed. New York: McGraw-Hill, 1988.

Gutfeld, Rose. "Earth Summit Has Put Bush on the Spot." *The Wall Street Journal,* April 7, 1992, A2.

Hoffman, W. Michael and Jennifer Mills Moore. "The Future Corporate Ethos." In *Business Ethics: Readings and Cases in Corporate Morality.* 2d ed., 607–634. New York: McGraw-Hill, 1990.

Jamieson, David, and Julie O'Mara. *Managing Workforce 2000: Gaining the Diversity Advantage.* San Francisco: Jossey-Bass, 1991.

Pearce, J. A., II, and E. C. Ravlin. "The Design and Activation of Self-Regulatory Work Groups." *Personnel Psychology* 40 (1987): 97–111.

Stevensen, Mark, and Victor S. Godden, eds., "Ethics and Energy Supplement." *Journal of Business Ethics* 10 (1991): 641–648.

Taylor, Jeffrey. "Global Market in Pollution Rights Proposed by U.N." *The Wall Street Journal,* January 31, 1991, C1.

Weaver, Paul H. "After Social Responsibility." In *The U.S. Business Corporation: An Institution in Transition.* Edited by John Meyer and James Gustafson. Cambridge, Mass.: 1988.

GLOSSARY

Accommodation stage the third phase in a firm's process in dealing with public crises related to unsafe products. This is the stage when the firm withdraws the product or defends its safety.

Acute crisis the second stage in a crisis during which actual damage is done and the crisis actually occurs.

Affirmative action a concept that focuses on active attempts by organizations to hire and promote individual members of groups that have been discriminated against in the past.

Agency stage the final phase in a firm's process in dealing with a public crisis related to unsafe products. This is the stage when the firm attempts to understand the safety issue and educate the public.

Altruist an ethical decision-making style based on providing benefits to others and contributing to the welfare of society.

Business strategy a level of corporate strategy formulation that deals with defining corporate strategy in terms of specific goals and business activities.

Capitalism an economic system governed by private and corporate ownership as opposed to government control.

Categorical imperative an ethical principle developed by Immanuel Kant that contends that individuals must act in ways they would universally wish all others to act in the same situation.

Chronic crisis the third stage in a crisis during which the firm undergoes a period of recovery, self-analysis, and healing.

Commercial speech a form of expression that refers to the type of language used in advertising and business interactions.

Compensatory justice a form of justice concerned with making amends to an individual for a past injustice.

Competitiveness the degree to which an individual or group can obtain or reach its goals as it engages in a rivalry with others in pursuit of the same goals.

Corporate internal decision structure the process by which corporate decisions are made about the organizational structure and the interpretation of established corporate policies.

Corporate strategy a level of corporate strategy formulation that deals with establishing broad goals and objectives upon which corporate policies and plans are based.

Convenantal ethic an ethical concept that focuses on the importance of social *relationships* among businesses, customers, and stakeholders.

Crisis resolution the final stage in a crisis during which the firm focuses on managing and resolving the crisis.

Cultural relativism a form of ethical relativism that holds that moral standards vary from one culture to another, and that individuals and firms should adhere to the moral standards of the culture in which their actions take place.

Defense stage the second stage of crisis management during which a firm's image could be at stake as it deals with intense and widespread publicity.

Distributive justice a form of justice concerned with the fair and equitable distribution of benefits and burdens.

Due process a course of action that follows established rules and laws of society.

Employment-at-will a common law principle that holds that the employer–employee relationship is strictly voluntary and that either party may end the relationship at any time.

Enterprise strategy a level of corporate strategy formulation that deals with the broad role of the firm in society and identifies the values the firm wishes to represent.

Ethical idealism a view of corporate social responsibility that contends that corporations can be responsible to society only if the corporation's actions are guided by a sense of moral duty toward stakeholder interests.

Ethical relativism an ethical framework that contends that each person has his/her own unique moral standards and that only these standards are relevant for judging his/her behavior. This framework dismisses the notion that universal rules for evaluating the morality of an action can exist.

Ethics code corporate policies and rules of conduct that attempt to guide the behavior of employees with respect to acceptable work practices.

Free market theory an economic theory that contends that the primary objective of business is to maximize profits. The marketplace is seen as the mechanism that will protect and regulate both consumers and producers.

Functional strategy a level of corporate strategy formulation that deals with translating the business strategy level into specific functional area goals and objectives.

Golden parachute contracts between a firm and its high-level executives designed to protect and compensate these executives in the event of a takeover, merger, or restructuring.

Greenmail the practice of firms purchasing their own shares from corporate raiders at prices above market value in order to prevent a takeover.

Individualist an ethical decision-making style based on individual reasoning processes, self-interest, and self-preservation.

Infomercial a form of TV advertising characterized by a documentary format, extended time frame, and more subtle sales techniques than conventional advertisements.

Insider trading the use of vital corporate information by a corporation member to obtain personal monetary gain.

Insight range the third stage in crisis management during which the firm must deal with the crisis and determine the extent to which the firm is at fault for the safety concerns relating to its product.

Justice an ethical principle concerned with equal opportunity and access to opportunities within society for all individuals. Moral judgements are based on the fair and equitable distribution of both opportunities and binders.

Keiretsu financially interlocked groups or cartels of Japanese companies, banks, suppliers, and other commercial parties who work together to enhance the business activities of each member firm.

Moral entitlement the belief that individuals or groups have an inherent right or privilege because they are a member of society.

Multinational enterprise a business organization whose operations are located in more than one country.

Myth a belief uncritically accepted by the members of a group, especially in support of existing traditional practices and institutions.

Naive relativism a form of ethical relativism that holds that only the self-interest and values of the individual are important for judging the morality of others' actions.

Neocapitalism a modified version of the traditional capitalist economic system. Neocapitalism is characterized by strong interrelationships among political, corporate, and human capital resource strategies.

Non-consequentialist ethic an ethical principle that does not focus on the outcome or consequences of an action when making a moral judgement.

Ombudsman a third party located within a firm whose function is to hear and address employee grievances with respect to immoral behavior within the organization.

Pragmatist an ethical decision-making style based on justifiable actions determined by a combination of interests in a context of specific situations. Pragmatists make decisions based on the needs of the moment and the specific consequences of those decisions.

Primary stakeholder individuals or groups who are directly involved in the operation and survival of the organization; for example, owners, suppliers, customers, employer.

Procedural justice a form of justice concerned with the fairness of the decision-making process, practice, and agreements.

Prodromal stage the first stage in a crisis during which the firm receives warnings or clues to a potential impending crisis.

Productionist individuals who advocate corporate social responsibility with a focus on sharing corporate profits with less fortunate members of society.

Progressivism a view of corporate social responsibility that holds that corporate actions should be guided by self-interest *and* a moral responsibility toward social change.

Pure speech a form of expression that refers to the general communication of ideas relating to politics, science, or art in the context of the marketplace.

Quality of work life (QWL) employee benefit programs designed to facilitate improvement in the quality of the business environment by responding to employee needs and values.

Raider individual who engages in corporate takeovers or takeover attempts. Raiders usually pursue hostile takeovers, which are strongly opposed by the management of the target firm.

Reaction stage the early stage of crisis management directly following the occurrence of a crisis. The firm must respond publicly to the crisis without the benefit of complete information or thorough analysis.

Retributive justice a form of justice concerned with punishing an individual or individuals for causing harm to another person.

Rights an ethical principle concerned with protecting the legal and moral rights of an individual or groups of individuals from being subjugated to the pursuit of societal well being.

Scientific management a management theory posed by Frederick Taylor that called for the separation of management and labor, as well as the necessity for the division of labor and for formalized chains of command.

Secondary stakeholder interested parties who are not directly related to the daily operation and functioning of the firm.

Sexual harassment a form of sexual discrimination consisting of unwanted verbal or physical behavior toward an individual such that rejection of this behavior directly or indirectly affects the individual's employment or performance and/or creates a hostile work environment.

Social audit a method for measuring and evaluating the social responsibility performance of a firm with respect to its social goals, policies, and programs.

Social contract a philosophical concept that pertains to beliefs and assumptions that characterize relationships between various groups within society.

Special interest groups groups or organizations who focus media attention on corporations they believe pose a threat to public welfare.

Stakeholders individuals or groups who have a vested interest or claim in the corporation or firm.

Stakeholder analysis an analytical approach that is concerned with the ways that different constituencies impact and affect business decisions and actions.

Stakeholder approach a form of analysis that focuses on observing and evaluating how business decisions as well as internal and external actions affect and are affected by constituencies.

Strategic business units divisions of corporations that focus on any one segment of the overall corporate product mix. The SBU is primarily responsible for all business activity undertaken by the firm within its market segment.

Takeover an attempt to gain control of a corporation by obtaining a majority share of corporate stock. Takeovers are characterized by stock purchases at a price much higher than the current market value.

Universalism an ethical principle that focuses on the means by which an action is taken, not the consequences of that action. This view holds that an individual's actions should be guided by a sense of moral duty toward other individuals' humanity.

Utilitarianism an ethical principle that focuses on the consequences of an act to judge whether it is right or wrong. This principle seeks to maximize the benefit and minimize the cost for all parties affected by the action.

Values beliefs and principles individuals use to guide their actions, behaviors, and their judgements of what is right and wrong.

Whistle-blowing the process by which an employee reports to a third party about a known or suspected wrongdoing engaged in by his or her employer.

Zaibatsu a group of large Japanese corporations whose members own controlling blocks of shares in other member firms. Each member firm has its own keiretsu organized around it.

INDEX

A. H. Robins Company, 134, 156
Accommodation stage, 161
Acquired immunodeficiency
  syndrome (AIDS), 3, 193–194
  and discrimination, 198–199
  moral issues with, 180
Acquisitions, 118–120
Action on Smoking and Health
  (ASH), 194
Acute crisis, 160
Advertising, 138–139
  and ethics, 143
  and free speech, 143–144
  and moral responsibility
  continuum, 139–140
  pros and cons on, 140–142
Aetna, 219
Affirmative action, 7, 199–200
  and compensatory justice, 200
  and reverse discrimination, 200–203
Age discrimination, 176, 179
Age Discrimination in Employment
  Act, 198
Agency stage, 161
Aging, of work force, 177–178,
  264–265
Air Quality Act, 155
Alcohol industry, 139, 142
Altruists, 78–79, 80
American Academy of Pediatrics, 141
American Cyanamid, 16, 150

Apple Computer, 117
Arco, 117, 156
Association, 9
AT&T, 14, 165, 206

Bakke case, 201–202
Bankruptcy of Manville Corporation,
  2, 86–87
Beasley, Robert, 19
Bentham, Jeremy, 66
Beshada v. Johns Manville Corporation,
  147
Board of directors, 122–123
Boeing Corporation, 3, 114, 124, 125,
  238
Boesky, Ivan, 121
Borg-Warner Corporation, 115
  values statement from, 100–101,
  114, 124
BP America, 150
Bradwell v. Illinois, 196
Bribe, in foreign negotiations, 58, 61
Bureaucratic administrator, 109–110
Burns, James MacGregor, 110
Bush, George, 228
Business
  ethical issues for, 7–8
  ethical reasoning in, 16–19
  future of ethics and, 252–253
  government regulation in, 165–166
  recent crises in, 2–3